The Neighboring Text

The

NEIGHBORING TEXT

CHAUCER, BOCCACCIO, HENRYSON

GEORGE EDMONDSON

University of Notre Dame Press

Notre Dame, Indiana

Library of Congress Cataloging-in-Publication Data

Edmondson, George, 1964–
The neighboring text : Chaucer, Boccaccio, Henryson / George Edmondson.
    p. cm.
Includes bibliographical references and index.
ISBN-13: 978-0-268-02775-9 (pbk. : alk. paper)
ISBN-10: 0-268-02775-7 (pbk. : alk. paper)
    1. English literature—Middle English, 1100–1500—History and
criticism—Theory, etc. 2. English literature—Old English,
ca.450–1100—History and criticism—Theory, etc. 3. Transmission
of texts—England—History—To 1500. 4. Historiography—Great
Britain—History—To 1500. 5. Chaucer, Geoffrey, d. 1400.
Troilus and Criseyde. 6. Boccaccio, Giovanni, 1313–1375. Filostrato.
    7. Henryson, Robert, 1430?–1506? Testament of Cresseid.
8. Troilus (Legendary character) in literature. 9. Trojan War—Literature
and the war. 10. Cressida (Fictitious character) I. Title.
PR275.H5E36   2011
820.9'358—dc22
2010052718

For Hazel-Dawn,

of course

CONTENTS

ACKNOWLEDGMENTS

Fittingly, for a work about texts and neighbors, this book has been shaped and reshaped—then shaped and reshaped again—by a number of different communities. It gives me great pleasure to acknowledge the members of those communities and to publicly thank all those who have supported this project and its author.

Luckily for it, and for me, this book began life as a dissertation directed by V. A. Kolve. Those fortunate enough to have had Del as a mentor, let alone a friend, know that mere words of gratitude cannot hope to repay his extraordinary generosity, his deep wisdom, his casual erudition, or his uncanny ability to provide the exact guidance one needs at the exact moment one needs it. For me, though, the task is made even more difficult when I consider that this book *really* began many years ago, in Del's undergraduate course on *Troilus and Criseyde* and the Dream Visions, and that mine was the last dissertation he directed before his retirement from teaching. What it was Del saw in my scruffy, slightly addled undergraduate self that made him want to encourage me to go to graduate school I'll never know, but I am eternally grateful that he did. I have tried my best, at any rate, to write a book worthy of its place in the Great Kolve Continuum.

Most of what is interesting and provocative in this book I owe to Kenneth Reinhard. Ken taught me almost everything I know about psychoanalysis, and every page here bears the mark of his influence, if not, alas, his brilliance. Some will describe my work as "Lacanian." I know that I am a Reinhardian.

I could never have conceived of this book if not for the example set by L. O. Aranye Fradenburg, and I am grateful to her for agreeing to serve as a member of my dissertation committee. In the end, however, the book owes its present shape mostly to the interventions of six people: Mark Miller, who didn't buy for a second the image of Chaucer as a "traumatized defender of the symbolic order" found in an earlier draft; Jonathan Crewe, who pointed out that this was actually a work of literary history; Klaus Mladek, whose influence on my thinking these past five years has been transformative in every way; Elizabeth Scala and Patricia Ingham, my readers for the University of Notre Dame Press, who suggested ways to improve the whole manuscript, and the introduction especially; and Peter Travis, who never minces words or withholds praise, and who has read and commented on every draft.

My colleagues at Dartmouth have fostered the sort of vibrant and welcoming community that every young scholar craves. For their unfailing support, I thank Ivy Schweitzer, Tom Luxon, Melissa Zeiger, Monika Otter, Brenda Silver, Colleen Boggs, Barbara Will, Don Pease, Lou Renza, Lynda Boose, Cleopatra Mathis, Cynthia Huntington, Marty Favor, Ernie Hebert, and Margaret Williamson. For taking good care of one of their own, I thank Soyica Colbert, Aden Evens, Bed Giri, Sam Vasquez, Tommy O'Malley, Aimee Bahng, Mishuana Goeman, Jeffrey Santa Ana, Darren J. Ranco, and Mary Coffey. Special thanks are due to Alex Halasz, Andrew McCann, Michael Chaney, and Michelle Warren, for reasons I am sure I don't need to explain to any of them. I could not have asked for three more supportive chairs than Peter Travis, Gretchen Gerzina, and Patricia McKee. Darsie Riccio has earned my eternal devotion for her expert efficiency, her forbearance, and her tact.

I am profoundly grateful for the intellectual, moral, and material assistance offered me over the years by numerous friends and colleagues. For all that they have done, I thank Elizabeth Scala, Patricia Ingham, Jeffrey Cohen, David Wallace, Rita Copeland, Robert Stein, Christopher Baswell, Frank Grady, Amy Hollywood, Stephanie Trigg, Tom Prendergast, Christopher Cannon, Bruce Holsinger, H. A. Kelly, Sylvia Federico, John Ganim, Ann Astell, Lisa Cooper,

Andrea Denny-Brown, R. A. Shoaf, R. James Goldstein, Geraldine Heng, Matthew Boyd Goldie, Eileen Joy, Jessica Brantley, Catherine Sanok, Christina Fitzgerald, Tom O'Donnell, Kathy Lavezzo, William Kuskin, Robert Meyer-Lee, Kathleen Biddick, Eric Santner, Adam Sitze, Carsten Strathausen, and Jeanne Baer. I am especially grateful to Dartmouth's Leslie Center for the Humanities and its director, Adrian Randolph, for sponsoring a manuscript review seminar on my behalf, and to Paul Strohm and Vance Smith for generously agreeing to comment on my work-in-progress. The book is stronger in every way as a result of their efforts. I am also extremely grateful to Barbara Hanrahan at the University of Notre Dame Press for her unflagging support of this project and for the patience, wisdom, and good humor she showed at a difficult time. Many thanks are due as well to Elisabeth Magnus, who edited the manuscript with delicacy and skill.

For helping me collapse the boundaries between inside and outside, mind and body, public and private, past and present, day and night, East Coast and West Coast, where I came from and where I've arrived, I thank Richard Lange and Kim Turner, Reagan Arthur and Scott Beck, Wes and Lisa Smith, Nancy Bracikowski and Klaus Schreiber, Darrell Hotchkiss and Jon Fox, Kristin O'Rourke, Bill Tutton, and, last but never least, Heather Lukes and Molly McGarry, who could just as well be included in the next paragraph.

I am eternally grateful to my father, Steven, my brothers, Brett and Jon, my sisters-in-law, Michelle and Karen, and my niece and nephews for their patience and understanding. My mother, Marjorie, taught me how to read when no one else could, and I deeply regret that she did not live to see me write a book of my own. Words can hardly express my gratitude to Jack, Shelley, and Jennifer Dumpert, and to Erik Davis, for fifteen years' worth of conversation, provocation, inspiration, affirmation, celebration, appreciation, and delectation. I owe my greatest debts—emotional, material, intangible—to my wife, Hazel-Dawn, whose love and support have made the whole thing possible.

An earlier version of chapter 1 appeared, along with parts of the introduction, as "Henryson's Doubt: Neighbors and Negation in the

Testament of Cresseid," in *Exemplaria* 20, no. 2 (2008), reprinted here by permission of Maney Publishing. Some of the language found in chapter 1 appeared as part of "Naked Chaucer," published in *The Posthistorical Middle Ages*, edited by Elizabeth Scala and Sylvia Federico. That material is reprinted here by permission of Palgrave Macmillan.

Introduction

I

There is a moment in Chaucer's *The House of Fame* that has long intrigued me. We are near the beginning of book 2: the golden eagle spotted by the dreamer ("Geffrey") at the close of book 1 has just swooped down and taken him up in its "clawes starke," and they are now soaring high above the world.[1] Geffrey is dumbfounded, to say the least; it takes a while for the eagle to recall him to his senses. He does eventually come around, however, at which point the eagle can at last explain the reason for this extraordinary turn of events. Jupiter, says the eagle, has taken pity on Geffrey for his years of thankless service "to Cupido the rechcheles" and his followers (668). Jupiter has considered Geffrey's many sacrifices, says the eagle: the long nights, the headaches, the hard work of making "bookys and songes and dytees" in praise of lovers and their "art" (622, 627). But Jupiter has considered other things as well:

> This is, that thou hast no tydinges
> Of Loves folk, if they be glade,
> Ne of noght elles that god made;
> And noght only fro fer contree
> That ther no tyding comth to thee,

But of thy verray neyghebores,
That dwellen almost at thy dores,
Thou herest neither that ne this;
For whan thy labour doon al is,
And hast y-maad thy rekeninges,
In stede of reste and newe thinges,
Thou gost hoom to thy hous anoon;
And, also domb as any stoon,
Thou sittest at another boke,
Til fully daswed is thy loke,
And livest thus as an hermyte,
Although thyn abstinence is lyte.

(643–60)

Ah, Geffrey. So dutiful, so selfless, so industrious! And now, as a re-ward for all of his "labour and devocion," this servant of Love's ser-vants is being escorted to the House of Fame—a place where he will be exposed to all the tidings he can handle, and then some (666).

Scholars have celebrated this moment for its self-deprecating humor and studied it for possible insights into Chaucer's working life as controller of customs.[2] I am drawn to it for what it has to say about the complexities of the neighbor relation. Geffrey's apparent indiffer-ence to the people dwelling at his very door would have made him, by late medieval standards, a perfectly decent neighbor, if not quite an exemplary one. Then as now, the "lowest common denominator of neighbourliness" appears to have been "the maintenance of an 'hon-est,' 'quiet' self-sufficiency and . . . abstention from behaviour liable to cause injury or provoke disquiet."[3] On the basis of those criteria alone, the bookish and retiring Geffrey would surely have made the ideal neighbor. And yet Geffrey's self-imposed isolation would also have marked him as something of an oddity within his immediate neigh-borhood. Exhibiting "certain passive qualities of restraint" was only the beginning; cultural norms also dictated that medieval neighbors actively participate in complex networks of reciprocity, obligation, and familiarity connecting them to the life of their local community.[4] They were not, at any rate, supposed to shut themselves up in their rooms—not even in London. They were not supposed to do what Geffrey has done by embracing books as his neighbors, rather than the people who dwell nearby.

And, besides, what have those books ever done for him? The eagle chides Geffrey for sitting at his books "domb as any stoon," poring over them until his look becomes "daswyd." If late medieval society defined neighborliness in terms of reciprocity and negotiation, then Geffrey seems to have gotten the raw end of the bargain. To hear the eagle tell it, he keeps giving to his books—giving his time, his attention, his energy, his (dare we say) love—when all he seems to get in return is stupefaction. Why would he want to do that to himself? What does he expect to get from his books that he would pursue it to the point of torpor?

This study concerns the strange form of intimacy evoked by the eagle's account of Geffrey's stunted social life: the intimacy of the neighboring text. We are not accustomed to thinking of the text as a neighbor. We refer to the text as a friend, perhaps, or a companion, or a commodity, or an object, or a portal, or a threat—but not as a neighbor. The same is true of our efforts to describe the relations among texts: we tend to speak in terms of progenitors and descendents, families and stemmata, whereas references to a "neighborhood" of texts, like attempts to draw out the "neighbor" relations among apparently disparate texts, are comparatively rare.[5] All the same, medieval literary studies has been developing a theory of the neighboring text for some time now. Medievalists influenced by postcolonial theory, for example, have worked tirelessly to dismantle the teleological, triumphalist, and, ultimately, nationalistic models of literary genealogy that for so long dominated our conceptions of literary history.[6] Ethan Knapp's observation that "perhaps no ideology is so central to the institution of literary history as that of filial piety" still largely applies, of course.[7] But in recent years, that once-dominant ideology has had to contend with an antagonistic model of literary relations in which the competing claims of various communities—adjacent, overlapping, dominant, and subordinate—get played out through the writing and rewriting, the imposition and appropriation, of certain shared narratives. In this scenario, neighboring becomes the very precondition of textual production, while texts themselves serve as a means of negotiating, contesting, and in some cases subverting the neighbor relation. Meanwhile, the ongoing ethical turn in medieval studies has revealed the many ways in which the late Middle Ages understood reading to be an ethical practice—a practice concerned with questions of the good life, with relation rather than being. We have long known, of course, that medieval readers turned to literature for instruction and correction.[8] We also recognize that "the logic that placed poetry 'under' ethics not only allowed for the freedom to read subversive classical poets such as Ovid, and often to recuperate them in Christian or simply practical moral contexts, but also allowed vernacular poets to explore the ethics of speech and silence, passionate love, friendship, social networks, and the conflict between the secular and the spiritual."[9] Moreover, if Mark Miller is correct, then there is reason to believe that medieval subjects, entirely capable of practicing a type of practical reason and thus of achieving a complex form of agency, actively willed their own participation in a normative system, rather than serving as passive receptors for the didactic lessons literature had to teach.[10] Of more immediate interest to the present study, however, is J. Allan Mitchell's recent argument that the fortuitous encounters, amorous (mis)adventures, and miraculous transformations so prevalent in medieval literature may also have instilled in readers an openness to the event—to the untimely experience of something at once *in* the medieval situation, a part of its everyday discourses, but not entirely *of* that situation, a product of its laws—that on its own established the potential for ethical subjectivity.[11] Building upon some of the insights gained from these and other developments, this study asks, in the first place, what would happen if we began to think about the relations between certain readers and certain texts as ones of neighboring, defined by proximity and carrying the weight of an event. At the same time, taking my cue from some of the recent work being done in manuscript studies, I pose a second question as well: What would happen if we pushed the matter further and, employing the same logic of "miscellaneity" that governed the seemingly random arrangements of medieval manuscripts, began to think about the relations among certain texts as ones of neighboring rather than of kinship?[12]

In both cases, we would be working with a model of relationality utterly central to late medieval society—more central, one could argue, than the models of kinship and genealogy that made up the "perceptual grid" for much of the period's historiography.[13] That the concept of neighborliness formed one of the foundations of communitarian life in the Middle Ages has long been recognized. But just how solid a foundation was it? An earlier generation of scholars tended to idealize the concept of neighborliness, as though harmony and cooperation somehow came more easily or naturally to medieval neighbors than to their latter-day counterparts. To be sure, the concept of neighborliness seems to have been so thoroughly inculcated in medieval subjects that it needed neither to be defined (there are no dictionary entries for the word *neighbor* before the eighteenth century) nor elaborated (there are no conduct books or instructional manuals explicitly devoted to the question of what it means to be a neighbor).[14] But as our understanding of late medieval communitarian life has deepened, the outlook of most historians has shifted accordingly, with the majority now insisting "upon the need to recognize [the typical medieval neighborhood's] heterogeneity, hierarchy and conflicts of interest, and to understand community 'not as an organic state, but as one negotiated and re-negotiated to suit the self-interests of its participants.'"[15] If there is anything like a critical consensus, it would be "that in medieval society neighbourliness was less a real, existing state of harmonious social relations than an ideal—a set of values aimed at fostering cooperation, a sense of collective identity and sentiments of community."[16] Everyone, it seems, knew what it meant to "be" a neighbor. The concept just didn't necessarily accord with the realities of daily life.

One of my wagers in this book is that a principle of neighborliness similar to the one described here might be extended, with some important qualifications, to the relations between medieval readers and texts. At the very least, I want to ask whether the norms that governed relations of propinquity in the communal sphere would also have informed the encounter between reader and text and, if they did, how that might then influence our understanding of literary history. First, though, we need to address a critical blind spot in one of the underlying principles of neighborliness itself. Mutual obligation presupposes mutuality, goodwill. But what if your neighbor exhibited neither? What if it were clear that your neighbor meant you harm? What if there was something about your neighbor that struck at the very nature of community, something with which you found it impossible to identify, or that called your own identity into question? What if your neighbor made you feel as though you didn't belong, that you were out of place? What if your neighbor were simply cruel? Would it be possible for you to obey the injunction, taught by the Bible and demanded by the practical necessities of communitarian life, to love that neighbor as thyself? Or would trying to obey that injunction merely compound your suffering?

As such questions suggest, there is an important distinction to be made between the ideal of neighborliness and the problematic of neighboring. Neighborliness is rooted in a Christian universalism wherein "the neighbor . . . is to be loved not for his 'own sake' but for the sake of God's unselfish love for his creatures, an unselfishness attested by Christ's gift of (his) life and death on behalf of the fallen."[17] Neighboring describes the particularity not only of the individual neighbor—his physical presence, his immediacy, his proximity—but also of the specific way(s) in which he manifests the deformative effects of having been created. From its inception, psychoanalysis has sought to understand the challenges that the problematic of neighboring poses to the ideal of neighborliness; and so it is mainly to the terms, concepts, and assumptions of psychoanalysis that I have turned in developing the methodology used here. In this I am guided by the conviction, well articulated by L. O. Aranye Fradenburg, Paul Strohm, Jeffrey Jerome Cohen, Patricia Clare Ingham, Elizabeth Scala, Sarah Kay, Sylvia Federico, Mark Miller, Erin Felicia Labbie, Britton J. Harwood, Peter W. Travis, and others, that psychoanalysis provides us with an especially useful framework for asking questions that the Middle Ages were either unwilling or unable (or perhaps just found it unnecessary) to ask about themselves.[18] In other words, I have turned to psychoanalysis because I think it can help us acquire a fuller understanding of late medieval European culture—even if it does so at the expense of some of that culture's fantasies about itself. And nowhere is this more the case than when treating the conjoined questions of the neighbor and of neighbor love, two subjects anatomized by Freud and Lacan as thoroughly as they appear to have been taken for granted by medieval theologians and the writers of conduct books.

Although the psychoanalytic understanding of the neighbor is not entirely new to the field of medieval studies—Fradenburg, for example, delves into the subject at various points in *Sacrifice Your Love*, and it makes an oblique appearance, under another name, as the "intimate stranger" of Cohen's *Of Giants*—it is still unusual enough, I think, to warrant some careful exposition.[19] The neighbor in psychoanalysis is not necessarily comparable, for example, to the biblical figure first encountered in Leviticus 19:18. Nor is it to be confused with the neighbor that Jesus, in his parable of the Good Samaritan, establishes as an ontological category: the subject as a loving, charitable neighbor to his fellow man, the subject who treats other people in what we might call a "neighborly" way.[20] The neighbor in psychoanalysis is a figure traceable instead to Freud's early experiment with cognitive science, the *Project for a Scientific Psychology*. There, in what has by now become, ironically, a well-known passage, Freud describes the process by which "a human-being learns to cognize" in relation to a figure Freud calls the *Nebenmensch* (the "next man," the "man alongside me," or, as the Standard Edition misleadingly translates it, "a fellow human-being"). "The perceptual complexes proceeding from this fellow human-being," writes Freud,

> will in part be new and non-comparable—his *features*, for instance, in the visual sphere; but other visual perceptions—e.g., those of the movements of his hands—will coincide in the subject with memories of quite similar visual impressions of his own, of his own body, [memories] which are associated with memories of movements experienced by himself. Other perceptions of the object too—if, for instance, he screams—will awaken the memory of the subject's own screaming and at the same time of his own experiences of pain. Thus the complex of the fellow human-being falls apart into two components, of which one makes an impression by its constant structure and stays together as a *thing*, while the other can be *understood* by the activity of memory—that is, can

be traced back to information from [the subject's] own body. This dissection of a perceptual complex is described as cognizing it; it involves a judgment and when this last aim has been attained it comes to an end.[21]

Drawing out the political implications of what seems, at first glance, like a speculative account of subject formation, Kenneth Reinhard notes how the divided nature of the *Nebenmensch* both enables and undercuts the fantasy of intersubjective relation on which community is founded. On the one hand, explains Reinhard, the *Nebenmensch* "represents any and every other person to whom the subject is bound in a relationship of competitive similarity, an imaginary 'equality' forced—more or less—as distributive justice in the social world by civil and moral codes." On the other hand, "The *Nebenmensch* is always *this* next person, always embodied in a particular person who fills the arbitrary place of the neighbor"; and in that respect it "materializes an uncanniness within the social relationship, an enjoyment that resists sympathetic identification and 'understanding,' linking the self and other instead in a bond of mutual aggression." The paradox of the *Nebenmensch*, continues Reinhard, is that it "embodies both sides of the reality principle." Acting "in the service of the pleasure principle," the *Nebenmensch* strives "to achieve constancy by enforcing the minimum level of restriction necessary to maintain both body and body politic." Meanwhile, "as the agent of the death drive"—the bearer of a "new and non-comparable" element that I judge to be "strange and even hostile on occasion"[22]—the *Nebenmensch* also "threatens to subvert the social order by manifesting the excluded scandal of the real that subtends it."[23] Like me and radically other than me, inhabiting the symbolic order of infinite substitutability and yet materializing the traumatic singularity of the real, the neighbor in its guise as *Nebenmensch* is simultaneously every "next person" within the community and the bearer of a strange enjoyment that makes community impossible. The *Nebenmensch*, to put the matter somewhat differently, is uncanny in the full, coincidental meaning of the term uncovered by Freud: the occupant of that precise juncture where the one sense of *heimlich*, "belonging to the house, not strange, familiar," shades into its opposite, "concealed, kept from sight, so that others do not get to know about it."[24] Familiar to me, yet possessed of a death drive "that ought to have remained secret and hidden but has come to light," the *Nebenmensch* embodies the peculiar arc by which *heimlich* "develops in the direction of ambivalence until it finally coincides with its opposite, *unheimlich*."[25]

In the first place, then, the *Nebenmensch* functions as a mediating figure through which the subject enters into the social and, beyond that, political fields. But space, defined by the proximity of the neighbor, is not the only dimension at stake in an encounter with the *Nebenmensch*. Because it involves memory, the encounter with the *Nebenmensch* also enlists the subject in a particular mode of temporality. In the Mirror Stage (as Lacan famously called it), the nascent subject anticipates a future self-mastery, first glimpsed in the coherent image of the counterpart—and attainable only through the eventual displacement of that counterpart. Imitative and aggressive, caught up in deferral, mimesis here keeps one eye on the negation of the other and one eye on the future. With the *Nebenmensch*, the nascent subject instead compares its memories of its own body with its impressions of the proximate other. Mimesis in this case takes a backwards glance, turning to the remembered past, to memory, in order to affirm subjectivity. At the same time, though, the subject isolates some *thing* in the *Nebenmensch* that disturbs memory, disrupting a narrative of selfhood based on specular identification and imitation. This thing is both new and noncomparable; it can be neither aligned with memory nor incorporated into a symbolic economy of exchange and substitution. In short, it falls out of the subject's history of becoming. As Freud would later recognize in *Beyond the Pleasure Principle*, the obstinate presence of this thing demands a radically different form of symbolization, with aims other than the mimetic and requiring no "special imitative instinct."[26] Though no less negative or concerned with mastery than in the Mirror Stage, symbolization in this case also becomes increasingly defensive and reactive: a way of protecting the imaginary comforts of memory from the real shock of the new and noncomparable.[27]

Although it would be another thirty years before Freud himself would explicitly substitute the "neighbor" of *Civilization and Its*

Discontents for the *"Nebenmensch"* of the *Project*, I follow Lacan in noting how uncannily the one figure anticipates the other in Freud's work. Indeed, Freud's description of the "next man" as "fall[ing] apart into two components," the satisfying object and the hostile object, perfectly captures the ambiguity that places the neighbor at the very center of the Western religious and philosophical traditions—and hence at the center of Freud's critique of those traditions. Located somewhere between familiarity and anonymity, between the family unit and the polis, the neighbor stands as that intimate other whose recognition we crave, and with whom we can partially identify, but who also displays a strange, potentially hostile desire—a death drive—that uncannily threatens the dream of community. There is an amorphous quality to the neighbor, a kind of liminality, that fundamentally confuses our approach to the neighbor both in theory and in practice. The neighbor is both intimate *and* strange, both proximate *and* remote, both reassuring *and* threatening; he rattles us even as he ratifies us.

But can such a figure help us to think about texts? Properly speaking, the figure I have been describing here is just that, a figure: "any and every other person" whom the subject might encounter at the point where individual bodies intersect with the body politic. But why is it, given that the place of the *Nebenmensch* is "arbitrary," filled by whoever happens to be alongside us, that its function could not be assumed by any and every other human-made *object*? Is there any reason why a material object, in particular one, like a text, that cultivates the illusion of a human voice expressing the thoughts and emotions of a particular human agent, could not present the subject with two distinct sets of "perceptual complexes," as Freud calls them: one a reassuringly familiar surface, the other a "new and non-comparable" element with which it is impossible to identify? Why should we hesitate to describe the relations between readers and texts as an ambivalent mixture of sympathetic understanding, misrecognition, and, in some cases, mutual aggression? If texts do not occupy the arbitrary place of the *Nebenmensch*, what place do they occupy?

I am not the first to raise these questions. Augustine, for example, seems to have been thinking along similar lines when he instructed his Christian readers to take the useful elements from pagan texts in the same way that the Israelites had absconded with the ill-gotten treasures of their oppressive Egyptian neighbors.[28] More recently, Paul Zumthor has noted that "our Middle Ages include a past that is both close and distant, foreign but familiar: isn't that a traditional definition of the 'neighbor,' the person whom, by turns, we exploit and love?"[29] Our relation to the past, Zumthor reminds us, is invariably a neighbor relation: one defined by conflicted gestures of identification and hostility, by an active parsing of the foreign and the familiar. And of course Zumthor, writing close to thirty years ago, may well have had in mind Lacan's groundbreaking essay "Kant avec Sade," which, as Reinhard has shown, "pursues a mode of reading . . . in which texts are not so much grouped into 'families' defined by similarity and difference, as into 'neighborhoods' determined by accidental contiguity, genealogical isolation, and ethical encounter."[30] All of these ways of thinking about the complicated relations between texts and readers, texts and texts, have done much to shape the methodology at work in these pages. But I would add to them this other observation, that a text can be a neighbor to its reader insofar as the recognizable surface of the text—the signs that make it legible as part of a particular cultural matrix—may also contain a "non-comparable" element that the reader, in his or her experience of the text, isolates as *Fremde*, as alien, hostile, and fascinating. The act of reading, like the "cognition" described by Freud, is thus construed as an ethical act, a parsing of the "good" and the "bad" that generates, as in the child's game of *fort-da* analyzed by Freud in *Beyond the Pleasure Principle*, more symbolization in response.[31]

Still, why speak of neighboring at all when some other model of affiliation—in particular, the genealogical model of textual lineage—might be more appropriate? One very good reason for questioning such lineal and successionist models of literary relation is their association with a conception of nationhood in which, as Patricia Ingham describes it, "nation figures as a relatively organic identity, a modern wholeness that can be traced genealogically back to a point of medieval origin."[32] As Ingham explains it, this way of formulating nationhood "depend[s] upon a progressive chronology, imagining the history of 'a people' as a teleological trajectory from early origins to a fully realized national present." What it elides, she argues, is the fact that "medieval community is imagined," in the Middle Ages themselves, "not through homogeneous stories of a singular 'people,' but through narratives of sovereignty as a negotiation of differences, of ethnicity, region, language, class, and gender."[33] In other words, the medieval origin in which teleological narratives of the nation claim to ground themselves is itself already fragmented by a host of competing, and indeed contradictory, narratives. But of course such fantasies of "communitarian wholeness" (as Ingham calls them) are not restricted to the nation alone. As Andrew Taylor has argued, the same logic lies behind the creation of any number of national literary canons, which in a similar fashion begin with the removal of what will later become "foundational" texts from a manuscript context that is anything but stable or determinative.[34] Indeed, one might go so far as to describe that context as a mixed community: multilingual, international, fluid, and seemingly arbitrary in its configurations. The fantasy of the stable canon, like the national fantasy of unification, continuity, and logical succession, seems intended to disavow a reality characterized instead by fragmentation, assortment, and chance proximity.

Taking this last insight as its starting point, this book aims to uncover a principle of neighboring evident, for example, in the logic of miscellaneity or in the ethnic and territorial disputes carried out through what Michelle Warren calls the practice of "border writing," but obscured through the cultivation of literary no less than national genealogies.[35] To do so, however, I will need to shift the terms of the discussion from those of (broadly) fantasy to those of (very broadly) ethics. In practice, this means that I will be less interested in exploring how different communities carry out the struggle for group identity by adapting and contesting certain narratives—in exploring, that is, how the writing and rewriting of specific stories becomes a way of writing certain groups into or out of the nation, or even of writing the nation itself into or out of existence—than in imaginatively recovering the moment of encounter between reader and text implied by literary production. As Slavoj Žižek has argued, it is never enough simply to unmask an ideological fantasy. One must penetrate to the enjoyment, to the *jouissance*, both orchestrated and masked by that fantasy.[36] Fantasy, as those familiar with the work of Fradenburg, Ingham, Cohen, and Federico well know, is what teaches us how to desire and thus, by extension, how to enjoy. Or perhaps it would be more accurate to say how *not* to enjoy. Because what fantasy mostly does is structure desire in such a way as to keep *jouissance* from putting an end to pleasure.[37] Lacan, using a formulation that I will return to several times in the course of this study, says that "what man demands, what he cannot help but demand, is to be deprived of something real."[38] Fantasy meets that demand by maintaining the fiction that we have been deprived of something in the order of the real: that someone else, some powerful figure or lost community, has absconded with *jouissance*, thereby relieving us of the distinctly unpleasurable burden of our own enjoyment. This is why, as Žižek argues so powerfully in *The Sublime Object of Ideology*, "the maxim of psychoanalytic ethics as formulated by Lacan ('not to give way on one's desire') coincides with the closing moment of the psychoanalytic process, the 'going through the fantasy': the desire with regard to which we must not 'give way' is not the desire supported by fantasy but the desire of the Other beyond fantasy. 'Not to give way on desire' implies a radical renunciation of all the richness of desires based on fantasy-scenarios."[39] The very opposite of ethical, fantasy constitutes an especially subtle way of transforming desire itself into a defense against the desire of the Other—that is, into a defense against the fact that the Other lacks, that the Other does not have *jouissance* safely in its possession. Better to fantasize that *jouissance* is lost, and so also, perhaps, recoverable, than to have to confront it directly, in oneself.[40]

The neighbor introduces an altogether different logic. Where fantasy strives to keeps us at a safe distance from *jouissance*, principally by cultivating the illusion that someone else (even a fantasy version of oneself) enjoys on our behalf, the neighbor instead brings us face to face with the very thing fantasy allows us to evade: a *jouissance* infinitely more disturbing and exciting than the paltry enjoyment one gains by participating in the rituals of sacrifice and renunciation that constitute communitarian life. Recall that, as Reinhard explains, the neighbor "embodies both sides of the reality principle," on the one hand helping the community "to achieve constancy by enforcing the minimum level of restriction necessary to maintain both body and body politic" while on the other hand serving "as the agent of the death drive"—the personification of the reality principle's cruel insistence on regulation, deferral, and sacrifice—and so threatening "to subvert the social order by manifesting the excluded scandal of the real that subtends it." To that extent, the figure of the neighbor extends the basic insight of postcolonial medievalisms not only that community is impossible, precluded from cohering by "an enjoyment that resists sympathetic identification and 'understanding,'" but that the fantasies of community remain trapped at the level of the imaginary—the economy of like and not-like—and its elaborate orchestrations of *jouissance*. Like the various and conflicting tales of King Arthur, tales that, in Ingham's words, "poignantly narrate the impossibilities, the aggressions, and the traumas, of British insularity," the neighbor is at once the building block of community and also its stumbling block, undermining the very dream of unity it inspires by pointing "to the complications of community, the disaffections and aggressions that inhabit, and threaten, union."[41] The neighbor, we might say, rounding it off to a formula, embodies the proverbial "hard kernel" of the real that one encounters once one has unmasked the ideological fantasy of the nation.[42]

That does not mean, however, that the neighbor will let us rest comfortably in the belief that antagonism defines the whole of the social order. Aggression is not the only response called forth by the neighbor relation, after all, any more than negotiation, contestation, and, in the last resort, lamentation are the only methods for dealing with that relation. On the contrary, the whole process of community formation is complicated by the imperative that, as Freud has it, "is known throughout the world and is undoubtedly older than Christianity, which puts it forward as its proudest claim": the imperative to love thy neighbor as thyself.[43] If psychoanalysis and medieval European ethical practice agree on anything, it is on the need to take that imperative seriously.

Freud himself had deep misgivings about the injunction to neighbor love. Subjecting it to a detached, almost brutal logic, "as though . . . hearing it for the first time," the founder of psychoanalysis concludes that, in essence, to be told to love thy neighbor as thyself is to be told to identify with the *thing* in the neighbor: to actively embrace the "hostile object" that the neighbor embodies.[44] Such behavior, from Freud's perspective, is in the final analysis deeply, tragically irrational because it runs so thoroughly counter to one's own self-interest—which is why, claims Freud, the twin commandments to love one's neighbor and one's enemies are, "at bottom," the same.[45] Yet what makes an already intolerable situation even worse, Freud argues, is that the aggression we would like to turn against the neighbor in response to his hostility toward us is instead turned inward, in the form of the self-punishing superego.[46] Not only, then, does the injunction to love the neighbor enjoin us to love the other as a reflection of ourselves, thereby demanding that we locate the truth of ourselves outside, in the other from whom we would just as soon flee. It also demands that we patiently tolerate, if not reward, even the hostility displayed by the neighbor toward us. In this way, the injunction to love the neighbor—a demand spoken, as it were, from the place of the superego—itself becomes hostile and aggressive, forcing us to suffer the more we try to live by it. The injunction, one might say, becomes at once the basis of civilization and the root of its discontent.

Freud is not just being uncharitable here. On the contrary, argues Lacan, "the whole Aristotelian conception of the good is alive in this man who is a true man; he tells us the most sensitive and reasonable things about what it is worth sharing the good that is our love with."[47] As Freud sees it, the injunction to love one's neighbor on the basis of nothing other than proximity is an ethical ruse, an affront to an economic model of ethics grounded on the assumption that love is a finite commodity, apportionable only to those with the most legitimate claims upon it. From Freud's perspective, all love, including neighbor love, is and ought to be narcissistic, reserved only for those in whom we find reflected an image of our own best selves: our closest relatives, our dearest friends, our heroes and mentors. To act otherwise is to violate a fundamental principle of ethics by failing to judge the good—those friends and family members legitimately deserving of our love—from the bad: those strangers who not only do not deserve our love but would, if given the opportunity, exploit us or do us harm.

Freud's wariness of the injunction to neighbor love—a wariness rooted, as Lacan points out, in an "Aristotelian conception of the good"—places him in some interesting company. Aquinas, for example, held that "the individual should love his own good more than he loves the good of his neighbor" and that, indeed, "an individual should always will a spiritual good primarily for himself and . . . should never endanger his own soul in order to secure that of his neighbor."[48] And then there are those practical-minded inhabitants of the medieval village, the ones who treated neighbor love as an economic matter subject to negotiation and adaptation. Where Freud diverges from these other parties is over the theological question of what it is we are being told to love in the act of loving one's neighbor as oneself. For medieval Christians, the imperative meant that one should strive to love one's neighbor as a means of loving the God who created that neighbor. "God," as the author of the *Speculum Christiani* so succinctly puts it, "is not louyde wyth-outen / thynne neghtbor. And thy neghtbor is not louyde wyth-outen God."[49] What makes that love possible, in fact, is not an adherence to the injunction per se but a translation of the positive commandment to love thy neighbor into a mechanism for obeying the negative commandments of the Decalogue. The *Speculum Christiani* makes this clear enough: "He that loueȝ his neghtbur, he not sleeȝ hym, ne lyeȝ to him that he loueȝ, ne couettys thynges of hym that he loueȝ, and he defouleȝ not hys wiyfe."[50] In the place of an inherently excessive and potentially inexhaustible imperative to do something without restraint, we instead get a long list of prohibitions, a guide to the many things we should not do to our neighbor in order to demonstrate our love for him and, through him, for God. Freud, taking the injunction more literally, understands it as a call to suffer, in every sense of the word, the peculiar traits that betray the effects of being a created thing, a creature subject to shaping forces largely beyond one's control. The literary critic Eric Santner makes this point when he writes that "the so-called formations of the unconscious can be understood . . . as the specific modes of expressivity of creaturely life," *creaturely life* here being a descriptive term for the "internal alien-ness" induced in us by our "overproximity to the mysterious desire of the other," an overproximity that keeps us in a constant state of becoming, of being forever subject to the forces of creation.[51] What is it, after all, to be in a position of radical subjection, creature to creator? It is to be constantly working to translate the enigmatic desire of the other "into more or less determinate demands—demands one can comply with, reject, fail at fulfilling, feel guilty about, and so on." This goes for the neighbor no less than for oneself: each of us is forced into the position of having to monitor, in a kind of infinite regression, a creatureliness in the other that is at least a reflection, and may well be a product, of our own creatureliness. Which is why, as Santner goes on to argue, it is the "never-ceasing work of symbolization and failure at symbolization, translation, and failure at translation, that constitutes the *signifying stress* at the core of creaturely life. My signifying stress is called forth—*ex-cited*—by my efforts to translate the signifying stress emanating from the other."[52]

Where before, in its medieval Christian iteration, the moral imperative to love thy neighbor as thyself served as a platform for obeying God's Ten Commandments, in its psychoanalytic version it has become a form of reading, a mode of hypervigilance in which we are constantly surveilling the neighbor, studying the neighbor to understand, or perhaps evade, our own creaturely existence. For Freud, in fact, it is an encounter with the "creaturely life" of the neighbor that establishes, and holds, the subject's being in the world. As Reinhard puts it, "Cognition emerges [for Freud] literally 'vis-à-vis' the *Nebenmensch*: some strange *Zug* (feature or trait, but equally line or stroke) in the neighbor's face both initiates and limits the comparison of its attributes with traces from earlier memories" archived in the subject's own body.[53] The power of that strange *Zug* is that it bears witness to what Santner would call, by way of Walter Benjamin, the "petrified unrest" of the neighbor's desire: to the agitation, the self-estrangement and unconscious suffering, that write themselves within one particular, and particularly striking, feature of the *Nebenmensch*.[54] What the *Zug* announces, in other words, is the presence of a *jouissance* that is in the *Nebenmensch* still more than or beyond the *Nebenmensch*: a neighbor internal to the neighbor, as it were. But insofar as we become fascinated (or disgusted, or obsessed) with the trace of the neighbor's *jouissance*, it becomes the basis of our own *jouissance*—the "nucleus," as Freud puts it, of the ego. The neighbor internal to the neighbor becomes, in turn, our own disturbingly strange and yet most intimate neighbor, the internalized remainder of an otherwise prohibited enjoyment, a "forbidden good."

What Freud's rejection of the Judeo-Christian injunction to love thy neighbor as thyself thus brings into view, according to Lacan, is that the injunction as such is not just irrational and impractical, a squandering of what ought to be reserved for our family and closest friends. The very excessiveness of the injunction, argues Lacan, forces us to take "the opening on to *jouissance*" that, as subjects bound by the pleasure principle, we otherwise seek to avoid. After all, if one is compelled to love even the "bad" neighbor *as oneself*, then one is also compelled to acknowledge that, as Reinhard puts it, "this neighbor also dwells within me; the ill will exhibited by the neighbor defines my own most intimate and disturbing *jouissance*."[55] For Lacan, our encounter with the neighbor is an ethical moment not simply because it forces us to recognize the proximate other as the site of *oneself* but because it presses us to acknowledge that the unfathomable desire in the other—the libido and aggression that we impute to the other—is in fact our own repressed desire coming back to us in ciphered form. Alenka Zupančič states the problem this way: "It is not simply the mode of enjoyment of the neighbor, of the other, that is strange to me. The heart of the problem is that I experience my own enjoyment . . . as strange and hostile."[56] If I have anything in common with my neighbor, it is that she too is estranged from her own most intimate desire, horrified by a pleasure of her own of which she herself is unaware,[57] and from which I, having judged it as corresponding with a primal affect I can no longer tolerate, would just as soon flee.

And yet, insists Lacan, recoiling from the enjoyment generated by the unbearable paradoxes of neighbor love is exactly what we should not do. In the first place, to flee from that enjoyment is invariably to demand either that the neighbor be disciplined for the strangeness of "his" *jouissance* or, in more extreme cases, that he be called upon to sacrifice his *jouissance* altogether. (In the most extreme cases of all, it is the neighbor himself who is sacrificed.) Furthermore, it is to reinforce the logic of the symbolic order by tethering *jouissance* to the transgression of the law, as if enjoyment could only be stolen by violating a commandment, as if the prohibition of *jouissance* were the only thing that ensured desire. But of course the injunction to love thy neighbor is not a commandment that could be broken. If that injunction works to support the law, it does so precisely by being an imperative, rather than a prohibition. Instead of commanding us not to do something, it enjoins us to love as our own the very *jouissance* we repudiate—a paradox so terrible that we instinctively recoil from it within the more placid confines of the symbolic order.[58] But that is not our only option. The much more radical proposition, Lacan contends, is to do what Freud does and take the imperative to love thy neighbor as thyself literally, recognizing that it cannot be exchanged for some other reading.[59] In short, it is to hear the imperative itself as something real, something immune to, and indeed disruptive of, the economy of compensation and exchange that defines the symbolic order.[60]

For Lacan, this literal understanding of the imperative to love thy neighbor as thyself is exemplified in "acts of the kind attributed to a certain Angela de Folignio, who joyfully lapped up water in which she had just washed the feet of lepers . . . or to the blessed Marie Alla-coque, who, with no less a reward in spiritual uplift, ate the excrement of a sick man."[61] To truly love the neighbor, one must do as certain female mystics would have done: make a judgment that the enjoyment in the neighbor is "bad" but still accept it, still take responsibility for it, even if it is not to one's taste.[62] Loving thy neighbor as thyself requires, ultimately, that one substitute oneself for the neighbor's *jouissance* even to the point of subjective destitution. It is to act, perhaps, as a servant of Love's servants, even though one is not a servant oneself. It is to search for tidings so that one can continue to tell the stories of lovers, even when one suffers for the effort. It is to love the *thing* in the neighbor so literally that one becomes thing-ly oneself, as "domb as any stoon."

My aim in turning to the figure of the neighbor is thus to formu-late a mode of literary history responsive to the event of reading: to the encounter with the neighboring text. This represents a historicizing practice in the sense that it ponders how the imperative to neighbor love—an imperative that the Middle Ages seem to have taken seriously as an ideal, if not always an attainable one—might have affected a medieval reader's response to the neighboring text, particularly when that reader was an engaged one like Chaucer. Would such a response entail anything more than gestures of reciprocity? What would a reciprocal gesture from a text look like, exactly? The text in question might be a neighbor in the original meaning of the term: a "near dweller," encountered in, or arriving from, a nearby place. But would that make it a good neighbor? Perhaps, then, as Reinhard has argued so forcefully, the neighboring text demands a more straightforward gesture of obligation: a willingness, on the reader's part, to take responsibility for its *jouissance*.[63] Heretofore I have treated such responsibility as an ethical practice. But it is also, as Freud implies in his account of the *Nebenmensch*, a matter of aesthetic judgment, a willingness to designate the "new and non-comparable" *thing* in the neighboring text as a precondition for taking responsibility for the *jouissance* associated with that *thing*. Such acts of critical neighbor love—that is, of loving the thing internal to the neighboring text literally, as oneself—are not limited to readers, however. The writing of texts might also be considered a form of neighboring, in both the ethical and aesthetic senses—that is, as the fulfillment of a responsibility for the *jouissance* of a text that one acknowledges as one's neighbor even when it might be regarded, in chronological terms, as the work of a precursor. Neighboring thus speaks to a different logic of textual relationality than that assumed by traditional genealogical models of literary history, a logic much closer in spirit to the miscellaneity—those seemingly random juxtapositions of spells with saints' lives, recipes with fabliaux, animal fables with penitential guides—that characterized medieval manuscript culture.

Confronting the neighboring text is always risky, because our will to critical judgment destroys the text in ways that reflect its own perceived ill will: its resistance to interpretation or systemization, its indifference to our desires, and, so often in the case of medieval literature, its intractable adherence to a worldview different from our own. We detect the strange *Zug* in the text, the illegible line or stroke impressed upon its features—upon the neighbor's features. But does the neighbor consider that *Zug* to be so strange? Who are we to isolate it, to single it out for our particular fascination? Then again, who are we to flee from it or to demand that the neighbor sacrifice it in the interests of the common good? The ethics of psychoanalysis compels us to take responsibility for what is ultimately our aesthetic judgment, our isolation of something we do not quite "like" about the neighboring text, something that disrupts our merely specular similarity, but whose obstinate presence reflects the ill will manifest in our own impulse to judge. In other words, the ethics of psychoanalysis asks us to love the neighbor as ourselves literally, to the letter, until we open ourselves to an enjoyment beyond the pleasure principle. It is my conviction that by doing so we will gain a fuller understanding, perhaps even an affective one, of late medieval culture.

II

There were many different directions this book could have taken.[64] It struck me, however, that a theory of the neighboring text seemed especially applicable to Boccaccio's *Il Filostrato*, Chaucer's *Troilus and Criseyde*, and Robert Henryson's *Testament of Cresseid*: three canonical texts of the late fourteenth and early fifteenth centuries whose relation to one another is usually figured in lineal, or at the very least associational, terms. As a matter of strict chronology, of course, the relation between these texts is undeniably lineal. And insofar as each one might be considered a translation of or response to another, their relation is certainly associational. What makes them neighboring texts is their shared concern with the matter of Troy.

Troy, as we have learned from the recent work of both Sylvia Federico and Marion Turner, signified a profound antagonism at the heart of fourteenth- and fifteenth-century English civic life, and London civic life in particular. As Federico puts it:

The Trojans were considered a noble society, but they were also considered lecherous and traitorous; their ultimate defeat was but a natural outcome of their unnatural desires. The troubling implication of this aspect of the Trojan legacy was that London, too, was full of deviant rulers whose passions would lead to the destruction of the city. . . . What Troy meant for London was split between prophesied glory of empire and doomed destruction by treason and lust. Similarly, how Troy made meaning in London was fragmented by the strategic, controlled uses of its associations, the uncontrollable excesses of these associations, and the inevitable clash these conflicting impulses produced.[65]

Such an argument cannot help calling to mind David Wallace's claim concerning the "absent city" of the *Canterbury Tales*. "There is no idea of a city for all the inhabitants of a space called London to pay allegiance to," writes Wallace; "there are only conflicts of associational, hierarchical, and antiassociational discourses acted out within and across the boundaries of a city wall or the fragments of a text called the *Canterbury Tales*."[66] As Federico describes it, however, the city in which Chaucer lived and worked was not so much absent as it was *impossible*, prevented from cohering not only by a multitude of antagonisms but by the fact that a ghost, the ghost of Troy, already occupied the symbolic place in which London hoped to emerge. Simply put, the impossibility of one city could not be thought of apart from the insistence of another. It wasn't that fourteenth-century London had arisen on the canceled ground of Troy; Troy canceled the very ground of London.

Richard II's role in what might be dubbed a culture of Trojan symptomatology provides a case in point. When issuing his proclamation for the international tournament held at Smithfield in October of 1390, for example, Richard seems to have gone out of his way to antagonize the Lords Appellant by rechristening London, in what Sheila Lindenbaum calls the king's "own chivalric language, 'le neufu troy.'"[67] Looked at one way, Richard's renaming of London can of course be seen as an important act of "genealogical" identification, since *Troy* could signify, to some ears, not only a point of mytho-historical origin but the epitome of chivalry: a noble city worthy of emulation for its honor and martial values. But Smithfield in the fourteenth century is not London proper; it is an adjacent space outside the city walls.[68] Richard's speech act, then, draws us immediately into the logic of the *Nebenmensch* by displacing any possible antagonism away from the fantasy space of transnational chivalric unification onto the city it-self, now associated, even in its typologically new state, with *Troy*, the watchword for treachery and failure. Not only, then, were any an-tagonisms internal to Smithfield stylized in the tournament's highly orchestrated militarism and contained within the enclosure of its lists. They were also displaced onto London through a formulation—*New Troy*—whose first term disavows the presence of antagonism, of ag-gression and disunity, even as its second term acknowledges it.

A similar dynamic is on display in Richard Maidstone's *Concor-dia facta inter regem Riccardum II et civitatem Londonie*. Maidstone's *Concordia*, as its title suggests, was written to celebrate—or, perhaps one ought to say, "insist upon"—the reconciliation between city and crown ostensibly brought about by Richard's royal entry into London in 1392. The poem, as Federico demonstrates at some length, tries des-perately to promote a corporate fantasy in which the once unruly and fractious city finds unity at last in its submission to the king, thereby restoring it to its proper status as "Trinovant."[69] But what the poem really ends up revealing, as Federico's analysis also suggests, is the intractable strain of antagonism within the civic symbolic order. One line in particular seems to inscribe this deadlock: "Hic licet accensus in te, Troia, parumper," which the poem's translator, A. G. Rigg, ren-ders as "Although his anger, Troy, blazed at you for a while."[70] This is surely accurate. For, indeed, Richard's anger did blaze for a while *at* Troy—that is, at London—in his sovereign suspension of the city's customary freedoms. Yet the Latin syntax also implies that Richard's anger blazed at London for a while *in* Troy, in the way his aristo-cratic fantasy of a New Troy implied the negation of the real-life city. The signifier *Troy* at this point signals the intrusion of the (Lacanian) real—the memory of Richard's aggressive desire, his sovereign gaze away from the city—not only into the structure of Maidstone's poem but into the fantasy structure of a unified corporate body it seeks to evoke. This can only draw the reader's attention to a fact that the *Con-cordia* tries desperately to evade yet everywhere reveals: "The really disruptive force in the community of London," as Pamela Nightingale puts it, "was the crown."[71] The embarrassment for Maidstone's poem all along is that Richard's literal and figurative entry into London, rather than reconciling crown and city, merely affirms Richard's status as a sovereign figure set apart from the corporate civic body. Inverting what had happened at Smithfield two years earlier, when the king had established the horizon of a transnational New Troy by excluding London, Maidstone's ideological fantasy of London as New Troy grounds itself in the radical exclusion of Richard II. Such are the poetics of antagonism.

Insofar as it articulates anything at all, then, *Troy* articulates the nagging worry that *Troynovaunt* is not so new that it can escape the internal problems associated with the Old Troy. "New Troy is supposed to be a perfected version of its point of origin," writes Turner, "but it also represents the contemporary, flawed capital. Troy and New Troy often tend to become confused in the late fourteenth-century imagination."[72] The paradox of *Troy*, at least when understood within the political discourse of London as "New Troy," is that it designates the impossibility of a complete exchange (New Troy for Old) even as it supports the translational logic of exchange itself. Yet to say that *Troy* is somehow within the political discourse of late medieval England is not to say that it is merely discursive, one signifier among many in a mobile army of signifiers. *Troy* functions, rather, as the ultimate self-canceling signifier, a signifier that immediately reveals, no matter where or how it is deployed, the production of the real through the everyday operations of the symbolic order. The usual (consoling) fantasy surrounding *jouissance* is that it is lost, prohibited, securely off limits: safely in the possession of an imaginary figure such as the notorious father of the primal horde, the Lady of courtly love, or even, as Jeffrey Cohen suggests, the Saracen other encountered, for example, in the Middle English romance *The Sultan of Babylon*.[73] And yet, as Žižek reminds us, "the trouble with *jouissance* is not that it is unattainable, that it always eludes our grasp, but, rather, that one can never get rid of it, that its stain drags along for ever—therein lies the point of Lacan's concept of surplus-enjoyment: the very renunciation of *jouissance* brings about the remainder/surplus of *jouissance*."[74] "New Troy" is supposed to be a "perfected version" of the thing it superseded, a civic body organized around the successful prohibition of all that undermined the city in whose symbolic place it stands: a Troy without Troy.

Yet the fact that Troy has not been left behind, that it continues to haunt the "New Troy" with images of lust, treachery, incest, aggression, self-destruction—that is, with all of the exciting, if also destabilizing, impulses gathered together under the sign of *jouissance*—underscores the fact that political subjects cannot get rid of *jouissance* even if they want to. This is not because *jouissance* isn't prohibited: *jouissance* is always prohibited to the extent that we cling, sometimes desperately and often at the price of our own discontent, to the fantasy that it is prohibited. But neither is it simply because our elaborate rituals of renouncing *jouissance* are themselves a source of endless, if also deeply pathetic, enjoyment. It is because the moment of lawmaking violence that creates *jouissance* is itself a transgression, an instance of cruel and excessive enjoyment that embeds *jouissance* in the very foundation of the symbolic order. What *Troy* marks, then, is not the idea of a community that might be but the impossibility of community as such—an impossibility crystallized in the excessive nature of the interdictions and injunctions meant to regulate communitarian life. The signifier *Troy* brings down the symbolic order from within, just as Troy itself was once brought down by all of the internal problems voiced by the first, uncanny term in the formulation *Troynovaunt*.

If medieval Londoners had reason to fear the pattern of self-destruction associated with the name of Troy, it was in part because medieval Trojan writings tended to draw every individual story into a larger, repetitive narrative of succession and implosion. Lee Patterson has christened this cycle of successive destruction "Thebanness," in reference to the legendary city that, long before Troy, established the template for civic ruination. One of the "two destructive patterns" that defines Thebanness, according to Patterson, is "a fatal recursiveness that undermines all progressivity upon which the ideals of secular history are based and condemns chivalric ambition, whether antique or modern, to an endless repetition."[75] By this reckoning, the medieval tradition of Trojan historiography not only enlists the writing of history in the service of what Walter Benjamin terms "natural history": the ceaseless, repetitive, invariably violent cycles in which human orders of meaning emerge and decay.[76] It also encourages us to treat literary history, by which I mean the theorization of relations among texts as they occur in and over time, as little more than a subspecies of a historical consciousness held in thrall to the logic of natural-historical succession. *Il Filostrato, Troilus and Criseyde,* and the *Testament of Cresseid,* by contrast, make up a neighborhood organized around the suffering and death of individual figures caught in the merciless grip of natural-historical cyclicality. What this means, in the first place, is that each of these texts presumes to intervene in the process of natural history by temporarily retrieving a particular story from out of an overarching narrative of cyclical, ineluctable ruin. Patterson's enormously influential analysis of secular historiography has bequeathed to medieval studies the fundamental Benjaminian principle that the repetitions inherent in natural history belie teleological and progressive accounts of human history. Yet it tends to downplay the equally crucial Benjaminian insight that natural-historical cyclicality, in its very emphasis on "natural decay, cultural ruin, and political disintegration," also holds open the possibility of redemption.[77] "The order of the profane assists, through being profane, the coming of the Messianic Kingdom," Benjamin writes in his "Theologico-Political Fragment." "The profane, therefore, although not itself a category of this Kingdom, is a decisive category of its quietest approach. . . . For nature is Messianic by reason of its total and eternal passing away."[78] Although they do so (as we shall see) to varying degrees and radically different ends, *Il Filostrato, Troilus and Criseyde,* and the *Testament of Cresseid* at least tarry with this idea that a redemptive interruption of linear history is made possible by the processes of natural-historical decay.

Another way of putting this would be to say that the neighborhood of texts isolated by the present study is constituted in part by a shared (if not always complementary) ambivalence about a model of historiography "which foregrounds the idea of burial" only so that its practitioners might distance themselves from the unquiet dead.[79] This "necrological" model of historiography, as Carla Freccero has labeled it, "aims at calming the dead who still haunt the present, and at offering them scriptural tombs" in exchange for their continued silence.[80] By contrast, the three texts studied in these pages remind us that sometimes, to paraphrase Freccero, the dead are not so much buried as buried alive, and that they might yet return, at the most untimely moments, to haunt us.[81] This may make it sound as though these texts have more to do with ghosts than with neighbors. If I have turned to the trope of the neighbor, it is largely because the neighbor keeps us grounded in the material world and its history, forever pulling us back into the real of lived experience. By this I do not mean just that there is an immediacy to the neighbor, a physical proximity that makes the neighbor impossible to ignore. I also mean that the neighbor forces us to confront the problematic fact of the real, the fact that there is some Thing about the neighbor with which we cannot identify but that we are nevertheless compelled to love as ourselves. In my view, the contemporary discourse of hauntology remains too caught up in gestures of affinity and identification, as if, by conjuring precursors from the past, we might be able to secure an identity in the present. The neighbor challenges that paradigm by being haunted by something that not only makes him a stranger to himself but also eludes our own attempts at identification. The neighbor is a vehicle for the ghost that dispossesses both of us.

Extended to the neighboring text, this idea of a haunted neighbor becomes tied to the idea of failed succession: to the ways in which the transmission of texts follows a discontinuous pattern, to the ways in which temporal succession leaves behind what Santner calls "deposits of suffering," deposits that are then encrypted in the textual artifacts that survive the demise of the historical form of life that once lent them coherence.[82] Those deposits of suffering, I want to argue, constitute a neighbor internal to the neighboring text, a neighbor that then disrupts the idea of a textual succession rooted in genealogy. This is especially so where the three texts in this study are concerned. For each one is structured around either the reanimation or the burial of characters that are, from the point of view of each text in the sequence, disturbingly present (or, better, overproximate) because of their radical absence from the place where they ought to be lacking. Yet by the very efforts of those texts to represent the death or burial of a particular character, each one ends up incorporating that character (in much the same way that "New Troy" incorporates *Troy*). In this way, then, each text in the series becomes a kind of tomb, albeit one containing a restless, displaced spirit. And in that, they end up entombing the form of literary history that I hope to conjure in these pages.

To aid us in visualizing the conception of literary history outlined here, I want to turn to a striking image from Lacan's *Ethics* seminar: the image of Jacques Prévert's collection of matchboxes. "It was the kind of collection that it was easy to afford at that time," recalls Lacan, "that time" being the era of Pétain (or, as Lacan so delicately puts it, "the time of 'Work, Family, Homeland,' and of belt-tightening"). He then goes on:

> It was perhaps the only kind of collection possible. Only the match boxes appeared as follows: they were all the same and were laid out in an extremely agreeable way that involved each one being so close to the one next to it that the little drawer was slightly displaced. As a result, they were all threaded together so as to form a continuous ribbon that ran along the mantelpiece, climbed the wall, extended to the molding, and climbed down again next to a door. I don't say that it went on to infinity, but it was extremely satisfying from an ornamental point of view.[83]

Although produced by Lacan as an example of "one of the most innocent forms of sublimation," this image of a chain of matchboxes linked by the sequential drawing of emptiness into an interior can also serve as a model for the sort of intertextuality—for the sort of literary history— I am trying to describe here. For consider: the ribbon of matchboxes can only advance, as it were, by the second matchbox pulling away from the first at the same time that it takes the other's drawer, now empty, into its own interior. Each matchbox in the chain is like a little tomb interring the emptiness of the one beside it. By the same process, though, the second matchbox's own drawer is displaced—an interior now turned exterior, an intimate space now made into something eccentric and excessive, held in suspension until it might become the empty, displaced interior of another matchbox.

In the first place, then, the matchboxes serve as an image of literary history as a segmented diachronic chain, with each individual unit in the chain possessed, as it were, by the emptiness it carries over from the unit that precedes it. Yet the little anecdote of the matchboxes might serve as a model for literary history in another way as well. Lacan makes it clear that Prévert's collection of matchboxes is determined by specific historical, material conditions. It is the only collection Prévert could afford, given the deprivations of the Pétain era. To that extent, the collection is embedded in lived history. At the same time, though, there is something completely random and eccentric about the collection. Why matchboxes, after all? The choice of object bespeaks the secret of Prévert's desire; it is something private, unknown perhaps even to the collector himself, yet on public display. The matchboxes hold no great cultural value in and of themselves. Rather, they are elevated to the position of the Thing—to the position of the absent cause of desire—by Prévert's act. It is Prévert, in other words, who blasts the matchboxes out of the "continuum of history,"[84] thus conferring upon them the dignity of the prehistoric Thing. But more than that, the act reflects an intuitive understanding of the deposit of suffering hidden and preserved within the object: of the fact that things can be profoundly Thing-ly. Lacan notes that the time in which Prévert assembled his collection was a time of "penitence" for France. It was a time, in other words, both of suffering and of the sorrowful recognition, by some at least, of France's complicity in that suffering. The collection of matchboxes is an oblique expression of suffering, shared and private, that designates the Thing within the situation. And Lacan, recognizing this fact many years later, acknowledges that Thing as his own. He sees in Prévert's expression of suffering— his understanding of the petrified unrest of the matchboxes as mute witnesses to natural-historical suffering—his own *extimate* truth.

I use the term *extimate*, coined by Lacan to describe that which is at once intimate and exterior to the human subject (a situation nicely summed up by Lacan's own characterization of *das Ding* as "something strange to me, although it is at the heart of me"),[85] to suggest how Prévert's collection of matchboxes exteriorized something intimate to Lacan that was nonetheless strange to him, just as it sublimated (or sublimed) that which was both intimate and strange to the collector himself. But I also use the term to evoke the contemplation involved in an encounter with the neighboring text, the way in which Prévert's matchbox collection makes evident, in an "extremely satisfying" manner, an eccentric and particular desire that one might otherwise not be able to comprehend. This is because the Thing as suffering—the Thing as *jouissance*, as the unsymbolized leftover or strange *Zug* detectable in the neighbor's features—is fundamentally on the side of death drive. In other words, the text as neighbor brings us into contact with the death we cannot otherwise contemplate, or that we can contemplate only through our encounter with the neighbor's own self-estrangement: the second death of utter eradication, beyond symbolization. And so to argue that an approach to the text as neighbor brings us into contact with the Thing is necessarily to make a corollary argument: namely, that the transformation of reading into an act of neighbor love enters us into the peculiar "space" of the Thing, the "space between two deaths."

That space, understood in the limited sense that Žižek has given it—as the troubled zone between physical death and some form of symbolic death, be it banishment or entombment, vilification or lamentation, the satisfaction or denial of last rites—has seen a recent influx of figures from the realms of medieval literature and culture. Lancelot, Tristan, Cligès, Richard II:[86] all have been said to inhabit the space between two deaths, taking up residence there beside such "original" occupants as Antigone and the ghost of Hamlet's father.[87] Perhaps the most relevant of these examples, at least for the purposes of the present study, is that of Richard II. Richard, as Paul Strohm has argued, can be said to have inhabited the space between two deaths for the thirteen years when his body, denied its rightful burial in Westminster, "lay out of place . . . at Langley abbey." "Richard's displaced burial . . . ," writes Strohm, "presented his foes and friends with a special crisis and opportunity. For, ominously or auspiciously, depending on one's loyalties and wishes, failure to secure his aura within an ordered succession prolonged its availability as a source of unease or a locus for desire. . . . Well might a Lancastrian, besieged by apparitions and rumors, hope to close the troubled space of their origin by returning Richard to his proper grave."[88] In Richard's displacement and reburial, I suggest, we find a particularly useful model for reinterpreting Chaucer's and Henryson's self-styled tragedies. For much like the Lancastrians, both writers found it necessary to return displaced figures, exiles from a prior—and, it seems, unsettled—order of meaning, to what were assumed to be their "proper graves." Very broadly, in other words, Chaucer's *Troilus* and Henryson's *Testament* might be understood as acts of symbolic interment—a settling of accounts—driven by ideological interests.

That, however, is about all that those two poems have in common with the political strategies of the Lancastrians. For very much unlike the Lancastrians, whose sole objective seems to have been to bury Richard as quickly, and as publicly, as possible, both Chaucer and Henryson (and, to a lesser degree, Boccaccio) show a keen interest in exploring what happens when a figure is left suspended in the "troubled" space between two deaths. Both, that is, seize upon their encounters with the neighboring text as an opportunity to tarry awhile with the Thing. In Chaucer's case, that meant thinking in more complicated terms about the relation of the historically minded (and situated) poet to the Other, and indeed about the fantasy of the Other itself. The necrological cultivation of the Other practiced, for example, by the Lancastrian propagandists is meant to serve exactly that fantasy. But could there be another model? And, if so, could it be sustained? These are among the more pressing questions taken up by Chaucer after his encounter with the neighboring text. For Henryson, meanwhile, the encounter with the neighboring text offered the chance to foreground the political dimension of neighboring and its connection to literary influence. Other fifteenth-century poets, as if trying to evade the burden of their own *jouissance*, helped to construct the idea of a father Chaucer. Henryson, by contrast, treats Chaucer not as an inimitable father figure keeping *jouissance* safely off limits but as a neighbor whose proximity makes it impossible either to evade *jouissance* or ignore its effects. The space between two deaths, as Henryson seems to recognize all too clearly, is a political space in the fullest sense of the term: a space in which one must come to grips with the Thing that makes community with the neighbor impossible.

Of course, just because a significant number of medieval figures can now be found inhabiting the space between two deaths does not mean that we should locate them there, or even that we should acknowledge the space itself. Lee Patterson, for example, has been outright dismissive of the whole idea, arguing that the very concept of a space between two deaths is "vapid" and therefore, one gathers, unworthy of use as such.[89] Obviously, I do not agree with this assessment in its entirety. All the same, Patterson raises a valid concern: if the concept of a space between two deaths amounted to no more than the observation that the time between death and interment can be an unsettled one, or that an unburied body is a distressing sight, or that it is awful to think of someone being thrown into exile, never to be heard from again, than it would indeed hold little critical value. This is why I intend to stress the aspect of the "second death" that Lacan derives mainly from the writings of the Marquis de Sade: the death, not of the body, but of the natural-historical cycle of emergence and decay from which the body between two deaths has been liberated. Again, it matters little whether the body in question happens to have undergone physical or symbolic death. The point is that these figures, because they refuse to go away, because they persist in pushing their various demands, threaten to undo the symbolic structure through which we comprehend not only life and death but also inclusion and exclusion, present and past, good and bad—the comprehensive structure, as Strohm terms it, of "ordered succession." Dead and yet uncannily present, these figures call on us to recognize the traumatic insufficiency or failure of the symbolic order; and in doing so, they rise to the position of the Thing as that which manifests the symbolic order's internal limit: the point at which, as in the *Nebenmensch*, the "satisfying object" of imaginary cohesion gives way to the "hostile object" of dissolution and annihilation. Having been violently extracted from the cycle of decomposition and regeneration, these bodies acquire, in turn, the power to disrupt the workings of the cycle itself. The second death, as Lacan puts it, is "death insofar as it is regarded as the point at which the very cycles of the transformations of nature are annihilated."[90]

On the one hand, this specter of annihilation is profoundly social and historical. Žižek, for example, suggests that "the empty place of the Thing"—a place that I shall describe variously in the following chapters as the future, the death drive, the neighbor's desire, the desire in the Other, the space between two deaths—is opened up by what he calls the process of "symbolization/historicization."[91] "The process of historicization implies an empty place," writes Žižek, "a non-historical kernel around which the symbolic network is articulated."[92] I take this to mean that our ongoing attempts to symbolize our experience as historically situated subjects inevitably run up against their own internal limits, their own points of failure. In short, it is our own processes of sense making that eventually isolate the Thing: that mute, immobile, nonhistorical kernel that not only remains immune to symbolization but insists on symbolization's failure. In this way, then, our collective impulse to historicization becomes central to our peculiar experience, as subjects, of the traumatic Thing. The cases of both Chaucer and Henryson, each of whom here apprehends the Thing through his encounter with a neighboring text in which the principal characters—Troilus, Cresseid—are subject to the process of historicization, provide two striking examples of this dynamic.

At the same time, however, the idea of a space between two deaths impinges directly upon the individual subject. "It is in the signifier and insofar as the subject articulates a signifying chain that he comes up against the fact that he may disappear from the chain of what he is," says Lacan.[93] This seems to imply two things. On the one hand, it seems to suggest that, because the subject is implicated in the signifying chain, the eradication of that chain—the annihilation of the symbolic order—implies the subject's own oblivion. The subject might disappear from the cycles of history—the cycles that are history—along with the symbolic order itself, which is nothing but those cycles, that chain. Just as disturbing, however, is the possibility that the dead are always on the verge of dying again: that the dead might be forgotten completely, that they might simply vanish, whether individually or collectively, from the accounting book of history. To be between two deaths is thus always to be facing the prospect of one's utter obliteration.

But perhaps it is best in this case not to draw too fine a distinction between history and the subject. For what the idea of a space between two deaths ultimately touches upon is the prospect that the signifying chain—the very logic of the symbolic order—might simply grind to a halt. Even more gnomically than usual, Lacan suggests that the space between two deaths "is the point where the false metaphors of being can be distinguished from the position of Being itself," which I take to mean that the space between two deaths is the space where a body might die forever, never having to undergo the second death, and so not come to be lacking.[94] The space between two deaths, the suspended lag before the arrival of one's second death, is the space in which the economy of lack that drives the symbolic order collapses, the space in which there is no lack and thus no being for the subject. Whereas the imposition of the symbolic order designates the Thing as that which lacks, the space between two deaths is the "empty" space of the Thing because it is the space where the Thing is found to be missing, like the mislaid Richard II, from the place where it ought to be lacking. In short, it is the space where both the symbolic order and the subject implicated by that order confront their limit and, in a very real sense, stop being.

For this reason, though I intend to follow Strohm (following Žižek) in stressing the ideological dimension of the space between two deaths, I also think it important to foreground the concept's subjective dimension: the fact that, at the risk of sounding mawkish, there is a Hamlet for every ghost, a subject who feels called upon to balance the Other's symbolic accounts. Although *Troilus and Criseyde* and the *Testament of Cresseid* seem to have been composed as something like acts of public service, with specific audiences of "loveres" or "worthie wemen" in mind, we should recall that the narrators of both texts, like their counterpart in *Il Filostrato*, present themselves as solitary, even isolated figures. The narrator of the *Troilus* speaks of his "unliklynesse," his difference from his own implied audience of lovers (1.16), while the narrator of the *Testament* describes himself as being alone, first in his chapel, then his room.[95] The narrator of *Il Filostrato*, meanwhile, turns his eyes away from the public places where he used to see his beloved, his heart reciting "to itself that unhappy verse of Jeremiah: 'Oh how solitary abides the city which before was full of people and a mistress of nations!'"[96] As much, then, as they are caught up, to varying degrees, in ideological maintenance, all three texts contain representations or reminders of the contingent encounters that led to their existence as texts. However much they might be implicated in the workings of a larger order, there remains something terribly lonely about each of the narrators that we will encounter here. Each one of them makes a judgment, an ethical gesture that is ultimately singular, contingent and, in one case, failed. And it is the results of those gestures, now open before us as neighboring texts, that we, as readers, are called upon to judge in turn.

MY OWN ACT OF JUDGMENT IS FAIRLY STRAIGHTFORWARD, though my argument follows something other than the obvious chronological order. In chapter 1, I take up the trope of the *Nebenmensch* to explore how the different treatments accorded Troilus and Cresseid in Henryson's *Testament*—resurrection for the one, entombment for the other—continue, at the level of mytho-history, the antagonistic neighbor relations between Scotland and England in the late Middle Ages. My reasons for starting with a chapter on Henryson (where one on Boccaccio would be more logical) are at once pragmatic and, in the broadest sense, theoretical. As a practical matter, placing a chapter on the *Testament* first allows me to concretize the central trope of this study, firmly tying literary neighbor relations to the social and political realities of the late Middle Ages. At the same time, by making use of the psychoanalytic principle of deferred action (which holds that the order of cause and effect is inverted, with cause emerging only secondarily, through the interpretation of its effects), the chapter foregrounds how Chaucer's *Troilus and Criseyde* is completed only after the fact, once Henryson's *Testament* has assumed responsibility for the *jouissance* from which Chaucer's poem ultimately recoils.[97] The full meaning of Chaucer's *Troilus* cannot be known, in other words, until Henryson embraces it—and, in the act of embracing it, partially destroys it—as a neighboring text. One of my aims in adopting this nonsequential chapter order is to replicate, in the structure of my own book, the disordered temporality of neighboring. That disordered temporality is at the center of chapter 2, where I ask what it means—for Chaucer, for literary history—that the narrator of *Il Filostrato* breaks with the examples set by his counterparts in Benoît de Sainte-Maure's *Roman de Troie* and Guido delle Colonne's *Historia Destructionis Troiae* and leaves Troilo, the figure whose death, in forecasting the fall of

Troy, guaranteed the eventual rise of England, unburied, suspended between two deaths. Finally, chapter 3 reads Chaucer's *Troilus and Criseyde* as a work both about the maddening paradoxes generated by the inherently excessive imperative to love thy neighbor as thyself and about the strategies, such as courtly love, that we employ to avoid having to confront the structural impasse that those paradoxes bring to light. Ultimately recoiling from the enjoyment crystallized in the imperative to neighbor love, Chaucer's poem (or, to be more accurate, its narrator) retreats into the logic of temporal succession enshrined by the medieval English chronicle tradition—but not before it has exposed the tragic cost of maintaining fidelity to an Other that does not exist. Linking the chapters together, meanwhile, is an ongoing concern not only with the problematic of neighboring itself—a problematic that encompasses identification, aggression, love, charity, and the possibility of a community organized around something other than sacrifice and exchange—but with how that problematic might help us grapple with the issues of spatiality, intertextuality, and temporality that both define and confuse the category of literary history.

CHAPTER I

Henryson's Doubt

Neighbors and Negation in the *Testament of Cresseid*

Robert Henryson's *Testament of Cresseid* is usually said to stand in a lineal or associational relation to Chaucer's *Troilus and Criseyde*. If Henryson's poem is not figured simply as a descendant of Chaucer's poem, then it is figured as a continuation, an imitation, a sequel, a dependent, a pretender, a worthy successor, a close companion, a rebellious offspring.[1] Even Gayle Margherita's "Criseyde's Remains," about as daring and original a reading of the *Testament* as one is likely to encounter, persists in defining the relationship of Henryson's work to Chaucer's as "filial."[2]

This chapter takes a somewhat different approach. Here I argue that the relation between the *Testament of Cresseid* and *Troilus and Criseyde* is best understood not in the passive terms of lineage and inheritance but in the more dynamic terms of neighboring. No one would deny that the two texts share a profound connection; Henryson, after all, could never have written the *Testament* if not for the prior existence of Chaucer's *Troilus*. But it does not necessarily follow from this obvious point that the texts are then bound to one another by a literary version of consanguinity. The language of the *Testament*, in fact, pushes us to understand its relation to *Troilus and Criseyde* less as lineal than as spatial and temporal—a relation of contiguity, contingency, chance proximity—and to read the *Testament* itself as a product not of family ties but of an ethical encounter. Specifically, it pushes us to read Henryson's poem as an encounter with *jouissance*, in two respects: as a poem that tries to take responsibility for the *jouissance* of its neighboring text and as a poem that, in assuming such responsibility, forces its reader to confront the *jouissance* at work in the paradoxes of neighbor love.

That is not quite so theoretical as it may sound. On the contrary, one distinct advantage of approaching the *Testament* and the *Troilus* as neighboring texts is that it underscores how literary neighbor relations can, in some instances, extend the part played by neighbor relations in the making and unmaking of specific communities, nations, and regions. As an especially complex example of what Michelle Warren calls "border writing," Henryson's *Testament* lays out the peculiar difficulties posed to the inhabitants of contested territories by the injunction to love one's neighbor as oneself. That injunction is challenging enough when one's neighbor is an ally. But what about when that neighbor is an enemy? Part of my argument here is that the *Testament of Cresseid*, as a product of the contentious neighbor relations between Scotland and England in the late Middle Ages, cannot help but confront the aggression inherent in the imperative to neighbor love. It is not just that the physical neighbors involved in this case are being aggressive; it is that such aggression is then compounded by the unreasonable call to love those same aggressive neighbors as oneself. That double aggression, and the suffering that follows in its wake, are reflected, I argue, in the *Testament's* treatment of Cresseid. Part of what the poem underscores in its twisted vision of Cresseid's fate (she is repudiated by Diomede, is sent into a kind of exile, is given leprosy by the gods, and then dies) is the impossibility of escaping *jouissance*. Our fantasy of *jouissance* is that it is safely prohibited, at once appropriated and preserved by the Father. But the *Testament* tells a different story. In Henryson's poem, no father figure—not Cresseid's father, Calchas; not father Chaucer; not the narrator—can protect the subject from the burden of *jouissance*. On the contrary, the poem repeatedly insists that we are forced, in our relations with the neighbor, to confront *jouissance* directly. And so that is what the *Testament* attempts to do: come to grips with the *jouissance* we encounter, not only in the physical neighbor, but in the injunction to love thy neighbor as thyself.

As Henryson's poem also makes clear, however, any attempt at coming to grips with the *jouissance* of the neighbor relation may easily spill over into the very aggression that the laws we install to govern that relation are meant to regulate. This comes across most obviously in the poem's characterization of Troilus. Among the more unusual twists in Henryson's *Testament* is the sudden reappearance, following his death at the end of *Troilus and Criseyde*, of Troilus, alive and well and riding with his garrison back to Troy. That setting is itself a powerful figure for neighboring, as it locates the culminating actions of the poem neither within the walls of Troy nor in the Greek camp, but in the shadowy borderland between the two. Far more significant, however, is the fact that the *Testament* brings Troilus, a figure whose death would foretell not only the demise of Troy but also, following the logic of *translatio imperii*, the eventual rise of England in Troy's symbolic place, back to literary life. It is by means of that reanimation, I argue, that the *Testament* manages to express, opaquely and perhaps unconsciously, all of the antagonism that seems to have defined the neighbor relations (or lack thereof) between England and Scotland in the later Middle Ages. For in suspending the death of Troilus, the *Testament of Cresseid* also manages to suspend, if only for an instant, and only at the level of metaphor, the emergence of Scotland's geographical and political neighbor to the south. Reanimating Troilus, the Scottish *Testament* disrupts the genealogical claims of a chronicle tradition that sought to trace the origins of England—and, ultimately, the conquest and absorption of Scotland—back to Troy.

But that is not the only way in which the *Testament* calls the future, the future that is Henryson's fifteenth-century present, into question. Ultimately, it is the treatment accorded Cresseid—the judgment passed upon her by the planetary gods, her subsequent entombment—that throws "a kind of temporal bomb" into the teleological historicism of the English chronicle tradition by encrypting the incomprehensible letter of the law, its cruel intractability, within the language of the *Testament* itself.[3] In other instances, the Scots pursued their aggressions against the English not only through violent conflict but also, as Katherine Terrell has argued, by appropriating and rewriting English narratives of history.[4] The *Testament* adopts a somewhat different strategy. In addition to entering into a struggle over narrative, Henryson's poem forces us to confront a *jouissance* that cannot be dispelled through narrativization. The fantasy of the English chronicle tradition, Terrell argues, is that political succession, like temporal succession, is inevitable: that time both marches on and, as it were, over Scottish claims to independence. Henryson's *Testament* instead forces us to tarry at the site of Cresseid's tomb, to linger awhile over its harsh inscription, to sense the materiality of its stone. In the process, the poem also invites us to experience the incomprehensible enjoyment of the law to the same degree as those subjects called upon to love an aggressive neighbor as themselves.

We can begin by looking at one of the odder moments in a poem defined, in some ways, by its odd moments. Hoping "to cut the winter nicht and mak it schort" [cut the winter night and make it short], the narrator of the *Testament* has just finished reading "ane quair" that we know, from his description, to be book 5 of *Troilus and Criseyde*. Still feeling somewhat restless, however, he takes up "ane vther quair" [another book] in order to "brek [his] sleip" [break his sleep]; and there he discovers a part of the story that Chaucer left out: "the fatall destenie / Of fair Cresseid, that endit wretchitlie" [the fatal destiny of fair Cresseid, who ended wretchedly].[5] Although the vaguely enigmatic nature of this scene is itself intriguing (why does the narrator want to break his sleep?), my immediate interest lies in the status of this "vther quair." To begin with, it is, as the narrator says, other: a text whose relationship to *Troilus and Criseyde* is one of proximate difference, of contiguity. Its very appearance seems almost magical: there, alongside "worthie" Chaucer's text, its equal and counterpart, sharing its principal characters and appropriating its verse form— yet still different in nearly every way (41). One has to be careful, of course, not to take the narrator entirely at his word. The whole thing is a put-on, an inside joke: the "vther quair" is in fact Henryson's own *quair*, his own text, written nearly a century after *Troilus and Criseyde* and in full awareness of its influence. Naturally, then, we want to attune ourselves to its anxieties, to the resistances and deceptions characteristic of the belated text. But we do not want to miss what the narrator is telling us, either. *Troilus and Criseyde* may precede his "vther quair," but it is not that text's precursor in any straightforward sense of the term. Instead, the *Troilus* precedes the *Testament* as the other always does, in logical time, already occupying the dialectical space where the *Testament* comes into being. *Troilus and Criseyde* does not give birth to the *Testament;* their relationship is not, as I have already suggested, filial. The *Troilus*, rather, neighbors on the *Testament*, occupying not only a contiguous physical position on the narrator's shelf but, more important, the same imaginative locus, the same place—call it the place where something happens to Troilus and Criseyde/Cresseid—in literary history. Likewise, the *Testament* is not, as is sometimes supposed, a mere continuation of *Troilus and Criseyde*, or a supplement to it. Neither is it a simple alternative to Chaucer's poem, as if we were being invited to choose which version of the story we might, as readers, prefer. It is an instance of defensive rewriting: a negation of that which occupies the place where it too emerges. By designating the *Testament* "ane vther quair," then, its narrator signals his knowledge that his text stands, not in any simple genealogical relation to *Troilus and Criseyde*, but in an ethical relation to it: a relation in which the one takes up the *jouissance* of the other. The two poems form part of a neighborhood, not a family.

This is a view substantiated, rather than undermined, by the two most obvious objections to it. The first is that fifteenth-century English and Scottish poets inevitably looked to Chaucer as their father or master. To be sure, a number of fifteenth-century poets, including Hoccleve, Lydgate, James I, and, in the early sixteenth century, Dunbar and Douglas, do pay homage to Chaucer as "maister deere / and fadir reuerent," "my maister Chauser," "venerabill Chauser," "O reverend Chaucere," and so forth.[6] But the same cannot accurately be said of Henryson, who never refers to Chaucer outside of the *Testament*—that is, never in a work not written in direct response to Chaucer's own— and then, as I have already noted, only as "worthie Chaucer glorious." I say "only" here not to suggest that *worthie* and *glorious* are not meant respectfully, since obviously they are. But neither do they imply the same sort of vertical relationship, filial or apprentice, as *fadir* and *maister.* Rather, they suggest an attitude of respectful recognition that, while mindful of Chaucer's reputation, stops well short of submission: a relative position, so to speak, of thirty, rather than ninety, degrees.[7] Chaucer was a figure—a text, a name, a memory—that Henryson's own poem had to acknowledge, had to *go through.* But this is not the same thing as claiming Chaucer's tutelage, let alone his paternity. The *Troilus* is not where the *Testament comes from.*

Instead, Henryson's poem turns Chaucer into a neighbor. To appreciate what makes this move so unusual—and also, I would argue, such an astute response to Chaucer's *Troilus*—it is first necessary to consider why Henryson's (rough) contemporaries would want to invent a "father Chaucer" in the first place. Seth Lerer has argued that "Chaucer—as author, as 'laureate,' and as 'father' of English poetry—is a construction of his later fifteenth-century scribes, readers, and poetic imitators," who developed the idea mainly in response to contemporary issues of governance and patronage.[8] Caught up as they were in developing post-Ricardian modes of power, Chaucer's followers needed an authority figure that would strengthen their own claims to authority or preferment while at the same time bolstering the prestige of their patrons. Unfortunately, the notoriously inept, marginalized, and self-deprecating Chaucerian persona presents no such figure. Faced with that dilemma, Chaucer's self-styled inheritors invented the fantasy of an exceptional father Chaucer that would make up for the shortcomings of the Chaucerian persona they encountered on the page. Here we should recall the fundamental psychoanalytic insight concerning the myth of the primal father. In Freud's myth, the primal sons rise up and kill their father so that they, too, can have access to the *jouissance,* manifest as unrestrained sexual enjoyment and tyrannical power, that the primal father had been reserving for himself. The cruel joke here, however, is that the sons, by killing the father, fail to gain access to the enjoyment they crave. Instead, fearing that one among them might try to assume the place of the now-dead father, they make a pact among themselves to establish orderly access to women and to power—a political act that, ironically, only makes it impossible for the sons to gain the illicit enjoyment they initially craved. But the other side of the primal father's murder is that it also installs the fantasy of the master or sovereign—the fantasy that there exists an exception to the rule of castration. This, I think, is ultimately what the poets of the fifteenth century were after in promoting the idea of father Chaucer: they made him inimitable, an exception, in order to retain the position of master that any of them, or any of us for that matter, might come to occupy. On the face of it, this sounds egalitarian. In practice, though, it merely serves a political structure organized around the sovereign by strengthening the fantasy that the cohesion of the community is grounded in an exception.

Henryson sees that fantasy for what it is: a way for Chaucer's imitators to disavow their own *jouissance*, manifest both as the formalized aggression of eulogy and as the attenuated enjoyment of bureaucratic language, by attributing it to a Chaucer who, like the murdered primal father, is more powerful dead and exceptional than alive and inadequate. For such writers, father Chaucer is a defense against having to assume the burden of the *jouissance* that the Chaucerian text otherwise forces them to confront. Henryson, meanwhile, perceives that Chaucer's own refusal of authority already dismantles the position of exceptional master that authorizes his would-be inheritors. Chaucer has not absconded with the *jouissance* reserved for the primal father. On the contrary, he retreats from it. And yet that retreat, that refusal of authority, is its own form of aggressive *jouissance*, since it means that the Chaucerian text goes out of its way to offer neither immunity from, nor a defense against, enjoyment. Henryson, alone among his fifteenth-century contemporaries, serves that *jouissance*—the *jouissance* of the neighboring text—by loving it, so to speak, as himself: an eruption of his own aggression.

The second obvious objection to reading the *Troilus* and the *Testament* in terms of neighborhood is that, for several centuries following its "unattributed inclusion" in Thynne's 1532 edition of Chaucer's works, the *Testament* was regarded not as a separate poem by Robert Henryson but as the conclusion to *Troilus and Criseyde*—its unacknowledged, yet logically "necessary," sixth book.[9] But Thynne's positioning of the *Testament* with the *Troilus*, far from establishing any simple genealogical relation between them, manifests, in a particularly graphic way, their inherently dialectical neighbor status. For if, on the one hand, Chaucer was regarded as the de facto author of both works, on the other hand it was Henryson's version of the story's conclusion, and its depiction of Cresseid as a leper, in particular, that would prove to be more influential in the following centuries. Chaucer as "auctor," as name, may have ended up overwriting, and thereby legitimizing, Henryson; but it was Henryson's *Testament* that managed to overwrite, assume the place of, the last book in Chaucer's text. In this odd way, then, the two poems, ranged alongside one another in an enormously influential edition of "Chaucer's" works, achieved a kind of interdependent equipoise—but only through an act of reciprocal negation.

"Neighboring" in this case might thus be said to extend a form of intertextuality peculiar to the fifteenth century: one in which a Scottish text depends upon a Chaucerian text for the completion of its meaning, but that in doing so presumes to complete the meanings of the Chaucerian text. Such texts "are 'inscribed,'" as L. O. Aranye Fradenburg puts it, "with a consciousness of their relations to other texts; they frequently take, as a subject of their discourse, the nature of literary revisionism."[10] Freely adopting a term from the work of Levinas, we might say that such texts are "obsessed": preoccupied both with and by the other.[11] Yet if Henryson serves as any indication, it would appear that, for fifteenth-century Scottish writers, literary revisionism constitutes more than just a simple act of rewriting, of "correcting" the other text; it constitutes an act of self-ratification, a movement of recognition and appropriation that enables being. And not just any being, mind you, but an explicitly national being, one grounded in "a richly complicated process of historical revisionism" in which, as Fradenburg goes on to argue, "Chaucer's text authorizes, and helps to articulate, the dream of a sophisticated vernacular poetry in 'Scottis.'"[12] Partly, then, through the *Testament*'s "inscribed consciousness" of *Troilus and Criseyde*, and partly through Thynne's editorial intervention, Henryson's text and Chaucer's became tied to one another, dependent upon one another, at least in the eyes of subsequent readers, for their completion. Yet it is precisely in the imposed nature of that interrelatedness—the fact that the two texts' coincidence is manufactured and not organic—that we discover their connection to be one of neighborhood rather than family, ethical encounter rather than blood ties.

One sees this even in something so apparently innocuous as the *Testament*'s depiction of the weather. Consider the poem's "overtly Caledonian setting."[13] "As in much late-medieval Scottish poetry," observes A. C. Spearing, "the real weather intrudes in opposition to the weather of literary conventions that had their origin around the Mediterranean, in such a way that the Scottish climate too becomes one convention played against others."[14] Opposition, intrusion, playing against: from its opening stanzas, the *Testament* generates a powerful sense not simply of differentiation but of inversion, as if it were appropriating the tropes of its neighboring text, Chaucer's *Troilus and Criseyde*, only in order to turn them back upon that text. Walter Scheps, in what he calls a "climatological reading" of Henryson's poem, is more detailed still. "Henryson's season," he writes, "is 'Aries, in middis of the Lent' (5), a reference which recalls from the most famous passage in Middle English Chaucer's 'Ram' which has 'his halve cours yronne'; however, instead of 'shoures soote,' Henryson describes 'Schouris of haill' that 'fra the north discend' (6). The reference to the north is significant. The arrival of Chaucer's April which kindles warmth and rebirth in England is replaced by a Caledonian spring of first extreme heat ('wedder richt feruent,' 4) and then penetrating cold from which the narrator can scarcely protect himself."[15] Scheps would have us read these details as indicative merely of Henryson's "sense of decorum," his understanding that a paradoxical "winterlie springe" most befits Cresseid's tragedy.[16] Decorum aside, though, the *Testament*'s self-consciously oppositional stance also seems to insist that its relation to Chaucer's poetry—*Troilus and Criseyde*, but also, if Scheps is right, the *Canterbury Tales*—is in fact a nonrelation, a *lack* of direct correspondence. Henryson's poem appropriates Chaucerian motifs, but only to modify or undo them; its invocations lead, ultimately, to negations. Viewed in this light, the "astronomically impossible" opposition between Venus and the Sun in lines 11 to 14 begins to seem not only like an "aesthetically necessary" gambit, as Scheps suggests, but also like an apt metaphor for Henryson's project of poetic inversion.[17]

Even in—*especially* in—its appropriations and revisions of Chaucer, then, the *Testament* reveals itself to be a profoundly late medieval Scottish text: a text that emerges in a place obsessed with its neighbor to the south, in an atmosphere where notions of autonomy remained inextricably tied to borders and intrusions, retributions and hostility—to all of the most unsettling aspects of the neighbor relation. Indeed, the chronicles of medieval Scotland contain more than just stories of English aggression: stories of battles and incursions, of lies and betrayals, of exploitations both great and small. They are shot through as well with the invective those aggressions aroused in the Scots. Here, for example, is a not untypical excerpt from Walter Bower's *Scotichronicon*, written in the 1440s. The English, warns Bower,

> know how to twist their faces away from their intentions, their words from their feelings, their language from their minds, and their discourse from their meaning. . . .
>
> And is it surprising if more than all other peoples they are intent on treachery . . . when indeed their kings have never been interested in keeping faith with the Scots? Therefore more than all other peoples under Heaven they are more involved in treachery. To nobody do they keep a promise they have made. . . . Hence even you, the Scottish people, though you exercise every precaution, though you are watchful in every way for your security and indemnity, . . . in these circumstances you must first of all defend your interests, because their malice is on the alert especially when they feel that in light of your abundant security you are not on your guard. Then at last they return to their artful wickedness.[18]

Bower's focus in this passage is of course local and topical, informed by a very specific set of conditions. Put aside the surface details, however, and his tone is uncannily close to that of Freud, who centuries later would scrutinize the moral injunction to love one's neighbor and conclude that, on the contrary, the neighbor

> has more claim to my hostility and even my hatred. He seems not to have the slightest trace of love for me and shows me not the slightest consideration. If it will do him any good he has no hesitation in injuring me, nor does he ask himself whether the amount of advantage he gains bears any proportion to the extent of the harm

he does to me. Indeed, he need not even obtain an advantage; if he can satisfy any sort of desire by it, he thinks nothing of jeering at me, insulting me, slandering me and showing his superior power; and the more secure he feels and the more helpless I am, the more certainly I can expect him to behave like this to me.[19]

Medieval Scotland may have been, like the rest of Western Europe, a nominally Christian nation, and the Scots themselves adherents, in principle, to the biblical ethic of neighbor love. But when the Scots thought about the English—and the chronicles suggest that they thought about them a great deal—they tended to do so, specifically, in those negative terms of the neighbor later articulated by Freud.[20]

To be fair, though, this obsession with the neighbor seems to have characterized life not only for the Scots but also for those English living along the country's northern border. The prologue to Sir Thomas Gray's mid-fourteenth-century *Scalacronica*, for example, reveals the extent to which Anglo-Scottish neighbor relations could shape even one's sense of history, including one's sense of literary inheritance. Part of "a border family, constantly involved in war with the Scots," Gray at one point got captured and was imprisoned in Edinburgh castle, where he "whiled away the time . . . by reading chronicles in rhyme and prose in Latin, French and English."[21] Inspired, Gray decided that he too would "'treat and translate in short' the chronicles of Britain and the 'gestes' of the English."[22] He then did what any self-respecting fourteenth-century writer would do: he had a dream vision. In this dream, the Sibyl ("a well-known figure in chronicle, liturgy and drama") led Gray into an orchard, where she pointed to a siege ladder leaning against a wall.[23] The wall, the Sibyl explained to him, represented the edifice of history, which Gray was to scale, stopping at each of the ladder's five rungs in order to look through a window at each of the authorities whose work he was to appropriate in the writing of his own chronicle: Walter of Exeter, the venerable Bede, the monk of Chester, and John of Tynemouth. Gray would not be allowed access to the fifth rung, the Sibyl told him, because there at the top were Henry of Huntington and Merlin, seers whose talent was to foretell the future, not recount the past. What interests me here is not only that this prologue, in using an architectural metaphor to spatialize the writing of history, transforms Gray's precursors from figures in the past to neighbors visible through windows in an orchard wall: intimate strangers to be observed and imitated, if never exactly known. Just as intriguing is the strikingly bellicose image of history as a wall to be scaled, literally, by a knight with a siege ladder. Not only does such an image evoke, through its associations with warfare and plunder, the aggression inherent in neighbor relations; it suggests how easily that aggression could, for those involved in the long struggle between England and Scotland, color even the act of writing with hostility and exploitation.

My first line of argument is thus that Henryson would have encountered *Troilus and Criseyde* at what might be called the place of the neighbor. This is a place charged, as the chronicle records of medieval Anglo-Scottish relations so amply demonstrate, with aggression and antagonism, treachery and exploitation. It is an impossible place, defined by what Slavoj Žižek describes as the lack of the social relation: the disruptive transversal of society by "an antagonistic split which cannot be integrated into symbolic order."[24] This is not to suggest that Henryson considered "worthie Chauceir" to have been himself personally hostile to the Scots (58). It is to suggest that, for a fifteenth-century Scottish poet, the Chaucerian text—a text already being promoted in Lancastrian circles as distinctly and definitively English—could not help but occupy the structural position of the neighbor, a position invariably connected, for the Scots, with an unrestrained enjoyment, a death drive, in the Other.[25] Reading back over the passage from Bower's *Scotichronicon*, for example, one cannot help but think how troubling it must have been, for Scots and English alike, to heed the biblical injunction to love one's neighbor as oneself when their neighbors were constantly out to exploit, impede, or even kill them. Bower, in fact, would surely be the last to dispute Freud's assertion that, "at bottom," the commandment to "Love thy neighbor" is "the same thing" as its "even more incomprehensible" obverse, "Love thine enemies."[26]

But that's not the end of it. Indeed, if that were the end of it, if the *Testament* amounted to a vehicle for neighborly aggression and nothing more, then I am not sure it would command our attention as it does. What I now want to suggest, then, is that Chaucer's *Troilus*, in occupying the vexed position of neighboring text, must necessarily have forced Henryson to struggle with—and, more than that, interrogate—the dilemma of neighbor love anatomized, often mercilessly, by psychoanalysis. Henryson himself never openly acknowledges that struggle as such. It is a struggle made legible only by its effects in the *Testament*, and by one effect in particular: doubt.

The *Testament of Cresseid* includes what is arguably the best-known declaration of doubt in all of medieval English and Scottish literature: "Quha wait gif all that Chauceir wrait was trew?" [Who knows if all that Chaucer wrote was true?] (64). That declaration might be understood, in the first place, as a small act of political resistance, akin to the skepticism with which certain medieval Scottish historiographers treated the English foundation myths derived from Geoffrey of Monmouth's *The History of the Kings of Britain*.[27] But we might also read it as a sign of resistance in the Freudian sense: a mode of defense that is also a form of repression. When Lacan claims, in *The Four Fundamental Concepts of Psychoanalysis*, that "Freud's method is Cartesian," this is in part what he means.[28] Freud, in fact, recognized early on just how powerful a role doubt could play in psychoanalytic practice. Initially, doubt "registers the impossibility of the real and thereby defends us against its intrusion into the symbolic."[29] *Oh*, we say when we sense that the real has gotten too close, *that can't be right*, or *That's impossible*, or *I'm not sure*, or some other variation on the phrase *I doubt it*. In this way, we act at the behest of the symbolic order by insisting, paradoxically, upon its "failure to say the real."[30] Rather than certify that the signifier has, at long last, hit upon the real, we instead enlist ourselves in the repetition—the endless attempt to say the real—that constitutes symbolization as such.

But if doubt serves as a defense against the real, it does so as a tacit admission of certainty: certainty that we have touched upon the real. Doubt (about the veracity of a particularly disturbing dream, say) doesn't arise from nowhere; it emerges at the point where authority, guaranteed by the power of interdiction and prohibition, fails. The opposite of radically skeptical, doubt in this respect is at once conservative, expressing the desire for more prohibition, the wish that the Other would do a better job of defending the subject against a confrontation with *jouissance*, and subversive, insofar as it registers our disappointment in the ineptitude of the Other. "Who knows if all that Chaucer wrote was true?" becomes just another way of saying that father Chaucer failed to enact a prohibition against *jouissance*. In an indirect fashion, then, the narrator of the *Testament* ends up neighboring on Chaucer's *Troilus and Criseyde*—that is, assuming responsibility for the *jouissance* of the neighboring text—in something like a literal fashion, by establishing a new boundary against the real. And in this case, that real is very much the narrator's neighbor, so proximate and intrusive that it makes him want to establish a clearer barrier between it and him. With doubt, one can be certain that something has gotten too close. Here that something is the *jouissance* of the neighboring text.

And yet what makes Henryson's text so fascinating is precisely that it *does* neighbor on *Troilus and Criseyde*, assuming responsibility for the *jouissance* of the neighboring text by absorbing that *jouissance* into its own structure, incorporating it, loving it as itself. The only complication is that, to effect such love, the *Testament* must turn to the apparently hostile strategy of negation. Joan Copjec explains the paradox of negation this way: "In order for the symbolic to evict the real and thereby establish itself, a judgment of existence is required; that is, it is necessary to *say* that the real is absented, to *declare* its impossibility. The symbolic, in other words, must include the negation of what it is not. This requirement is not without its paradoxical effects, for it means ultimately that the symbolic will be filled not only with itself, since it will also contain this surplus element of negation."[31]

Paradigmatic of this dynamic is the foundational dream of psychoanalysis, Freud's dream of Irma's injection. The manifest content of this dream, for those who might not be familiar with it, can be summarized as follows. Freud dreams that he is in a large hall receiving guests when he spots his patient "Irma," whom he takes aside and reproaches for not accepting his "solution" to her as-yet mysterious ailment. She complains of pains in her throat, her stomach, her abdomen. "It's choking me," she says. Freud, alarmed, convinced that he must be "missing some organic trouble," takes Irma to the window and, despite her "signs of recalcitrance," peers into her mouth. There, Freud is shocked to discover "a big white patch" and, in another place, "extensive whitish grey scabs on some remarkable curly structures." "All at once" Freud calls in his mentor, Dr. M., who, though he "looks quite different" than in waking life, nevertheless confirms Freud's findings. By this point, Freud's friends Otto and Leopold are also standing beside Irma, Leopold "percussing her through her bodice," pointing out a "dull area" on her left side and some "infiltrated" skin on her shoulder. Dr. M. says that it must be an infection, at which point Freud and the others are "directly aware" of the infection's origin: "Otto had given her an injection of a preparation of propyl, propyls . . . propionic acid . . . trimethylamin"—Freud can now distinctly see "the formula for this printed in heavy type." The dream then ends with Freud thinking that such injections "ought not to be made so thoughtlessly" and that "probably the syringe had not been clean."[32] One of the pivotal elements in this dream, as Copjec points out, is doubt: doubt about the conflicting diagnoses of the dream's "three sorry figures of authority," Dr. M., Otto, and Leopold. Ostensibly, these authority figures are summoned to prevent Freud from being engulfed by the *jouissance* condensed in the mysterious white patch in Irma's mouth. Instead, their failed judgments, by allowing for doubt, make it possible for Freud to move toward *jouissance*, to assume responsibility for *jouissance*, rather than ceding it to the Other. It is for this reason, argues Copjec, that Freud "does not simply flee from the unconscious or from the real of Irma's desire: *he holds on to them*."[33] Freud's triumphant pronouncement of the solution to Irma's mysterious ailment—*trimethylamin*—at once affirms the symbolic order by declaring the impossibility of the real, and yet maintains the real (and, by extension, the possibility of *jouissance*) by including its negation within the symbolic order.

Freud's dream, I want to argue, can help us to understand not only why the *Testament*'s narrator wonders aloud if all that Chaucer wrote was true but also why he admits to doubt about the "vther quair"— that is, about Henryson's own poem:

Nor I wait nocht gif this narratioun
Be authoreist or fenȝeit of the new
Be sum poeit, throw his inuentioun,

Maid to report the lamentatioun
And wofull end of this lustie Creisseid,
And quhat distress scho thoillit, and quhat deid.

(64–70)

[Nor do I know if this narrative be authoritative or fabricated anew
by some poet through his invention, made to report the lamentation and woeful end of the beautiful Cresseid, and what distress
she suffered and what manner of death.]

Copjec reminds us that, because "the symbolic must inscribe its lack of
foundation in the real," the process of negation "also thereby inscribes
the real itself, since it is precisely there where we do not know, that
enjoyment, *jouissance* (a pleasure in the real) arises. *Jouissance* is a kind
of 'secondary gain' obtained where knowledge fails."[34] Like Freud, the
narrator of the *Testament* refuses to cede responsibility for *jouissance* to
the fantasy of the Other. There is no hiding from the burden of *jouissance* here; instead we are made to confront it in all of its strange and
disturbing proximity, as a neighbor. At one point in *The Four Fundamental Concepts of Psychoanalysis*, Lacan alludes to what he calls, somewhat misleadingly, the "colophon of doubt," noting that doubt acts as
a marginal sign alerting us to the presence of the real.[35] Here, then,
is the *Testament*'s colophon—or, more precisely, manicule—of doubt,
a part of the text that directs us to a confrontation with the real. We
cannot run from the *jouissance* that passes between Chaucer's text and
Henryson's; neither one will screen us against that encounter. Rather,
we are called upon to struggle, as the narrator of the *Testament* struggles, with the sudden overproximity of a *jouissance* he has but doesn't
want: the *jouissance* that, embedded in the unbearable paradoxes of the
neighbor relation, binds his "vther quair" to Chaucer's.

This struggle culminates, as we shall see, in the *Testament*'s revival
of Troilus. Mostly, though, and more dramatically, it gets played out
around the contested figure of Criseyde/Cresseid. It is a curious fact
about Criseyde, as Gayle Margherita points out, that the first mention
of her in Chaucer's poem "refers to an event that in fact never occurs in
the narrative: her death."[36] As the narrator writes:

For now wil I gon streght to my matere,
In which ye may the doble sorwes here
Of Troilus in lovynge of Criseyde,
And how that she forsook hym er she deyde.

(1.53–56)

From the very beginning, the *Troilus* narrator tips his hand, letting us know that Criseyde will end Chaucer's poem where Troilus begins it: suspended in the disjointed lag or interval that Lacan calls "the space between two deaths." The crucial difference, however, as we shall see in the next chapter, is that the ending of *Il Filostrato* represents Troilo's death at the hands of Achilles while saying nothing of his interment. Boccaccio's poem neither mourns its Troilo nor memorializes him; his death, never subject to any sort of ritualization or symbolization, assumes no meaning other than as a warning against "fickle" young women.[37] Troilus thus "enters" Chaucer's poem demanding exactly the type of "symbolic" death he goes on to receive, first in his apotheosis to the eighth sphere, then, moments later, in his world-denying laugh.[38] Criseyde, on the other hand, will end up being granted a form of symbolic death only: exile, estrangement, ill repute. She is, as she herself already knows, as good as dead, at least in the eyes of posterity. "Allas," she says,

of me, unto the worldes ende,
Shal neyther ben ywriten nor ysonge
No good word, for thise bokes wol me shende.
O, rolled shal I ben on many a tonge!
Thorughout the world my belle shal be ronge!

(5.1058–62)

Her death is foretold, her epitaph all but written, fixed "unto the worldes ende." But she is not yet physically dead.

In one of its many inverted repetitions of *Troilus and Criseyde*, then, the *Testament of Cresseid* begins with its own eponymous character, rather than Troilus, having entered the space between two deaths. Yet there is another, more important, way in which the *Testament* repeats and inverts *Troilus and Criseyde*: in setting out to "liberate" Cresseid from the space between two deaths, the *Testament* narrator sets out to negate the neighboring text's unsettled, and unsettling, desire. He does so, in the first place, by filling out what he apparently regards as the neighboring text's unbearable silence, describing for us just what happened to Criseyde/Cresseid beyond Chaucer's poem:

> Quhen Diomeid had all his appetyte,
> And mair, fulfillit of this fair ladie,
> Vpon ane vther he set his haill delyte,
> And send to her ane lybell of repudie
> And her excludit fra his companie.
> Than desolait scho walkit vp and doun,
> And sum men sayis, into the court, commoun.
>
> (71–77)

[Once Diomed had fulfilled all his appetite, and more, on this fair lady, he set his whole delight on another and sent to her (Cresseid) a declaration of divorce and excluded her from his company. Desolate, she then walked up and down and, some men say, into the court, commonly/common court.]

The narrator here sets about to clarify, as it were, the terms and conditions of Cresseid's symbolic death: her repudiation and banishment, her exclusion, even (some men say) her descent into promiscuity.[39] Perhaps the most striking detail in this passage is the written, the legalistic, nature of Cresseid's banishment. Diomed, as it turns out, does not just spurn Cresseid; he issues a "lybell of repudie," a formal declaration or bill of divorce. At the moment of Cresseid's passage into the *Testament*, the signifier is deployed as a kind of barrier between her and the communities of both Trojans and, now, Greeks. Not only has her good name been ruined, degraded until it becomes a watchword for unfaithfulness; a formal declaration of repudiation has been issued against her.

Cresseid is now an outcast; soon she will become a leper. Yet even in her most abjected state, Cresseid is never fully "thrust aside" by the narrator's (or Diomed's, or the planetary gods') "'unshakable adherence to Prohibition and Law.'"[40] As a practical matter, if nothing else, Cresseid's ordeal accurately reflects the legal procedures current in fifteenth-century Scotland.[41] Not only, then, is her characterization in the poem legally determined; her status as an excluded outsider is still very much a legal status. The law, so to speak, still manages to count Cresseid, even when there is no more that it can do to her.[42] But in a much larger sense, Cresseid is explicitly marked *by* the law, by language, as "maculait," stained and polluted (81). Paradoxical as it may sound, the symbolic order absorbs her into itself at the very moment it appears to reject her. This is because, to return to Copjec one last time, "it is necessary to *say* that the real is absented, to *declare* its impossibility. The symbolic . . . must include the negation of what it is not," thereby incorporating into its own structure something other than itself.[43] If the *Testament* seeks to negate the enjoyment associated with Cresseid, it must do so not by rejecting it outright but by acknowledging it, saying it, prohibiting it—in other words, incorporating it within the poem's own, highly legalistic language.[44]

By far the most prominent sign of that incorporation, and of the "paradoxical effects" it generates, is Cresseid's leprosy.[45] Although Gayle Margherita and Felicity Riddy both make the essential point that Cresseid's leprosy moves her, as she herself puts it, into the register of the "abiect odious," and thus into the register of that which is rejected by the symbolic order, there can be no escaping how thoroughly *symbolized* leprosy already was—and thus how thoroughly the sentence of leprosy subjects Cresseid to the defining power of symbolic law. "Cresseid's leprosy is a particularly suitable punishment for her promiscuity," writes Saul Brody in his classic study of leprosy in medieval literature. "Not only does it ravage her beauty, but what is more, because leprosy was commonly understood to be a venereal disease, a consequence of lust, it makes her past sinfulness apparent to her and to all who see her."[46] If anything, Cresseid's leprosy draws her more fully into the symbolic order than ever before, since the affliction would have been immediately legible as a sign of lechery: a moral interpretation, a judgment. And indeed, Henryson's poem works overtime to stress the legalistic, the statutory, nature of Cresseid's disease. Saturn, for example, is described as "lawfullie" depriving Cresseid of her beauty and "mirth," while Cynthia descends to "red ane bill on Cresseid quhair scho lay, / Contending [the] sentence diffinityue" [read a verdict against Cresseid where she lay declaring the definitive sentence] of physical decay (332–43). And when Cresseid, having awoken to find herself humbled and deformed, gains her father's permission to go "in secreit wyse" to "ȝon hospitall at the tounis end" [in a secret manner to yonder hospital at the town's end] and finish out her days as a miserable beggar, another "lipper lady" pointedly advises her to "go leir to clap thy clapper to and fro, / And leif efter the law of leper leid" [go and learn to clap your clapper to and fro, and live after the law of the leper folk] (479–80).[47]

Live after the law of the leper folk: It sounds so definitive. And yet the use of *leif* in this context could not be more bitterly ironic, considering "that medieval lepers were sometimes treated, in religious and legal terms, as if they were . . . dead while alive."[48] The "law of the leper folk" condemns Cresseid to a "life," one might say a bare life, between two deaths, and so does nothing to resolve the matter of the neighboring text's desire while doing everything to emphasize the law's cruelty.[49] If anything, in fact, the sentence of leprosy fails to achieve what appears to be the poem's larger aim; for it only ends up generating the very real it means to evict. That paradox gets compounded, as Spearing and Margherita (among others) observe, by the fact that Cresseid seems to get punished less for lechery than for blaspheming the gods. On this point, at least, Cupid is emphatically clear:

> . . . quha will blaspheme the name
> Of his awin god, outher in word or deid,
> To all goddis he dois baith lak and schame,
> And suld haue bitter panis to his meid.
> I say this by ȝone wretchit Cresseid,
> The quhilk throw me was sum tyme flour of lufe,
> Me and my mother starklie can reprufe,
>
> Saying of hir greit infelicitie
> I was the caus, and my mother Venus,

Ane blind goddes hir cald that micht not se,
With sclander and defame iniurious.
Thus hir leuing vnclene and lecherous
Scho wald retorte in me and my mother,
To quhome I schew my grace abone all vther.

And sen ȝe ar all seuin deificait,
Participant of deuyne sapience,
This greit iniure done to our hie estait
Me think with pane we suld mak recompence;
Was neuer to goddes done sic violence:
Asweill for ȝow as for my self I say,
Thairfoir ga help to reuenge. I ȝow pray!
(274–94)

[Whoever will blaspheme the name of his own god, either in word
or deed, does both dishonor and shame to all gods and should have
bitter pains as his reward. I say this in reference to yon wretched
Cresseid, who through me was sometime the flower of love, yet
who can starkly reprove my mother and me, saying I was the cause
of her great unhappiness and calling my mother, with slander and
injurious defamation, a blind goddess who cannot see. Thus she, to
whom I show my grace above all others, would blame her unclean
and lecherous lifestyle on my mother and me. And since you are all
seven deified, partaking of divine wisdom, this great injury done
to our high estate we should recompense, I think, with pain. Was
never done to a goddess such violence: as much for yourselves as for
myself I say, therefore, lend your support to vengeance, I pray you!]

Cresseid is not given leprosy as a punishment for lechery; she is given
it, as she herself later concludes, because she blames the gods, in whom
she once had faith, for her having fallen into lechery, and because she
regrets having ever made sacrifices to them.[50] "My blaspheming now
haue I bocht full deir" [My blaspheming have I now bought full dear],
says Cresseid. "Allace, this day; allace, this wofull tyde / Quhen I
began with my goddis for to chyde!" [Alas, this day; alas, this woeful

turn of events, when I began to chide my goddess] (354, 356–57). In Cresseid's case, the punishment literally does not fit the crime.

But it is not just Cresseid's sentence that sows confusion, applying the usual sign of lechery to what appears to be an act of blasphemy instead. Despite what Cupid says, and what Cresseid herself admits, the exact nature of the crime committed remains a mystery. Was it Cresseid's infidelity to Troilus, her alleged promiscuity, her blasphemy, her vanity? "All these," observes Riddy, "at some point or other in the poem, are brought to the fore as things for which she deserves to be punished."[51] Cresseid, it seems, is being punished for everything all at once and nothing in particular. Precisely because of such confusion, however, I am not sure that the exact nature of Cresseid's crime, be it lechery or blasphemy or vanity, is the thing at stake here. At stake is Cresseid's association with the incomprehensible *jouissance* of the law, a *jouissance* manifest most explicitly in the injunction to love thy neighbor as thyself. The judgment leveled against Cresseid reduces her, as I suggested earlier, to the level of bare life. And yet the poem, by depicting that judgment in all its cruelty, might be said to issue its own form of judgment against the law, thereby pushing us to confront, in the image of Cresseid's leprous flesh, "something rotten in law" itself.[52] Indeed, it is surely significant that leprosy, the outward sign of punishment written, as it were, upon Cresseid's suffering body, does not necessarily correspond to her supposed transgression. Leprosy is supposed to signify a life of lechery. But in Cresseid's case it may also signify something else, something for which leprosy would seem an arbitrary punishment at best. Or it may signify nothing more than that the law will do as it pleases. Here, then, at the point where the law asserts itself most forcefully, making full use of its powers of isolation and proscription, we instead find the signifier once again signaling its inability to name the real, to authorize itself by grounding itself in the real. Circling whatever enjoyment Cresseid embodies without ever hitting it, the signifier of leprosy instead fills the symbolic order with the very real it means to indict and evict. It does so, however, not in the usual way, by "turn[ing] in circles around the real that is lacking in it," but by going one step further and insisting that the real that ought to be lacking is not lacking at all but is in fact all too evident in the operations of the law meant to prohibit it. What is lacking in this case, in other words, is lack itself; and the materialization of that lack of lack (which might also be described as an overproximity of the real that should be lacking) is Cresseid's leprosy. If is true, as psychoanalysis repeatedly insists, that "the essence of our enjoyment . . . is *to deprive someone else of his or her enjoyment*," then here we have a striking example.[53] Not content to depict the workings of the law and leave it at that, the *Testament* instead makes us feel the full weight of the law's irrational and inconsistent *jouissance*. In this case, at least, the law betrays its own enjoyment when it punishes Cresseid for hers.[54]

To the long-standing question of whether the *Testament*'s outlook is fundamentally pagan or fundamentally Christian—that is, fundamentally about the cruelty of the law or fundamentally about the power of redemption to fulfill and even supersede the law—we can thus answer: pagan, with a Christian supplement. That the planetary gods are excessively cruel in their punishment of Cresseid is admitted even by the poem's narrator, who complains:

> O cruell Saturne, fraward and angrie,
> Hard is thy dome and to malitious!
> On fair Cresseid quhy hest how na mercie,
> Quhilk was sa sweit, gentill and amorous?
> Withdraw thy sentence and be gracious —
> As thow was neuer; sa schawis through thy deid,
> Ane wraikfull sentence geuin on fair Cresseid.
>
> (323–29)

[O cruel Saturn, ill-humored and angry, severe is thy judgment, and too malicious! Why have you no mercy on fair Cresseid, who was so sweet, gentle, and affectionate? Withdraw thy sentence and be gracious—not that you ever have been; so much is evident through your deed, a vicious sentence delivered on fair Cresseid.]

The planetary gods, whose so-called parliament is little better than a kangaroo court, personify the cruelty of the law as such, its unremitting and non-negotiable character. In that, at least, the *Testament* is entirely conventional. "There are innumerable English, French, Italian, and German poems in which a sin against love or an insult to Venus and Cupid is punished by a quasi-legal court made up of the pagan gods," notes Denton Fox. What sets the *Testament* apart, Fox argues, is the "unusual degree" to which Henryson "makes the descriptions of the gods important for the meaning of the poem."[55] It is no mistake, I think, either that Henryson goes out of his way to make us experience the pagan gods as living things, beings tied directly to the workings of the natural world, or that he has the gods come to Cresseid in a dream. As if undoing the palinode to Chaucer's *Troilus and Criseyde*, Henryson sets his poem in a time before monotheism, in effect suspending "a certain atheistic message" (as Lacan puts it) "at the heart of Christianity itself."[56] God is not yet dead at the moment of Cresseid's punishment, and so Cresseid has no recourse to the transmissive scheme instituted by monotheism's deposition of paganism's living gods. Cresseid cannot, in other words, be interpellated into a structure where *jouissance* has been replaced by the collective internalization of guilt over the murder of the primal father—a structure, in short, where the prohibitions of the dead father are more powerful than the living father had ever been. Instead, Cresseid is forced to suffer the nearness of a *jouissance* that the law "both produces and prohibits."[57] In this scenario, there is no dead father to delimit *jouissance*; there is only the real of the law in all its immediacy. And that real comes to Cresseid where it always comes: not within a waking world dictated by the economy of the pleasure principle, but in a dream that cannot be doubted. In her dream, Cresseid confronts the *jouissance* that is her most intimate neighbor.

Given, then, that the law in the *Testament* is shown to be both cruel and excessive, designed to pursue vengeance rather than justice, it is all the more interesting to note that Cresseid is punished by the planetary gods—exposed, as it were, to the full weight of the law— only after she has returned to the house of her father, Calchas. In fantasy, at least, it is the Father who preserves the possibility of one day attaining *jouissance* while at the same time relieving us of the burden of having to assume the *jouissance* we actually encounter in and as our neighbor. But with the punishment meted out to Cresseid in the

Testament, Henryson dissolves that fantasy. In short, there is nothing the Father can do to protect Cresseid from the cruel *jouissance* exhibited by the law. But why stop with Cresseid? Could we not say the same thing about the *Testament* narrator as well? The narrator can doubt Chaucer all he wants, but in the end he is forced to serve a *jouissance* he can neither abide nor escape, the overbearing, overproximate *jouissance* of the neighbor. Ultimately, the weight of the law bears down on the narrator as much as it does Cresseid, albeit in a slightly different manner. Cresseid is made to suffer for her transgression of the law; the narrator suffers because of the demand that he follow the inherently transgressive (in that it prohibits nothing while commanding us to act without restraint) injunction to love the neighbor as himself. Cresseid experiences *jouissance* in a way that mirrors and displaces the narrator's own experience of the very law he seeks to avoid.

All of which may help to explain why the narrator describes himself, at the beginning of the poem, in terms that anticipate Cresseid's symptoms as a leper. Lamenting that the "greit cald" not only has prevented him from praying to Venus in his "oratour" as he had intended, but has driven him to take refuge in his chamber by the fire, the narrator wistfully notes that

> Thocht lufe be hait, ȝit in ane man of age
> It kendillis nocht sa sone as in ȝoutheid,
> Of quhome the blude is flowing in ane rage;
> And in the auld the curage doif and deid
> Of quhilk the fyre outward is best remeid.
> (29–33)

[Though love be hot, yet in a man of age it kindles never so soon as in youths, in whom the blood flows in a rage; and in the old the desire is dull and dead, for which the best remedy is an external fire.]

Like Cresseid, whose "heit of bodie" is taken by Cynthia as part of her punishment-disease, the narrator "has a preponderance of the cold and dry qualities, and so is unfit for love," according to Denton Fox (334).[58] Likewise, much as Cresseid refuses to pay homage to

Venus and Cupid, the narrator neglects, because of the cold, to pray to Venus's "hie magnificence," opting instead to pass into his chamber and read *Troilus and Criseyde* (26). And although *doolie* was apparently one of Henryson's favorite adjectives, according to Fox, the narrator's use of it to describe both the season in which he writes and also Cresseid's dream-vision of the planets seems more than coincidental.[59] These may be only echoes, of course.[60] And yet, when taken together, the correspondences between Cresseid and the narrator—their shared symptoms, their transgressions, minor and major, against Venus—suggest that, on some level, the narrator identifies with the enjoyment that Cresseid embodies. Betrayed by his own metaphors, the narrator reveals the figure of the neighbor's *jouissance* to be that of his own closest neighbor as well: his *jouissance*. And the law his poem uses to punish that figure becomes, in turn, a way of fleeing the aggression of the neighbor that dwells within him, and that in the very place of the vanished Law adds its weight to that which prevents him from crossing a certain frontier at the limit of the Thing.[61] One possible explanation, then, for why the narrator works so hard to repudiate Cresseid is that she confronts him, in the place of the neighbor, a place occupied by Chaucer's "quair," with the embodiment of a desire that he recognizes as his own repressed desire, and from which he recoils as emphatically as he did the bitter cold of his "oratur" at the beginning of the poem. "[Q]uhat euer men deme or say / In scornfull langage of thy brukkilness, / I sall excuse *als far furth as I may* / Thy womanheid, thy wisdome and fairness" [Whatever men judge or say in scornful language concerning your fickleness, I shall excuse *as far as I can* your womanliness, your wisdom and fairness], the narrator promises Cresseid (85–88, my italics). But for him there is no crossing the frontier of interdiction signified by that "may." Not only does he recoil from the *jouissance* he might experience by transgressing against a prohibition he imagines will allow him to forgive Cresseid only so far. He also recoils before the injunction to love the neighbor as himself, an injunction that, if followed to the letter—that is, until it touched upon the real—would force him to embrace the *jouissance* that is also in him. Instead, the narrator goes to the opposite extreme, attempting to reestablish the barrier—or, to put it in terms better suited to the world of Anglo-Scottish relations, the border—between his most intimate neighbor and himself.

In a sense, though, that effort only deepens the connections among Cresseid, her narrator, and, lurking somewhere behind them, Henryson. Obviously, these three figures occupy very different positions in respect to the poem we call the *Testament of Cresseid*. And yet they have this much in common: none of them can avoid the burden of the law, because all three occupy a weak position at best—and a vulnerable, even threatened position at worst—in relation to a more powerful neighboring entity, be it author or nation or divinity. None of them, in other words, is secure from *jouissance*. And so we find that the poem begins to experiment, in its treatment of Cresseid, with different strategies for keeping *jouissance* at bay—that is, with supplementing an Other that has fundamentally failed to sustain the fantasy of prohibition. Inevitably, though, those strategies end up mirroring the plight of the narrator, who flees the cold of his chapel (where, as it happens, he hoped to pray to Venus to aid him in his efforts at love) only to encounter the neighboring text. Far from protecting Cresseid or the narrator or even Henryson from the pressures of the neighbor relation, those strategies only bind them more closely to it, and in a way that emphasizes the added burden that the injunction to love thy neighbor as thyself places upon those living along the borders of a contested region, under constant threat of invasion and destruction.

This pattern establishes itself in the *Testament* through a series of set pieces subjecting Cresseid to the basic modes of legal practice: interpretation and judgment. First, there is the so-called Complaint of Cresseid, in which Cresseid, surveying the ruin of her beauty in lines that "transfer the *ubi sunt* theme from the dead to those living dead, the beggars," offers herself as an exemplum to her imagined counterparts.[62] "O ladyis fair of Troy and Grece," she intones,

> attend
> My miserie, quhilk nane may comprehend,
> My friuoll fortoun, my infelicitie,
> My greit mischeif, quhilk na man can amend.
> Be war in tyme, approchis neir the end,

And in ʒour mynd ane mirrour mak of me:
As I am now, peraduenture that ʒe
For all ʒour micht may cum to that same end,
Or ellis war, gif ony war may be.

(452–60)

[attend my misery, which none may comprehend, my fickle fortune, my unhappiness, my great misfortune, which no man can
amend. Beware in time, the end approaches near, and make a mirror of me in your mind: as I am now, it is possible that you, for all
your might, may come to the same end, or else worse, if any worse
there could be.]

Even in Cresseid's own view, the value of her experience lies in its
moral interpretation: the fact that it can be translated not only into a
precept but also into a mechanism for greater self-regulation. Women
should make a mirror of Cresseid in their minds not in order to identify with her outright (although clearly they are meant to see in her
a reflection of what they might become) but to use her as a warning against inconstancy. Women should hold an image of the leprous
Cresseid in their minds, in other words, so as to prohibit themselves
from transgressing as she did. Her image is itself a kind of barrier
against the Thing it materializes.

Cresseid's actions in and around her written testament betray a
similar tension. For some readers, those actions—Cresseid's admission of guilt ("Nane but my self as now I will accuse"); her divestment
of all her worldly possessions, including her physical body—represent
the pinnacle of Cresseid's moral development. But they might also be
viewed as a kind of backsliding. The problem here has mainly to do
with Cresseid's willingness to accuse herself of betraying Troilus. Fundamentally, that self-accusation enlists Cresseid in a structure that, as I
argued near the beginning of this chapter, Henryson seeks to circum-
vent by refusing to buy into the fantasy of father Chaucer: a structure
that perpetuates the prohibition of *jouissance* through the collective
internalization of guilt for the murder of the primal father. However
noble Cresseid's willingness to accept guilt may appear, its practical

effect is to interpellate her in a transmissive scheme that not only plays into the logic of temporal succession underpinning English imperialist ambitions but also establishes, through a narrative of guilt and betrayal, a barrier between Cresseid and the neighboring *jouissance* that she, above all, suffers. And while her divestment of worldly possessions may, like her bequeathing of her corpse "with wormis and with taidis to be rent" [to be rent by worms and toads], reduce Cresseid to the level of bare life, it also subjects her to that most mundane of legal procedures, the distribution of property. In her last act before dying, Cresseid fulfills the expectation of the law by sacrificing *jouissance* to what Lacan derisively calls "the service of the goods." If this constitutes, as some would have it, a "gaining of wisdom," it comes at a heavy price.[63]

As with the sentence of leprosy, however, this program of incremental symbolization does not quite succeed, because the (Lacanian) real still persists, this time in the intrusive presence of Cresseid's disembodied voice. Riddy, for example, makes the intriguing suggestion that Cresseid is nothing *but* a voice: a series of speech acts—diatribe, complaint, testament—providing "discontinuous subject positions."[64] If, however, we are going to characterize Cresseid as a voice, it would be helpful to recall that the voice is, like the gaze, the Lacanian object *par excellence:* the "object *a*" as the cause, the wellspring, of the subject's own desire, her own attempt to symbolize the elusive desire in the Other. That what Cresseid says amounts to little more than a series of generic commonplaces matters little; the crucial point is that her disembodied voice itself exerts a powerful fascination that goes well beyond the words it happens to be speaking. Indeed, one might go so far as to say that the words put in Cresseid's mouth, words that move her from one mode of subjectivity to another without ever fixing her in one, are put there specifically to screen against the deathless, timeless *jouissance*—the suffering—that pulses behind them. Cresseid's words may debase her, may even condemn her. But as long as she continues to speak them, as long as she continues to occupy the privileged position of the voice as object, then the powerful desire she (dis)embodies has yet to be fully evacuated from the poem.

And so the *Testament* tries to negate that desire once and for all, with Cresseid's entombment. The importance of this entombment is not simply that it completes the cycle that the *Testament* set out to complete, moving Cresseid from symbolic to bodily death, transferring her from the space between two deaths, the space of the destabilizing outcast, to that of the fully memorialized corpse. It is that it translates Cresseid's suffering, her symbolic and literal deaths, into a moral inscription: "'Lo, fair ladyis, Cresseid of Troy the toun, / Sumtyme countit the flour of womanheid, / Vnder this stane, lait lipper, lyis deid'" [Lo, fair ladies, Cresseid of Troy the town, sometime counted the flower of womanhood, under this stone, late a leper, lies dead] (607–9). By this point, not even Cresseid's own voice remains; it has been supplanted by the omniscient voice of an abstract Other, a battery of signifiers instructing us how to read Cresseid's life story. The implied "voice" of the tomb literally speaks over Cresseid, covering her with chiseled words that would make her mean something legible within the terms of the symbolic order.

But what do those chiseled words really mean? A. C. Spearing observes that "in such passages" as the one inscribing Cresseid's epitaph "not a word is wasted, and each successive phrase or clause has the effect of a hammer-blow. Their ideal form is precisely an epitaph, compressed by the limited space of the tombstone and made durable by the very hardness that resists the chisel. Chaucer's style has important origins in courtly speech, but Henryson's, at least in cases like this, strongly implies writing."[65] Spearing is absolutely right, I think, to emphasize the materiality of Cresseid's epitaph: the durability and resistance of its lettering, the hardness of the stone on which it is chiseled. But I would go further still and claim that the very purpose of Cresseid's epitaph is to draw our attention to its materiality. The writing on Cresseid's tombstone is characterized by a kind of inertness. No one is apt to appropriate it for a competing narrative that contests the meaning of Cresseid's death; there isn't going to be a second, subversive gravesite. The poem leaves us no choice but to dwell upon this particular epitaph—not in spite of but because of the fact that it remains as impenetrable and unyielding as the stone on which it is written. Its connotations are plain enough—beware Cresseid's sad fate, beware mutability, beware vanity—but its directive is unclear. Are we meant to pity Cresseid, judge her, identify with her, lament her passing, recoil in horror? The wording of the epitaph, "famously elliptical" as it is, does not provide much in the way of instruction.[66] But that, I want to argue, is precisely the point: Cresseid's epitaph, its wording at once literal and indirect, its lettering etched upon the insistently material medium of stone, comes as close as possible to approximating a particular way of experiencing the imperative to neighbor love.[67] On the one hand, we are like the "fair ladyis" summoned by the epitaph's invocation, called upon less to comprehend the meaning of Cresseid's epitaph than to contemplate the physical reality, the unavoidable proximity, of the tombstone itself. But of course we know more about the circumstances that brought Cresseid to be a leper laid under that stone than those "fair ladyis" ever could, and that knowledge—knowledge about the tragic events that the compressed form of the epitaph manages both to crystallize and to elide—only deepens our incomprehension before the stone itself. From our perspective, not only does the stone turn Cresseid's suffering into an occasion for contemplation; it also literalizes the intractability of the law that caused that suffering in the first place. Note that the wording of the epitaph is neither prohibitory nor hortative, but a strange conflation of both: prohibitory in the sense that it alerts us to the wages of transgression, hortative in that it appeals to us to imagine ourselves in Cresseid's place, to join her in her lonely leper's grave. The effect is to experience the epitaph as one experiences the injunction to love thy neighbor, as a call both inescapable and incoherent. The epitaph doesn't directly command us not to do something. One can either heed its summons or not. And yet to heed that summons is to do so excessively, to the point that one ends up suffering the law as Cresseid has suffered it. In short, the quality of the tombstone, its hardness and inertness, insists that we take its wording literally, to the letter—that is, until we experience it as something real, beyond the reach of negotiation or exchange. Cresseid's tombstone is the consummate neighboring text.

A project that began with doubt has now taken us to the edge of Cresseid's tomb. But it cannot be said to end until the poem's final lines, where the narrator explains why he has made his poem:

Now, worthie wemen, in this ballet schort,
Maid for ʒour worschip and instructioun,
Of charitie, I monische and exhort,
Ming not ʒour lufe with fals deceptioun:

Beir in ȝour mynd this sore conclusioun
Of fair Cresseid, as I haue said befoir.
Sen scho is deid I speik of hir no moir.

(610–16)

[Now, worthy women, in this short poem, made out of charity for your honor and instruction, I admonish and exhort you, mix not your love with false deception: bear in your mind this sore conclusion of fair Cresseid, as I have just now told it. Since she is dead I will speak of her no more.]

Its condescending tone notwithstanding, the language here evokes, at the very end of the poem, a potentially radical form of neighbor love, one much closer to that envisioned by Lacan in *The Ethics of Psychoanalysis*. Noting that "one would have to know how to confront the fact that my neighbor's *jouissance*, his harmful, malignant *jouissance*, is that which poses a problem for my love," Lacan almost reluctantly concludes that "it wouldn't be difficult at this point to take a leap in the direction of the excesses of the mystics." "No doubt the question of beyond the pleasure principle, the place of the unnameable Thing and what goes on there, is raised in certain acts that provoke our judgment," admits Lacan, "acts of the kind attributed to a certain Angela de Folignio, who joyfully lapped up water in which she had just washed the feet of lepers . . . or to the blessed Marie Allacoque, who, with no less a reward in spiritual uplift, ate the excrement of a sick man."[68] The fit between the two texts, Lacan's seminar and Henryson's poem, is not an exact one, of course. The narrator is asking his female readers to recoil from the example of Cresseid as much as to identify with it: to remember Cresseid without going so far as to allow her to accord, as Freud claims the Thing never does, with the memories of their own bodily actions. Nevertheless, the narrator does ask "worthie wemen" to bear in mind the "sore conclusioun" of Cresseid specifically, in effect asking them to meditate upon Cresseid's reduction to the thingliness of bare life. What is more, he exhorts them not to mix their love with false deception, a plea obviously intended to discourage women from betraying men in the way Cresseid is accused of betraying Troilus, but that in context might be taken as the model for a form of neighbor love in which we encounter the Thing in a direct, unmediated fashion, rather than reducing love to a matter of mutual reflection.

If this makes it sound as though the burden of neighbor love falls disproportionately on the most vulnerable and least powerful members of the poem's audience, that is because the *Testament* seems determined to make exactly that point: the imperative to love thy neighbor imposes more suffering upon the weak than the strong. Still, there may be more to the narrator's direct appeal to women than just that. Monitory as they are, the narrator's words nevertheless envision a community bound by something other than the internalization of guilt for, and ambivalent identification with, the figure of the dead father. Cresseid is dead, of course—so dead that the narrator shall "speik of hir no moir" (616)— but there is no indication that her death perpetuates the fantasy that *jouissance* is thereby suspended. On the contrary, women should bear in mind the sore conclusion of Cresseid for the very reason that any of them could suffer the same fate and come to embody the Thing. Rather than a closed community bound by the common identification with an exceptional figure, the set of women evoked by the narrator is open and potentially infinite, structured in such a way as to accommodate even future readers willing to bear in mind a suffering that, paradoxically, "nane may comprehend." The last line of the poem may sound final. And yet it is as if the narrator himself understood that neither Cresseid's testament nor his own admonishments held the power to redeem her. Cresseid's redemption is tied, rather, to the acts of neighbor love performed by an infinite, unbounded set of worthy women.

But that love is connected, in turn, to Cresseid's physical decay. Were Henryson writing strictly about, and not simply during, the fifteenth century in Scotland, we would be obliged to limit our understanding of redemption to the one that medieval Scots themselves would have possessed: the Christian belief in salvation through Christ. But the fact that Henryson restricts his poem to a pagan setting (never invoking, as Chaucer does at the end of *Troilus and Criseyde*, the Resurrection), while at the same time emphasizing Cresseid's physical ruin, invites us to seek out an understanding of redemption as something immanent and potential, rather than fulfilled—an understanding provided, in our own time, by Walter Benjamin. For Benjamin, redemption depends upon the erosion of the earthly kingdom, since it is only the inevitable decomposition of the physical world that will allow for the advent of the heavenly kingdom. That is why the realm of the profane is invested, as Benjamin sees it, with what he elsewhere calls a "weak messianic power": its inevitable ruin only clears the way for the world's redemption. Crucially, though, redemption is not therefore referred to the future. Rather, the proximity of the profane thing marks, in its ongoing, if at times imperceptible, decay, the intrusion of messianic time into the present.[69] In her ruination, then, Cresseid is already on a path to redemption, but that path has nothing to do with either admonishment or guilt. It leads, moreover, to a future that, in its very intrusion into the present—not as a promise but as a neighbor—falls out of the logic of temporal succession. In laying her under a stone, the *Testament* not only delivers Cresseid over to a potentially infinite neighborhood of women. It also delivers her from historical time.

This (implicit) version of charity, the last we encounter in the poem, stands in notable contrast to what some consider the *Testament*'s emotional climax: Troilus's first act of charity toward the leprous Cresseid (the second being his later building of her tomb). This is, to be sure, a poignant moment. Riding back to Troy one day, Troilus's garrison passes a group of lepers who, upon seeing the knights, cry out for alms. Moved by pity, Troilus rides over to the group, unaware that Cresseid is sitting among them. At that moment, Cresseid happens to look up, and something in her face reminds Troilus of his former lover, even though "scho was in sic plye he knew hir nocht" [she was in such a plight that he knew her not] (501). Momentarily shaken, Troilus recovers enough that

> For knichtlie pietie and memoriall
> Of fair Cresseid, ane gyrdill can he tak,
> Ane purs of gold, and mony gay iowall,
> And in the skirt of Cresseid doun can swak.
> (519–22)

[For knightly compassion and in memory of fair Cresseid, he took a belt, a purse of gold, and many a glittering jewel, and flung them down into Cresseid's lap.]

He then rides away without a word. But the narrator is not done. After Troilus has gone, Cresseid turns to the other lepers and asks, "Quhat lord is ʒone . . . haue ʒe na feill, / Hes done to vs so greit humanitie?" "ʒes," says one of the lepers,

> "I knaw him weill;
> Schir Troylus it is, gentill and fre."
> Quhen Cresseid vnderstude that it was he,
> Stiffer than steill thair stert ane bitter stound
> Throwout hir hart, and fell doun to the ground.
>
> Quhen scho ouircome, with siching sair and sad,
> With mony cairfull cry and cald ochane:
> "Now is my breist with stormie stoundis stad,
> Wrappit in wo, ane wretch full will of wane!"
> Than fel in swoun full oft or euer scho fane,
> And euer in hir swouning cryit scho thus,
> "O fals Cresseid and trew knicht Troylus!"
>
> (533–46)

["Have you any knowledge what lord is yonder that has done us so great an act of kindness?" "Yes, I know him well. It is Sir Troilus, gentle and generous." When Cresseid realized that it was he, there shot a bitter pain, stiffer than steel, throughout her heart, and she fell down to the ground. When she recovered, with sighing sore and sad, with many a worried cry and cold *Ach*: "Now is my breast beset with stormy pains, wrapped in woe, a hopeless wretch!" Then she fell in a swoon several times before she finally stopped, and always as she swooned she cried out thus: "O false Cresseid and true knight Troilus!"]

The emotional impact of this sequence derives, as some have argued, from the fact that the lovers' encounter is neither a reconciliation nor a reunion but "a nonrecognition scene," an ironic moment in which, despite their proximity, "not ane ane vther knew" [neither one knew the other] (518).[70] And yet it is not a total nonrecognition scene, because the leper that Troilus sees before him momentarily calls to mind "the sweit visage and amorous blenking / Of fair Cresseid" [the sweet visage and loving glances of fair Cresseid]. Commenting on that disruption of memory, the narrator notes how "the idole of ane thing in cace may be / Sa deip imprentit in the fantasy / That it deludes the wittis outwardly, / And so appeiris in forme and lyke estait / Within the mynd as it was figurait" [the image of a thing in some cases can be so deeply imprinted in the imagination that it deludes the five senses and so appears in the same form and similar condition as it had been figured in memory] (503–11). If Troilus cannot recognize the leper on the ground below him, it is not only because she is unrecognizable but because his vision is clouded by the fantasy of his lover as she once was. He remains, in the broadest possible sense, blind to the suffering before him—blind to the Thing—because his vision of his momentary neighbor can only accord with memory, while negating the real.

Troilus's act of charity, in other words, follows precisely the moment when the *Testament* makes most literal the *lack* of relation, the asymmetry, between its protagonists: the moment when it has become impossible for Troilus to identify with Cresseid as a figure of suffering. "In any encounter there's a big difference in meaning between the response of philanthropy and that of love," Lacan argues in his reading of the legend of Saint Martin and the beggar. "Saint Martin shares his cloak, and a great deal is made of it," says Lacan. "Yet it is after all a simple question of training; material is by its very nature made to be disposed of—it belongs to the other as much as it belongs to me. We are no doubt touching a primitive requirement in the need to be satisfied there, for the beggar is naked. But perhaps over and above that need to be clothed, he was begging for something else, namely, that Saint Martin either kill him or fuck him."[71] Admittedly, Lacan's language at this point may strike some as needlessly profane, if not a little puerile. Indeed, it almost seems as if Lacan were trying to enact, and not merely describe, the shocking encounter with the Other's desire. Nevertheless, Lacan's provocative style is no reason to dismiss what really matters in this passage, and that is its evocation of a radically new ethics. Philanthropy, the sharing of what is, after all, meant to be shared, is neither difficult nor ethical, Lacan implies. On the contrary, philanthropy is less an act of sacrifice than an act of interpretation, a way of maintaining the illusory integrity of the ego by reading the disturbing nakedness of the other as a cry for sameness, an excuse to clothe the other in the same cloak as oneself. In any encounter with the other, we invariably confront a desire that is ultimately unknowable and, as Lacan's strong language makes clear, potentially horrible: a confused eruption of aggression and libido. To truly show respect for the other, then, we must abjure a piety that only serves to screen us from the horror of the other's intimate desire. Our task instead, Lacan implies, is to acknowledge ownership of that same desire—to love it, as we would love our neighbor, as our self. But philanthropy does exactly the opposite, translating the enigmatic desire that threatens us into legible, manageable need. Philanthropy, that is to say, functions as nothing less than a means of denying, through a violent insistence on merely specular identification, the unfathomable Other in the Other's desire. As in the case of Saint Martin, philanthropy aims literally to cover up the libido and aggression, the killing and the fucking, that confront us in our neighbor relations. Whatever its stated purpose, then, Troilus's act of charity can be read as an attempt to deny, by draping it in the recognizable terms of moral condemnation, the Other desire he encounters in Cresseid. Troilus's magnanimous gesture, we are to believe, makes the symbolic whole, principally because it is meant to counteract the lack of relation between Chaucer's text and Henryson's implied *by* desire. But if there is indeed a "difference in meaning" between philanthropy and love, as Lacan suggests, then we see that difference here. For the wholeness brought by Troilus's charity is ultimately hermetic, closed off, rooted in a negation that takes the guise of a forced mirroring, an imaginary ratification extracted from the other. However sublime the act itself, the practical effect of Troilus's charity is to screen against the desire in the Other by translating Cresseid, the embodiment of that desire, into two texts—a testament, an inscription—that aim to substantiate the cultural values epitomized by the "trew knicht Troylus."

It is at this point that we begin to touch upon the profound mythoideological implications of the *Testament*'s disinterment of Troilus, implications that suggest the difficulty of separating literary neighbor relations from medieval Anglo-Scottish neighbor relations in general.

Recall not only that England traced its origins to Troy—that, indeed, London fashioned itself the "New Troy"—but that the fate of Troy was traditionally tied to that of Troilus. When the latter had died, so the legend had it, the former was doomed to fall. Crucially, however, that myth of origins held true only for the English; the Scots had a very different view. There was, in fact, as R. James Goldstein has demonstrated, something of an ongoing "war of historiography" between the English and the Scots in the Middle Ages.[72] "The opening salvo" of this war, according to Goldstein, "was fired in 1291 when Edward I attempted to establish his claim to suzerainty in Scotland through an 'appeal to history.'" Initially, this was an appeal "that relied to a remarkable extent on chronicle history." In 1301, however, Edward, in a letter to Pope Boniface VII defending his claim to the Scottish throne, extended the official historical narrative "to include legendary history, basing [his] account, directly or indirectly, on Geoffrey of Monmouth's widely circulated *The History of the Kings of Britain*."[73] We needn't concern ourselves with the exact details of Edward's argument. Suffice it to say that, through a deft conflation of Anglo-Norman and "Trojan" law, Edward managed to trace his claim back not only to Locrine, the firstborn son of Brutus, who acquired Albany (Scotland) after defeating his brother's usurper, but also to Dunwal, king of the Britons, who received Scotland in surrender from its rebellious king and then passed its crown to his elder son. What matters for us at this point is the Scottish response. "The earliest Scottish texts in the war of historiography," according to Goldstein, are the *Instructiones* and *Processus* of Baldred Bisset, one of the canon lawyers sent to plead the Scottish case at the papal curia. There are two prongs to Bisset's argument. On the one hand, he seeks to discredit Edward's "appeal to the legendary history of the Britons" by pointing out that the king's "historical argument is largely based on 'unproven fictions [*figmenta*] about an obsolete distant past,'" rather than on those recent events that, in the Scots' view, clearly demonstrate their independence. However, since Edward insists on bringing it up, Bisset is only too happy "to play the game of legendary history," as Goldstein puts it. Thus Bisset's "primary attack on British legends rests not on the suggestion that they are false," as Goldstein goes on to explain, "but on the claim that they contain half-truths at best." Sure, concedes Bisset, "the descendants of Brutus once ruled the entire island." But in the intervening centuries, "the Britons were conquered by the Saxons, who in turn fell before the Danes." Then, "when the Saxons finally overcame the Danes they were conquered once again, by the Normans." Meanwhile, Bisset argues, "the Britons who occupied Albany were later conquered by the Picts, who in turn were conquered by the Scots." Oh, and one more thing: William never conquered the kingdom of Scotland.[74]

Note that, like Henryson, Bisset begins by cultivating doubt about an English text. Who knows if all that Edward wrote was true? More intriguing, though, is the countermyth of Scottish origins, described here in a report to Edward I from one of his representatives at the papal court:

> Then, sir, in order that credence be not given to the documents, histories, and deeds described in your statement, they say that allegations like those recounted in your narrative are put out of court by the true facts, and they endeavor to demonstrate their assertion by chronicles and narratives of a contrary purport. Brutus divided between his three sons the island once called Britain, and now England, and gave to one son Loegria, to another Wales, and to the third what is now called Scotland, and made them peers, so that none of them was subject to another. Afterwards came a woman named Scota, daughter of Pharaoh of Egypt, who came via Spain and occupied Ireland, and afterwards conquered the land of Albany, which she had called, after her name, *Scotland*, and one place in that land she had called after the names of her son Erk and her husband Gayl, wherefore that district was called *Ergaill* [Argyll], and they drove out the Britons, and from that time the Scots, as a new race and possessing a new name, had nothing to do with the Britons, but pursued them daily as their enemies, and were distinguished from them by different ranks and customs, and by a different language.[75]

Like Henryson and his "vther quair," the Scottish canon lawyers produce an "other" story that, running parallel to the English version, seeks to undo any genealogical relation between the two. In this version, the Scots and the English are fundamentally neighbors: intimate others occupying the same space—geographical, imaginary, historical—with each one trying to negate, to overwrite, the other.

This suggests that the *Testament*'s reanimation of Troilus, which culminates in his acts of charity toward Cresseid, in particular the building of her tomb, realizes more than just "the jilted lover's fantasy" of triumph and magnanimity—of having the last word.[76] It might also be read as part of a larger critique of the English chronicle tradition and, beyond that, as an allegory of the troubled intersection between the "war of historiography" and the paradoxes of the neighbor relation. We have noted that the death of Troilus serves as the precondition for the eventual rise of England. But let us note as well that Cresseid, like Scota, the mythological founder of Scotland, is a daughter. Is it so far-fetched to suggest that Henryson may have been drawn to the story of a suffering daughter, a daughter who cannot be protected from the depredations of the law, because of its uncanny parallels with Scottish concerns about England's imperialist ambitions? It is as if, in the encounter between Troilus and Cresseid, England and Scotland were encountering one another at the level of their mutually exclusive foundation myths. Just as England longs to drape Scotland, so to speak, in the same chronicle as itself, so Troilus is blinded by fantasy—the fantasy of historiography—to the suffering and humiliation he sees before him. Incapable of loving the neighbor as himself, he instead responds with charity—that is, with a gesture meant to answer the suffering of the other by "re-creating her according to the 'reassuring image of my own narcissism.'"[77]

And what of Troilus himself? If, as I will go on to argue in the final chapter of this book, *Troilus and Criseyde* can be seen as pursuing an English ideological fantasy of overwriting Troy by symbolically interring Troilus—in short, of establishing the symbolic as a barrier against the Thing—then the *Testament of Cresseid* can be seen as realizing, however unconsciously, a specifically Scottish ideological fantasy: that of creating a barrier against the aggression of the English neighbor. And it accomplishes this not simply by interring Cresseid, thus negating the desire of that neighbor, but by reviving the embodiment

of the English legendary Thing: the Troy-Thing. Whether intention-
ally or not, the *Testament*, by insisting on the existence of Troilus in
a continuous present, disinters, revives, that which must remain dead
and buried so that the English New Troy may go on existing on its
canceled ground. So long as Troilus remains alive, then for that suspended period of time Troy has never fallen, or has yet to fall, and
so, according to the logic of imperial translation, England has never
existed, never arisen in Troy's empty place. Cresseid, meanwhile, persists, in negation, within Henryson's poem. Her future redemption
disrupts the genealogical scenario grounded in Troilus's death.

CHAPTER 2

Fremde and Neighbor

On Chaucer's Encounter with Boccaccio's *Il Filostrato*

In the previous chapter, we saw how Henryson's *Testament of Cresseid* reacted to the encounter with the neighboring text by negating,
through an act of textual interment, the "new and non-comparable"
element it had isolated in Chaucer's *Troilus and Criseyde*. That act of
interment, I argued, could be interpreted as an especially radical form
of neighbor love. Specifically, it could be interpreted as Henryson's
attempt to take responsibility for the *jouissance* that is one's closest
and most disturbing neighbor. In that respect, the *Testament* might
be said to "complete" the work of *Troilus and Criseyde* by naming,
through an act of critical and aesthetic judgment, the enjoyment from
which Chaucer's poem ultimately recoils: the enjoyment generated by
the inherently excessive imperative to neighbor love. But as we shall
also see, the *Testament*'s interest in burying the undead desire of the
neighboring text, insofar as it mirrors and inverts *Troilus and Criseyde*'s treatment of its titular characters, also ends up throwing into
high relief the compromises with historiography made by Chaucer in
his own work. In the next two chapters, we shall trace the path by
which Chaucer came to risk the form of neighbor love realized, and
then betrayed, in *Troilus and Criseyde*. And we shall do so by first

considering, at length and in depth, his encounter with Boccaccio's *Il Filostrato.*

I

The *Chaucer Life-Records,* as usual, tell us very little. In 1372, Chaucer traveled with two Italians, John de Mari and Sir James de Provan, to Genoa, on a trading mission.[1] Exactly why Chaucer, then an esquire in Edward III's court, was chosen for such a mission remains unclear. Our best guess is that it was for his knowledge of Italian, which he had likely acquired, in his youth, from the Italian merchants who frequented his father's house on business. The same trip, which ended up lasting until May 1373, also took Chaucer to Florence, for reasons that are still obscure. Likely he was sent there to meet with members of the powerful Bardi banking family, with whom Edward III had various dealings. Once again, he was probably chosen for his knowledge of Italian, although we do not know for certain. About all one can say regarding this first visit, based on the evidence of the poems, is that Chaucer seems to have acquired—or read, or heard, or at the very least heard about—Dante's *Commedia.*

Five years later, beginning in May 1378, Chaucer was back in Italy, this time in Lombardy, as part of a diplomatic mission to Bernabò Visconti and the English mercenary Sir John Hawkwood. This mission, undertaken to cultivate an alliance with Bernabò in England's ongoing disputes with France, was not particularly successful. Indeed, the whole thing would amount to little more than a handful of scattered documents—letters of protection, receipts, memoranda—if not for the fact that Chaucer just happened to encounter, perhaps in Bernabò's own library, Boccaccio's *Il Filostrato.*

Beginning with C. S. Lewis, who long ago conjured up the indelible image of a donnish Chaucer "feeling the charm" of *Il Filostrato*'s "narrative power" yet finding himself, "at many passages, uttering the Middle English equivalent of 'This will never do!'," the tendency has been to imagine that encounter as something like a shock to the system: a medieval English poet's first experience with the new and the strange.[2] For some critics, moreover, that imagined shock has come to stand as a metaphor for Chaucer's experience with Italy as a whole, which they compare to that "of English academics in the United States in the 1950s or early 1960s," to "'the open-mouthed response of Eastern Europeans when confronted in the late 1980s with the wealth of the West,'" and, most fanciful of all, to "Gawain's accommodation at Bertilak's castle."[3] If there is an exception to this pattern, it is David Wallace, who argues that Chaucer would in fact have felt at ease with the productions of "Italian literary cultures," including *Il Filostrato*, since he would have encountered them "within a familiar international nexus of capital, mercantile activity, and warfare."[4] Chaucer, as Wallace pointedly reminds us, was not some innocent abroad. On the contrary, he belonged, like Petrarch and Boccaccio before him, to a transnational courtly elite and had traveled far—to France and Spain, as well as to Italy—in the service of two kings. Never mind his ties to the London merchant community and the royal household; that Chaucer even had access to Bernabò's library should tell us something about the kind of circles he moved in, the preferment he enjoyed. He also knew Italian, as the work of both Wallace and Barry Windeatt amply demonstrates.[5] At the very least, he seems unlikely to have recoiled from *Il Filostrato* in quite the twittering way Lewis imagines.

But does this mean that Chaucer never recoiled from Boccaccio's poem at all? Generally speaking, Wallace makes a powerful case for recognizing the continuities between "Renaissance" Italy and "late medieval" England: two historical periods that just happened to have been unfolding, simultaneously, in the late fourteenth century. Nevertheless, to emphasize only Chaucer's affinity with the literary culture that produced *Il Filostrato* is, I think, to duck the question of why he then, to invoke Lewis once more, "did" something to Boccaccio's poem: why he altered and reworked so much of it, and to such radically different ends. If Chaucer would have recognized *Il Filostrato* as the product of his own transnational courtly culture, why then did he bother to change it at all?

One of my aims in this chapter is to explore that question—in essence, the question of Chaucer's unknowable intentions—by offering a construction, in the psychoanalytic meaning of the term: a story, conjectural and quite possibly erroneous, meant to hold the place of a history too fragmented to be recollected. In psychoanalysis, constructions are deployed less to explain something than to do something; their purpose, as Freud puts it, is to "make out what has been forgotten from the traces it has left behind."[6] Ordinarily, this would be a piece of the patient's early history. Here it takes the form of a forgotten moment in literary history, the moment of what I want to call, following Kenneth Reinhard, "originary non-relation" between Chaucer as a medieval reader and *Il Filostrato* as a Trecento text.[7] When Chaucer traveled to Italy in 1378, he did so as part of an ultimately unsuccessful diplomatic mission. Since it seems unlikely that he also went with the specific aim of reading *Il Filostrato*, his encounter with Boccaccio's text should be viewed as contingent rather than necessary, accidental rather than premeditated. That is not to say it was extraordinary. On the contrary, my construction is predicated on the assumption that Chaucer's act of reading Boccaccio's poem was as mundane as is any act of reading, the outcome of a complex set of everyday, material realities. All the same, it was eventful, a transformative moment in Chaucer's career as a poet. It is that paradoxical encounter, at once mundane and eventful, that I hope to construct.

To that end, I want to begin by suggesting that it was precisely *because* he and Boccaccio moved in interconnected cultural and linguistic milieus that Chaucer felt compelled to transform *Il Filostrato* as he did. For with *Il Filostrato*—a work written in a language that had been familiar to him since childhood and yet was not his own; the expression of a literary culture he understood but that was nonetheless alien to the literary traditions he knew best; an object neither wholly familiar nor entirely strange—Chaucer encountered something more than just another text. He encountered a text that psychoanalysis allows us to recognize as his neighbor: a prior, proximate other falling apart into two components, one recognizable and "satisfying," to use Freud's terminology; the other *Fremde*, foreign or alien, and also, as Freud puts it, "hostile."[8] It is this particular understanding of Chaucer's relation to *Il Filostrato*—a relation of neighboring in the fullest sense, defined by an encounter with a figure, the *Nebenmensch*, that is both the universalized embodiment of community and the particular agent of its uncanny disruption—that comes through when one places Wallace and Lewis alongside one another, as conceptual supplements. Wallace, for his part, by foregrounding Chaucer's wholesale involvement in the political currents of late fourteenth-century Europe, reminds us that neighbor relations are anything but abstract. Rather, they unfold in a world populated by multiple bodies joined together in bodies politic governed—more or less—by codes of distributive justice. If *Il Filostrato* were not embedded in the network of Lombardian power or legible as the product of a social order recognizable to Chaucer as an extension of his own—if Chaucer had not participated, as minor diplomat and astute observer, in the international nexus Wallace describes—then it could never have come to occupy the arbitrary place of the neighbor.

Recall, however, that resemblance is not all there is to the neighbor. There is also a profound uncanniness, insofar as the *Nebenmensch* materializes the "complex of perceptions through which subjective reality divides into the representable world of cognition and the 'unassimilable' element that Freud calls *das Ding*, 'the thing.'"[9] However familiar the *Nebenmensch* might be, he nonetheless harbors something *Fremde*, something alien and hostile to the subject: an intimation of "the death drive in its pure state." The only question is, whose death drive? Consider the following excerpt from Gower's *Mirour de l'Omme:*

> But no matter who may gain profits, it is amazing, it seems to me, to see the Lombards in our country, who, though they are foreigners, try to claim to dwell in our country just as free and welcome as if they were born and brought up with us. But it is to beguile us that they pretend to be our friends, and their intention underneath is to plunder us of our gold and silver.
>
> These Lombards cheat us; they exchange their straw for our grain. For two goods they give us four evils. They bring us their fustian, and they deprive us, with false hand, of our rich, royal gold nobles and of our pounds of fine sterling metal. This is one of the principal causes that our country is barren. But, if my advice were taken, may God never save me if we would have such fellows as our neighbors.[10]

The challenge posed by the neighbor, as Gower's diatribe makes all too clear, is that his actions manifest a death drive that is also our own death drive, an expression of our own aggressive impulses, our own will to exploit those who, falling outside the categories of kin and citizen, collapse the distinction between proximity and strangeness. As Lacan succinctly puts it: "My neighbor possesses all the evil Freud speaks about, but it is no different from the evil I retreat from in myself. To love him, to love him as myself, is necessarily to move toward some cruelty. His or mine?, you will object. But haven't I just explained to you that nothing indicates they are distinct?"''' The whole problematic of neighboring is thus on display not only in the fact that Gower's language expresses all of the aggression he imputes to the Lombards. It is also there in the way that he would deny the status of "neighbor" to those who, neither kin nor stranger, most thoroughly embody the term—the way he retreats from the "neighbor" in himself by condemning the behavior of his physical neighbors. How Chaucer would have reacted to the spectacle of the man he calls "moral Gower" attacking a community to which he himself was connected through his father's business dealings, one can only imagine. The important thing for us, at this point, is that it suggests something about the atmosphere in which Chaucer would have encountered Boccaccio's text for the first time.

It is this uncanny aspect of the neighbor that, more than anything, makes me reluctant simply to abandon Lewis. For as problematic (or embarrassing) as parts of Lewis's essay surely are, its vision of a Chaucer agitated by *Il Filostrato* suggests two models for pursuing this study's most ambitious aim, which is to reorient the course of literary history in the late fourteenth and early fifteenth centuries around the uncanny figure of the *Nebenmensch*. The first model is that of an ethical Chaucer, a Chaucer who emerges, after his encounter with *Il Filostrato*, only through his struggle to maintain fidelity to a particular act of judgment, a parsing of the good—those aspects of the poem that he could understand "by the activity of memory"—from the bad: the Thing. Lewis, it is true, may reveal more about his own prejudices than about Chaucer's when he imagines the latter responding to "certain passages" in *Il Filostrato* by exclaiming, "This will never do!"

Yet his strange act of ventriloquism also invites us to consider whether Chaucer, recoiling from "an enjoyment that resists sympathetic identification and 'understanding,'" might have written *Troilus and Criseyde,* not in simple imitation of *Il Filostrato,* but in response to the "mutual aggression" that bound his text to Boccaccio's.

The second model suggested by Lewis's essay, one closely related to the first, is that of a discontinuous, ultimately reactive temporality: a way of thinking about heterogeneous time. When Chaucer traveled to Italy, we now realize, he not only journeyed through physical space, working his way across the Channel and (most likely) over the Alps. He also traveled through and across different periods in historical time, shuttling back and forth between an English Middle Ages and an Italian Renaissance, underway simultaneously in the late fourteenth century. Lewis, I would argue, was already thinking in terms of just such a disjointed temporality when he proposed that "the process which *Il Filostrato* underwent at Chaucer's hands was first and foremost a process of *medievalization.*"[12] By this, Lewis meant that Chaucer wrote his poem as a kind of corrective to Boccaccio's, translating it into what would have been, for Chaucer, the more familiar terms of historiography, rhetoric, doctrine, and, most problematically in the view of later critics, courtly love. This suggests that "medievalization" amounted to nothing more than an aesthetic process, an imposition of genre and form. But one might push Lewis's claim further and say that Chaucer, in recoiling from something foreign and inassimilable in *Il Filostrato,* affirmed the synchronic period in historical time known to us, today, as the Middle Ages. Put in terms of the *Nebenmensch*—foregrounding, as it were, the temporal dimension of the subject's encounter with the *Nebenmensch,* the dimension involving memory and an experience of the new—one might say that Chaucer affirmed the situation he understood against the only thing that is ever truly foreign and other, ever truly "new and non-comparable," to use Freud's description of *das Ding,* at the level of time: the future.

To imagine Chaucer adopting such an affirmative stance is not the same as imagining him standing in simple opposition to a diachronic conception of sequential time. For one thing, the synchronic state I have in mind, rather than existing in isolation from other time periods, establishes itself specifically against an apprehension of the future—that is, against a future already impinging itself upon the present scene. Such a future, at once detectable "within" the present but not reducible to its terms, may not represent an absolute rupture, but neither can it be described as a mere continuation. A continuation requires, obviously, that there be something to continue. The paradox of the future that I am attempting to describe here is that it flares up within the present, thereby making the final constellation of that present impossible. Full but not whole, the late medieval present constructed itself, as a synchronic state, against the incursion of a future whose very arrival precluded its cohesion as present time.[13]

This might make it seem as though Chaucer's response to the future dimension of *Il Filostrato* were entirely reactive, perhaps even negating. And indeed, if we were to restrict ourselves to Lewis's concept of "medievalization" alone, that would be the only way of reading it. It is for this reason that I find myself drawn to Gregory Stone's intriguing, and now largely forgotten, claim "that certain literary texts in the late Middle Ages . . . have a presentiment of the idea of the Renaissance, and they don't like this idea."[14] Whatever the shortcomings of Stone's overall argument, this particular claim seems worth salvaging if only because it can help us conceive of Chaucer's response to *Il Filostrato*, as to Trecento Italian cultures generally, as something other than slack-jawed wonder or specular identification. We still tend to think of the early modern period as somehow having invented the Middle Ages. Stone, like Lewis, inverts that sequence, allowing us instead to imagine a scenario in which a writer like Chaucer helped to create the English Middle Ages, as a synchronic state, by affirming a judgment leveled against the future. Chaucer's affirmation of himself as a "medieval" subject, a subject in the middle, poised between past and future: that is what constitutes the ethical heart of his experience with Boccaccio's text.

Another way of putting this is to say that Stone's thesis helps us recognize how Chaucer's encounter with *Il Filostrato* marked the beginning of his fidelity to an event: the untimely event of the future. Suppose that the "familiar international nexus of capital, mercantile activity, and warfare" in which that encounter took place defined what might be called, following Alain Badiou, the "situation" of the late fourteenth century in Europe.[15] The question I am trying to pursue here is why, if *Il Filostrato* were simply a recognizable part of that situation and nothing more, Chaucer took it upon himself to alter it and not merely replicate it. One possible answer to this question would be that Chaucer's otherwise unremarkable encounter with *Il Filostrato* somehow managed, like every genuine event, to exceed the situation that gave rise to it. Drawing, once again, on the trope of the neighboring text, we might say that most of *Il Filostrato* was legible according to the terms of late fourteenth-century literary culture. If nothing else, it at least resembled other works that Chaucer could call to memory. But it also, to judge by the fact that Chaucer felt compelled to "do" something to it, contained an element, a *thing*, so radically new and noncomparable according to the laws of the late medieval situation that it called the situation itself into question. One might go further, then, and say that Chaucer recognized *Il Filostrato* as *his* event, by which I mean that it was he alone who grasped the fact that *Il Filostrato* was not entirely reducible to the laws of the situation he knew. In writing *Troilus and Criseyde*, Chaucer signaled that, much like Troilus after he first sees Criseyde in the temple, he no longer found it possible to relate to the situation from any perspective other than that of the event.

Yet if Stone's thesis makes it possible for us to read Chaucer's act of writing *Troilus and Criseyde* as a way of maintaining fidelity to the event of the neighboring text, it also allows us to recognize the unexpected forms fidelity itself might take. Fidelity, as Badiou defines it, is a refusal to give way. "Never forget what you have encountered": that is the maxim of fidelity.[16] As I see it, Chaucer's reworking of *Il Filostrato* constitutes just such an act of fidelity, of not forgetting. But what does it mean not to forget? Chaucer's decision to revisit his encounter with the neighboring text by writing his own version of that text—in short, Chaucer's act of repetition—suggests that simply struggling to work through an event might also represent a way of maintaining fidelity to that event: of not forgetting, even unconsciously, what one has encountered. Fascination, obsession, excitement, anxiety, negation, even pulling back: these, too, register that one cannot forget what one has encountered, that one must return, in time, to the untimely moment of the event. In this way, repetition emerges as an ethical gesture equal to the invention championed by Badiou.

This is why I would amend Stone's claim that "certain late-medieval texts" (among which I would like to include *Troilus and Criseyde*) mourn the "death of the troubadour": Stone's term for the way those texts resisted the ascendance of an individualized Renaissance "narrative" over a collective medieval "lyricism." Properly speaking, mourning is an act of forgetting, a process of renunciation that culminates in the acceptance of compensatory objects in the place of whatever is lost. As Stone describes it, however, the texts he has in mind resisted the idea of an emerging Renaissance in much the same way that Freud says the ego revolts against the death of the love object.[7] That is, they refused to renounce their own historical "idea"—to accept whatever it was the future had to offer and "move on" from their synchronic moment. Such a disposition sounds much closer to melancholia than to mourning. But it is a peculiar form of melancholia, one in which the medieval present itself becomes the unmournable lost object. Refusing both the promise of future compensation and the anticipation of future loss, this is a melancholia that can do nothing more than contemplate the ruin of the present situation in the wake of the event.

Although I draw my terms from psychoanalysis, my larger point here is really a literary-historical one. Chaucer's repetition of *Il Filostrato* as *Troilus and Criseyde*, I want to propose, was an instance when literary history "advanced," moved forward diachronically, not just by pulling back, but by staying rooted at the point where temporal movement had been arrested. In subjecting *Il Filostrato* to a process of "medievalization," Chaucer took literary history out of sequence, recoiling at the very moment when one might expect, however naively, to find linear development. But why did he choose to "medievalize" Boccaccio's poem, to "do" something to it, in the first place? What was it about *Il Filostrato* that seems both to have attracted and repelled Chaucer? What did he perceive in that particular text that made him want to repeat it, but with a difference? My immediate answer to these conjoined questions is that Chaucer was, to borrow a term from Eric Santner, profoundly *ex-cited* by *Il Filostrato*.[18] What I mean by this is not simply that Chaucer felt inspired by Boccaccio's poem, that he felt moved by it to push his own art in new directions. What I mean is that his encounter with *Il Filostrato* exposed him "to the peculiar 'creativity' associated with the threshold of law and nonlaw"—that he found himself "delivered over," as Santner puts it, to the space of "'sovereign *jouissance.*'"[19] It was not just that Boccaccio's poem was a novel take on the matter of Troy—that much was undeniable—or that it was written, not in the elevated manner of the courts, but in the style of the *cantari*, the songs of the street.[20] The peculiarly creative aspect of *Il Filostrato* that most *ex-cited* Chaucer, I mean to argue, was the identification between its narrator and Troilo: the substitution of the pre-Christian protagonist of the story for its latter-day teller. I am not suggesting that Chaucer simply disapproved of that identification. My point, rather, is that he was "called forth" by enigmatic messages emanating from the other, messages that he then took it upon himself, quite literally, to translate. Responding to the eventful nature of his encounter with the other's desire, Chaucer made an ethical decision, parsing the neighboring text into those elements that corresponded to what he could understand "according to memory" and that which he isolated as *Fremde*, as foreign and vaguely unsettling: the *Filostrato* narrator's conjuration, in the name of the future, of a dead figure from the pre-Christian past.

II

Assuming that the manuscript of *Il Filostrato* available to Chaucer was one that included the Proem (not all surviving copies do, although the copy that Bernabò had in his library does), he would have found an expression of identification between the narrator and Troilo on one of its very first pages.[21] Explaining to Filomena, his ostensibly absent mistress, why he has put the story of Troilo into verse, the narrator writes that the best way he could think of to regain her love and so secure his "future well being" was to be able, in the person of someone as emotionally overcome as he was, to relate his sufferings in song. And so—I am paraphrasing—he began to turn over in his mind, with solicitous care, "old stories" in order to find one that he could make into a likely shield for his secret and amorous suffering. Nor did any one more suitable for such a need come into his mind than that of the valorous young Troilo, son of Priam, the most noble king of Troy, to whose life his had been very similar after his mistress's departure insofar as it was sorrowful (Pr. 10–12).[22] Unremarkable as it may appear to us now, the identification declared here between the narrator and his pre-Christian counterpart was in fact boldly innovative, an example of what Donald Howard once characterized as Boccaccio's contribution to the "birth" of fiction as we know it.[23] That very innovation can be seen as problematic, however, precisely because identification, as psychoanalysis has taught us, forms the basis not only for subjectivity but also for ideology. Here I rely on the crucial distinction Lacan draws between imaginary identification, in which the would-be subject tries to assume an outside, specular image, and symbolic identification, in which the subject assumes her place in the symbolic order by identifying with what she perceives to be the Other's desire.[24] It is these symbolic identifications, in particular, that act as the linchpins of ideology, not only because they enable us, as subjects, to transcend the aggression inherent in imaginary identification with the counterpart by establishing what Reinhard terms "the common-places of a community," but also because, more sinisterly, they foster "community spirit" by encouraging us to direct our aggressions against those considered to be outside the community.[25]

I make this point to draw attention to the role that identification had typically played in the medieval tradition of Trojan historiography. Symbolic identification is obviously at work, for example, in Benoît de Sainte-Maure's *Roman de Troie*, the probable source text for *Il Filostrato* and a work available, along with its Latin redaction, Guido delle Colonne's *Historia Destructionis Troiae*, to Chaucer. The difference is that Benoît (and Guido after him), rather than identifying with any one character in his vast work, identifies with its supposed originator, Dares, regarded in the Middle Ages as the most trustworthy and accurate historian of the Trojan War. As Benoît explains:

This Dares of whom you hear now was fostered and born in Troy. He dwelt there, and did not leave till the army had departed. Many a deed of valor he did himself both in assault and in battle. He was a wondrous clerk and learned in the seven arts. Wherefore he saw that the matter was so great that neither before nor since has there been a greater; thus he was minded to preserve the memory of these deeds. He wrote the history of them in Greek. Each day he wrote it thus, as he beheld it with his eyes. Everything they did in the day, either in battle or combat, that night this Dares wrote it all, as I tell you. Never on any account would he refrain from saying and setting forth the truth. Therefore, though he was of the Trojans, he did not on that account show more favour to his own people than he did to the Greeks. He wrote the truth of the story. For a long time this book was lost, so that it was not found or seen. But Cornelius discovered it in Athens and translated it. By his wit and skill he turned it from Greek into Latin. We must believe him and hold his story true far rather than him [i.e., Homer] who was born a hundred years or more later, who knew nothing indeed, except by hearsay. (3–4)[26]

What Benoît seems most drawn to here is a kind of presence: the ability to report, accurately and without bias, the events of the war just as they happened at the moment they happened. The *Roman* is not suffused with the same profound sense of loss that permeates *Il Filostrato* and *Troilus and Criseyde*. Dares' lost work has been recovered, and so the past too has been recovered, in all its detail. By aspiring to the place of Dares, then, Benoît also aspires to the authority of the former's all-encompassing, utterly trustworthy eyewitness account of the war. In the *Roman*, we are assured, the "words" ("les moz") of the story as Dares established them are "[e]nsi tailliez, ensi curez, / Ensi asis, ensi posez, / Que plus ne meins n'i a mestier" [so fashioned and wrought, so set down, so arranged, that none of them, greater or less, is out of place]. "Ci vueil l'estoire comencier" [I shall begin the story here], insists Benoît,

> Le latin sivrai e la letre,
> Nule autre rien n'i voudrai metre,
> S'ensi non com jol truis escrit.

Ne di mie qu'aucun bon dit
N'i mete, se faire le sai,
Mais la matire en ensivrai
(Pr. 134–40)

[I shall follow the Latin closely, I shall put in nothing, but as I find it written. Nor do I say or add any good word, even had I the skill, but I shall follow my matter] (4).

It may be that Benoît's performance in this and similar passages amounts to no more than an elaborate put-on. But the reason the put-on works is that it plays on the medieval conception of the historian as "someone who narrates or reports events which actually occurred in the past," just as it accords with the medieval understanding of history as having been "written only by those who had witnessed the things about which they wrote."[27]

One reason, then, that Benoît would seek to identify with Dares' symbolic position is that the latter was thought to possess, and thus also to confer, the legitimacy of presence. From a psychoanalytic perspective, however, Benoît's identification with Dares can also be viewed as essentially symbolic (as opposed to imaginary), with Dares occupying the structural position of the Father and providing Benoît with a text-based ego ideal: that "guide beyond the imaginary" from whose vantage point the subject stands in judgment of itself, measuring itself, usually negatively, against the Other's ideals.[28] If, in imaginary identification, "we imitate the other at the level of resemblance," according to Slavoj Žižek, "in symbolic identification we identify ourselves with the other precisely at a point at which he is inimitable, at the point which eludes resemblance."[29] And so we find that the trait in Dares with which Benoît identifies, the trait by which he seeks to ratify his own work, is the one thing that he can never imitate: Dares' now impossible position as eyewitness to the past. Any exact mirroring, then, is out of the question; Benoît can only aspire to a promise, the promise to let Dares' words be his guide in the writing of his own text. Put another way, Benoît can aspire to the authoritative place of Dares only insofar as he commits the process of symbolization/

historicization—in this case, the ongoing, retroactive accounting of the trauma of the Trojan War—to the strict maintenance of the symbolic order: the fixing of signifiers in their proper places.

Here we begin to get a sense of why Chaucer, as someone approaching *Il Filostrato* as a "historical poet," would likely have been "excited" by the *Filostrato* narrator's avowed identification with Troilo.[30] Simply put, that identification makes clear *Il Filostrato*'s estrangement, if not outright separation, from the genealogically based community of Trojan historiography. Ordinarily, the texts in that community were bound by a common identification with the figure of Dares. Through the identification between its narrator and Troilo, *Il Filostrato* announces instead that it *neighbors on* that community, connected with it less by consanguinity than by mere contiguity. The *Filostrato* narrator may, like Benoît or Guido, turn to "old stories" for his material; but his identification with Troilo means that such "turning to" is where his own poem's relationship to those stories ends. Beyond that, they remain mutually estranged, committed to different desires. Indeed, while *Il Filostrato* might be said to acknowledge, however obliquely, its debt to other texts, it can hardly be said to complement them. Boccaccio may have "read widely in Trojan matters." Yet he did so, according to Wallace, "not to create a consistent historical account, but to serve his own, highly individual purposes."[31] Whatever it was Boccaccio wanted from the matter of Troy, it wasn't the comforts of historiography.

Instead, Boccaccio's poem does something much more radical: it "blasts" the story of Troilus and Criseyde "out of the continuum of history," to borrow a typically evocative phrase from Walter Benjamin.[32] Before *Il Filostrato*, the story of Troilus and Criseyde had functioned as a minor, if tragic, subplot within the much larger cycle of Trojan mytho-history. While hardly neglected by previous writers, the story of Troilus's love for Criseyde had been at least muted—subordinated to the larger thematic interests of the Trojan cycle, inserted, so to speak, into the edifice of official, monumental history. Neither epic nor chronicle, the Trojan cycle had long functioned, in its medieval iterations, as the consummate "natural-historical" narrative, a story about the sequential, cyclical, inevitable, and ultimately violent rise and fall of ruling powers. The *Filostrato* narrator, rather than simply reinscribing that tradition, "decompletes" it instead, in effect isolating a single element of the cycle from the implacable rhythms of natural history. *Il Filostrato* does not merely reorient the Troy story, nudging it in the direction of romance. It starts the history of Troy, and thus the mytho-history of medieval Europe, over again, beginning it at a new point: the point at which the sequential order of natural history has been suspended in favor of the love story. Acting more like a (post) modern archivist than a medieval historian, the narrator of *Il Filostrato* disordered the late medieval present by reviving a dormant future: a future latent in materials overlooked, or rendered moribund, by the writing of official history.

Almost immediately, however, the narrator begins to compromise his potentially radical gesture. In Benjamin, the historical materialist works to redeem something specific—an era, a life, a work—by blasting it out of the false continuity of official history. His purpose is to "recognize," in a moment of temporal arrest, "a revolutionary chance in the fight for the oppressed past," holding open "the straight gate through which the Messiah might enter."[33] The narrator of *Il Filostrato*, by contrast, conjures Troilo in what can only be described as a bid for self-preservation:

> Moved by more useful advice, I changed my proposal and wished to let it [i.e., the "sorrow engendered" in him by Filomena's absence] be disclosed and to give it an outlet from my sad breast with some suitable lamentation in order that I might live and be able to see you again and might by living remain yours a longer time. No sooner did such an idea come into my mind before the way to implement it occurred to me; this occurrence, which seemed inspired by a secret divinity, I took as the most sure sign of future well-being. And the way was this: I wanted to be able, in the person of someone emotionally overcome as I was and am, to relate my sufferings in song. (Pr. 11)

What matters here is not that the narrator does indeed go on living while Troilo, his hapless counterpart, dies. This is to be expected, after all; Troilo always dies. What matters is that, in this particular case, Troilo might be said to die—or be made to die again—precisely so that the narrator can assume his place as the one suffering, made prostrate, for love. Troilo dies so that the narrator might gain an identity.

But then, had that not always been the motivation, to some extent, behind the medieval obsession with retelling the story of Troy's destruction? To give credit where credit is due, Boccaccio does seem to get at one of the more uncomfortable aspects of the Trojan cycle by reminding us, however obliquely, that Troy and its inhabitants were repeatedly dying, in French, in Latin, and in English, so that the territories of medieval Europe could secure their "identities" as nations. This is no doubt one reason why the narrator's identification with the suffering figure of Troilo feels so risky: it cannot help but raise the question of the *jouissance*, the enjoyment, that his predecessors stood both to gain and to lose in their identification with Dares. Benoît and Guido had each, to borrow a phrase from Žižek, "bet on Father." That is, each of them had avoided "the impasse constitutive of desire"—the impasse by which desire leads, not to satisfaction, but to the revelation that *jouissance* is impossible—by assuming a symbolic identification with the Name-of-the-Father that transforms the inherent impossibility of enjoyment into its prohibition.[34] That way, they were able to "protect" themselves from the burden of surplus-*jouissance*, the *jouissance* evident everywhere within the workings of the law, by attributing all *jouissance* to the symbolic position of the exceptional Father. *They* don't derive any enjoyment from the violence of the Trojan cycle; *they* don't experience the *jouissance* associated with destroying Troy and its inhabitants yet again, as if to insist that, yes, this time the Trojans really are dead enough for their "descendants" to lay claim to their inheritance. *They* are only following the lead of their authority (even when they aren't, which is often). This pretense, by which medieval narrators of the Trojan cycle turned Dares, the fiction that allowed them to report the past, into a mechanism allowing them to disavow their own present enjoyment, Boccaccio lays bare by having his narrator identify with Troilo.

It is not just the naked fact of that identification that seems risky, however. It is the symbolic weight attached to the figure with whom the narrator chooses to identify—and also, more potently, the manner in which he pursues that identification. Initially, at least, the choice of Troilo may strike one as unremarkable, even harmless: the narrator, a pathetic figure, finds a way to express his suffering through the experiences of another pathetic figure. Is that not a basic definition of semiautobiographical fiction? Ordinarily, yes. But what makes the difference in this case is our knowledge of that pathetic figure's earlier death. For centuries, "the constant feature" of the Troilus figure, according to Piero Boitani, had been "his death at the hands of Achilles." In both the classical tradition "and that part of the medieval tradition which is directly or indirectly influenced by it," Troilus, as Boitani goes on to argue, "is not primarily a character but a 'function.' He is his death and the fall of Troy in that war which, being the first and most famous of all, constitutes the archetypal World War."[35] Traditionally, the meaning of the Troilus figure had been, not just his death, but the symbolization of that death as a harbinger of the fall of Troy. Now, though, that figure has been transformed into something radically different: a "shield" for the "secret and amorous sufferings" of a young man laid low, as he claims Troilo also was, by love. Deracinated from the (admittedly deadly) form of life that vitalized him for so long, the Troilus figure now finds himself thrown into the very midst of natural history: a symbolic form, a relic, persisting beyond the death of the form of life that once gave it meaning. One might, for this reason, profitably describe the narrator of *Il Filostrato* as a sort of allegorician, in the Benjaminian sense: actively separating signifiers from their original signifieds, employing an associative mode "in which the link between figure and meaning is experienced as a human construct" and thus subject to the erosive cycles of natural history.[36] Yet, as such, he makes what Benjamin contends is the allegorician's tragic mistake: not content to "faithfully rest in the contemplation of bones"—that is, to gaze in horror upon the ongoing catastrophe of natural history—he instead "faithlessly leaps forward to the idea of resurrection," asserting the robustness of his own moment by reanimating the dead.[37]

What I am proposing here is that the narrator, going a step further than the simple reanimation of Troilo, "undeadens" him instead. Santner, as part of his ongoing inquiry into what he calls, following Benjamin, the "creaturely" dimension of human life, argues that the "ex-citation" produced by the subject's encounter with the enigma of the desire in the Other "is neither simply livening nor simply deadening but rather . . . undeadening; it produces in us an internal alienness that has a peculiar sort of vitality and yet belongs to no form of life." "What is undeadening in life," Santner goes on to conclude, "is thus not exposure to lawlessness as such but rather the meta-juridical dimension of the law"—that is, to the violent imposition of the law that is also, at the same instant, the law's suspension.[38] Troilo is a peculiar case of such undeadening: a figure reanimated so as to be undeadened, rendered agitated and excited, made prostrate, by an encounter with the metajuridical dimension of the law. I have described the narrator's identification with Troilo as "creative." By this I mean not only that it was innovative but that its innovativeness signaled the narrator's remapping of a situation grounded by Trojan mytho-history. The narrator, that is, deliberately undeadens Troilo by exposing him to a sovereign act: the suspension of the generic "laws" (as it were) that had traditionally governed medieval historiography and, by extension, Troilo's significance.[39] In Benoît's *Roman*, for example, Troilus, the fierce warrior, dies a fierce warrior's death (one involving decapitation and the defilement of his corpse), and his sacrifice is honored accordingly, as Guido will later put it, with "anguished lamentations" and a "rich tomb"—details notably absent from *Il Filostrato* (27.4–8).[40] Again, though, it is not just that Boccaccio's poem denies Troilo the symbolic interment ordinarily accorded him in the historiographic tradition; it is that it offers him no recognizable symbolic interment at all. Rather than dying *for* something, or receiving funerary rites appropriate to his sacrifice, Troilo's sudden, unremarkable death in *Il Filostrato*—"Achilles one day slew him wretchedly after he had already killed more than a thousand" (8.27)—offers little more than an end to his "ill-conceived love" [il mal concetto amore], his "wretched sorrow" [miserabile dolore], and his "vain hope" [speranza vana] (9.28). What it does not end, however, is Troilo. To be sure, Troilo is now physically dead. And yet the question, like the body, remains: Is that end really an end? If the traditional meaning of the Troilus figure simply *was* his death, then what happens when that death goes missing its final symbolization: its monumentalization as part of the "rich tomb" of history?

This is a question that assumes new urgency in the poem's next section, when the narrator appends to Troilo's death the following moral: "O youths, in whom amorous desire comes surging with age, I pray you for the sake of God that you restrain your ready steps to the evil appetite and that you mirror yourselves in Troilo's love which my verses have displayed above because, if you will read them in the right spirit, you will not lightly have trust in all women" (8.29).[41] This eleventh-hour exhortation has sometimes been taken as evidence that *Il Filostrato* functions, *in toto*, as a condemnation of foolish love.[42] But while it might be true that the narrator offers Troilo as a "negative *exemplum*" in which other amorous youths might mirror themselves, judging themselves thereby from the prohibitory perspective of the ego ideal, it is also true that the narrator refuses, rather conspicuously, to follow his own advice.[43] On the contrary, instead of mirroring himself in Troilo and restraining his ready steps, the narrator identifies with the counterpart's suffering to the point that he takes the other's place—becomes the new embodiment of that suffering. "O happy you who will see her which I, sorrowing wretch, cannot do!" the narrator says to his poem in its final part. "And when with joy you have been received into her hands, humbly commend me to her high worth, which alone can give me salvation" (9.5). Then, a few verses after: "If while she is listening to you, you see that her angelic face shows a little charity or she sighs for my toil, pray her as much as you can that it may please her to return here now or to command my soul to take itself away from me because, wherever it must go from here, death is much better for me than such a life" (9.7). The striking thing about these passages is that they reveal a narrator who wants to possess, not the authority of historiography, as did Benoît and Guido, but the very suffering and death of the figure he has undeadened. The narrator could have followed the example of his predecessors and identified with Dares, the self-appointed chronicler of temporal events. Instead, he opts to identify with a figure, Troilo, who is fully subject to the vagaries of those events: a figure whose time is limited, who is always living on borrowed time. To put it bluntly, the *Filostrato* narrator identifies with a figure that is fated to die, a figure whose future, indexed by the poem's own repeated references to the "burning" of both Troy and Troilo, is one of doom.

That identification conveys two, apparently contradictory, messages. The first, which amounts to a highly stylized threat, warns the absent Filomena not to let the narrator end up like Troilo, lest *she* end up being compared to the faithless Criseida. The second, which amounts to a condemnation of Filomena before the fact, signals the narrator's awareness that his warning is in vain, since his absent mistress not only will not be returning but may never have been possessed by him in the first place. (Here one should recall that, as Giulia Natali points out, the narrator seems never actually to have touched Filomena, only to have looked at her.)[44] Adopting a fundamental strategy of the melancholic, the narrator here betrays, in his tacit acknowledgment that he will not obtain the "pity" from his mistress that he needs to "live longer," "an intention to mourn that precedes and anticipates the loss of the object," introjecting his libidinal attachment for the object so that he might "adhere to it at least in its absence" rather than have to confront the fact that it is actually unobtainable. "From this point of view," as Giorgio Agamben puts it,

> melancholy would be not so much the regressive reaction to the loss of the love object as the imaginative capacity to make an unattainable object appear as if lost. If the libido behaves *as if* a loss had occurred although *nothing* has in fact been lost, this is because the libido stages a simulation where what cannot be lost because it has never been possessed appears as lost, and what could never be possessed because it had never perhaps existed may be appropriated insofar as it is lost. . . . Covering its object with the funereal trappings of mourning, melancholy confers upon it the phantasmagorical reality of what is lost; but insofar as such mourning is for an unobtainable object, the strategy of melancholy opens a space for the existence of the unreal and marks out a scene in which the ego may enter into relation with it and attempt an appropriation such as no other possession could rival and no loss possibly threaten.[45]

Confronted by a fundamental lack in the Other, which in this case manifests itself in Filomena's absence, her silence, her lack of a clear mandate or communication, the narrator responds by disavowing that lack, transforming it instead into a loss that he does not have to sacrifice: a loss that he can retain as if loss itself were something one might possess. The narrator's refusal to entomb Troilo, then, is no mere oversight. Rather, it functions as a phantasmatic way of disavowing the lack represented by Filomena's absence. Ultimately, the end of Troilo, which represents lack on a grand scale—the lack that guarantees the rise of later empires—is no end at all, but a translation of the narrator's impending doom into the fullness of loss.

III

Leaving aside, for the moment, what all of this suggests about the narrator's ethical position, I want to ask a more pressing question: Where does all of this leave Troilo? On the one hand, he has been rendered, yet again, physically dead; but, unmourned and unmemorialized as anything other than a warning against inconstant young women, he ends *Il Filostrato* having yet to be interred: an exposed pagan figure denied the achievement of his usual symbolic destiny. Indeed, if the traditional meaning of the Troilus figure *is* his death, as Boitani claims, then Boccaccio has changed that meaning so as to make it illegible within the medieval tradition of Trojan historiography. Granted, Troilo gets killed in battle, as he always must, and, yes, the narrator asks his readers to "piously make a prayer for [Troilo] to Love that he may repose in peace in the region where he dwells" (8.33). But even this last request, though it may take Troilo's burial for granted, can be seen as problematic, since unlike Benoît and Guido, both of whom were careful to describe Troilus's interment, the narrator here displaces the responsibility for Troilo's peaceful repose away from himself and onto the reader. Yet we have been shown nothing to convince us that Troilo is, in fact, at peace. And what if the reader refuses the narrator's request? What happens to Troilo, and to Troy, then?

In other words, what would it mean to say that the ending of *Il Filostrato* finds Troilo not so much dead as suspended in the "space between two deaths"?[46] As Žižek glosses it, this space is a "gap"— the unsettled interval that obtains between biological death and its proper symbolization—whose emptiness can come to contain "either sublime beauty or terrifying monsters": either the splendor of the banished Antigone or Hamlet's father's restless ghost.[47] But there are other dimensions to the space between two deaths that should also concern us. One of these has to do with the question of identification. The quality that makes both Antigone and Hamlet tragic figures is that they identify with, assume as their own, the suffering of two figures—Polynices and Hamlet *père*—caught in the gap between biological and symbolic death. In other words, it is only when they identify with figures whose own deaths have yet to be symbolized, only when they seek to close for the other the gap between real and symbolic death, that Antigone and Hamlet themselves move to the inherently tragic space between two deaths. For it is then that both characters, having voluntarily forsaken their places in their respective communities, become not only unintelligible to those communities, outcasts whose desire runs so counter to the common good as to become terrifying and bewildering, but the very instruments of their undoing. Hence the other dimension of the space between two deaths that should concern us: the dimension of what might be called, for lack of a better term, implication. As Lacan's own emphasis on the role of the Chorus in *Antigone* makes clear, the space between two deaths inevitably involves communities: other subjects whose symbolic universes are imperiled, if not annihilated, when the space between two deaths is held open.[48] This is not simply to say that the very fact a space between two deaths exists to be filled denotes a failure of the symbolic order, a failure on the part of community to enact a symbolic ritual. It is to emphasize that when the Thing, the intrusive embodiment of the symbolic order's failure, emerges in the space between two deaths—when Antigone or the two Hamlets, all of whom are beyond caring about the common good, pursue their desire to the point of destruction—the remaining community can be saved only at the cost of its radical reorientation. As Žižek puts it, "The very existence of the symbolic order implies a possibility of its radical effacement, of 'symbolic death'—not the death of the so-called 'real object' in its symbol, but the obliteration of the signifying network itself."[49] No longer is the word the death of the Thing it names; the Thing is the death of an order of words. The success of Antigone and of the Hamlets is the ruin of their erstwhile symbolic communities.

To be sure, no one is likely to mistake *Il Filostrato* for *Antigone* or to confuse its protagonist (or, for that matter, its narrator) with Hamlet. On the contrary, what distinguishes *Il Filostrato*'s opening of the space between two deaths—what tells us that it is neither a classical text nor an uncannily modern text uncomfortably aware of the classical tradition, but a Trecento text that exploits "old stories" in a novel way—is the fact that the narrator acts to *move* Troilo to that space. The *Filostrato* narrator, unlike Antigone or Hamlet, cannot really be described as working for the other. He does not seek to free the other from the space between two deaths and so to enter that space himself. Instead, he relocates an already dead other to the space between two deaths in order that the other might be made to work for him. Polynices lay unburied, food for carrion eaters; Hamlet the elder had died, as he so memorably puts it, "unhouseled, disappointed, unaneled," sent to his account with all his imperfections on his head (*Hamlet* 1.5.77–79). Troilo, by contrast, had already been mourned, in Benoît and in Guido, by all of Troy, while his corpse had been interred with honor in a rich tomb. Where Hamlet and Antigone are haunted, the *Filostrato* narrator conjures. All things considered, then, that narrator presents us, as I am arguing he did Chaucer, with an ethical muddle. On the one hand, going to the space between two deaths, refusing to give way relative to desire, represents an ethical gesture of the highest order.[50] There is a reason we find it difficult, as readers, fully to comprehend either Antigone or Hamlet: They occupy an ethical register that most subjects, "content" to sacrifice desire to what Lacan calls the service of goods, work all their lives to avoid. But whereas Antigone and Hamlet refuse to give way on desire in order to do their duty to the other, the narrator does his duty to no one but himself—despite his disingenuous warning against foolish love. In going to the space between two deaths, the narrator of *Il Filostrato* somehow manages to drain that act of its ethical content.

Again, this is not necessarily to compare the figure that *does* end up occupying the space between two deaths—Troilo—to either Antigone or Hamlet, let alone Hamlet's father's ghost. He is nowhere near so frightening, so mechanical. Troilo, I would venture, is more akin to another, less intimidating manifestation of the Thing. This is the vaguely tragicomic father in a dream interpreted by Freud in *The Interpretation of Dreams*: the father who was alive only because he did not know that he was dead.[51] The upsetting, and also the pitiable, thing about Troilo in *Il Filostrato*, that is to say, is his imposed amnesia: the fact that he has no idea he has already been killed, repeatedly, in Virgil, in Benoît, and in Guido, to name but the most prominent examples available to Chaucer. Troilo is not like Antigone or the ghost of Hamlet's father. He does not carry a mandate, does not come demanding a settling of any symbolic account. He is, instead, unwittingly disinterred, his story made to repeat itself after it has already found its ending, and for reasons little connected to his classical function. For this reason, then, Troilo's continued suspension between two deaths could only seem, at the very least, awkward and uncomfortable, the unresolved outcome of an ethical transgression: the transformation of a pathetic ghost into a specter sent to haunt an absent mistress.

But it was also something more. In "Ethics and Tragedy in Psychoanalysis," Alenka Zupančič notes that, as Hegel once put it, "the force of the great tragic characters of antiquity consists in the fact that they have no choice: they *are* what they will and accomplish from their birth on, and they *are* this with all of their being."[52] Such a characterization is equally applicable, or should be, to a classically derived figure like Troilo: a figure, as I have argued, who "is his death and the fall of Troy"; a figure whose very name, *Troilo*, "contains both the beginning and the end of Troy."[53] Troilo, with all of his being, was meant to be both the life and death of the city whose very name existed, as a diminutive, in his own. More than being merely awkward, then, Troilo's particular Thing-ly status, his affinity with the father who "had really died, only he did not know it," would likely have resonated for Chaucer on not only an ethical but also an ideological level. Stated baldly, Troilo's continued suspension between two deaths would have amounted to the destabilizing intrusion, at the level of the signifier, of Troy, the mythical foreclosed origin of the medieval West, within a late fourteenth-century, Christocentric symbolic order.

Why that intrusion should have mattered to Chaucer may be explained, in part, by what Sylvia Federico has called the "desire for Troy" current in late fourteenth- and early fifteenth-century fantasies of English nationhood.[54] That desire, Federico argues, was essentially utopian: "a means," as she puts it, "of creating a past, present, and future in accord with specific ideals and also a means of mobilizing that imagined historicity in gestures of self-invention and self-definition."[55] This is, I think, an accurate enough way to describe the approach taken by some of Chaucer's English contemporaries, who found in Troy what Federico elsewhere calls a "site of desire": that is, a repository of desire, a place toward which various desires tended, and by which their ends were more clearly defined.[56] Chaucer's encounter with Troy as a site of desire in *Il Filostrato*, by contrast, comes much closer to the encounter with the *thing* in the *Nebenmensch* theorized by psychoanalysis. For in this particular instance, Troy did not represent an empty space in which Chaucer might have realized his own dreams and longings, his own "desire." It was not the endpoint for a vision, whether utopian or otherwise, of what England (or, more specifically, London) might become. More traumatically, Troy, in its diminutive embodiment as Troilo, the "Little Troy," instead confronted Chaucer with the "site"—the locus, the embodiment, the near-palpable presence—of a strange desire lodged in a neighboring text. Like some of Chaucer's associates, in other words, the narrator of *Il Filostrato* betrays a desire for Troy. The difference, however, is that the desire here is not forward-looking, rooted in a lack that keeps the signifying chain in motion—that opens a direct path to the future. To apprehend desire meant, in this case, that Chaucer was then led to apprehend, not just a lack in the field of the Other, but the lack even of the foundational lack that establishes the Other. For with Troilo unburied, not yet subject to the second death, the place of lack was suddenly, and paradoxically, occupied: possessed, in every sense of the word, by the ghost of the very figure whose absence lay at the foundation of England. Acknowledging that possession, Chaucer also acknowledged that he and his English contemporaries were, for the time of Troilo's disinterment, dispossessed of the place of lack.

To grasp this point, I want to turn to the homology Lacan develops between the Thing, *la Chose*, in seminar 7, *The Ethics of Psychoanalysis*, and "cause" in seminar 11, *The Four Fundamental Concepts of Psychoanalysis.* "Cause is to be distinguished from that which is determinate in a chain, in other words the *law*," says Lacan. "There is cause only in something that doesn't work."[57] "Cause," in other words, is precisely that which marks the point of failure in the symbolic order: the point where the law proves unable to overwrite the Thing—the point, in short, at which the "something that doesn't work" turns out to be the symbolic order itself. Cause, to put the matter another way, *is* the traumatic rupture, the sudden overproximity of the Thing, *la Chose*, against which the symbolic order is constantly being arrayed. This is worth bearing in mind, I would argue, because of what Lee Patterson has written regarding the legacy of Benoît's *Roman de Troie.* The *Roman* "matters for an understanding of *Troilus and Criseyde*," writes Patterson, because

> it establishes the terms in which later Trojan historiography attempts to understand its subject. That the originary moment of secular history should be an overwhelming catastrophe is itself an unsettling fact, but that it should also be a catastrophe whose causes are obscure, whose events stand in a painfully enigmatic relation to the individual, and whose ultimate meaning resists decipherment—these are qualities that made the Trojan story a continual anxiety for the medieval historical consciousness, and run counter to, or subterraneously undermine, the uses of Trojan descent and *translatio imperii* in the service of secular interests.[58]

According to Patterson, the enduring legacy of Benoît's text—the principal reason it continued to hold a powerful fascination well into the fifteenth century—was that it brought medieval Europe face to face with the trauma of its own originary, yet frustratingly "lost," cause: the catastrophic destruction of Troy. There is a powerful psychoanalytic truth to Patterson's assessment. Yet he overstresses, I think, the "ultimate" meaninglessness of that destruction. True, the rupture of cause is itself enigmatic and, because it persists outside of the symbolic order, inherently without the meaning that only symbolization can confer; but it is precisely because cause as such cannot be signified that the symbolic order emerges, almost dreamlike, in its place. The symbolic order, that is, amounts to little more than a provisional response to cause, a way of answering to its trauma. To argue, then, that the "ultimate meaning" of Troy's downfall "resists decipherment" is to miss that point. According to the dominant historiographic tradition, the downfall of Troy gave rise to the medieval European symbolic order, was the cause of that order; and in this sense it is fraught with meaning, however retroactively constructed. Its meaning, to put it bluntly, *is* fall, *is* destruction, *is* death—which is why its return within the order erected against it, the order contingent on its fall, proves so unsettling.

Here, then, where Troilo's suspension between two deaths translates into an encounter with Troy as cause, Chaucer may also have been "ex-cited" by *Il Filostrato*; for it is at this point, where an opening of the space between two deaths exposes one to such trauma, that the notion of what Lacan calls the "second death" comes fully into play. Earlier I noted, through Žižek, that "the very existence of the symbolic order implies a possibility of its radical effacement, of 'symbolic death.'" The simple fact that an order of language exists, as Chaucer himself seems to have known only too well, logically means that it also could disintegrate, become incomprehensible—that it could *not* exist in any meaningful sense.[59] But how is it, exactly, that one comes to apprehend such nonexistence—in essence, the implied nonexistence of the socio-symbolic big Other? As Žižek explains it, any symbolic order can catch a glimpse of its own contingency, since every "reference to the empty place of the Thing . . . enables us to conceive the possibility of a total, global annihilation of the signifier's network: the 'second death,' the radical annihilation of nature's circular movement, is conceivable only in so far as this circular movement is already symbolized/historicized, inscribed, caught in the symbolic web—absolute death, the 'destruction of the universe,' is always the destruction of the *symbolic* universe."[60] The Thing, because it is never truly dead, annihilates, undoes, "nature's circular movement" of generation and decay. However—and this is the crucial point—such an annihilation makes sense for us only because the "natural" cycle is always already overwritten by the symbolic. The destruction of the universe is the destruction of the symbolic universe precisely because the universe exists for us only insofar as we symbolize it. Thus the Thing, by overturning nature's cycles, its laws, implies the "annihilation of the signifier's network" established precisely that we might comprehend, if not conquer, that same cycle. For this reason, then, an encounter with the Thing, in whatever manifestation, carries with it profound social, ideological, and political implications—precisely because its traumatic eruption intimates the death of all three of those orders.

It is Chaucer's reaction to that encounter that I am trying to clarify here. Chaucer, I want to claim, maintained fidelity to the lost cause of the medieval present, something he detected in his encounter with the neighboring text. Mostly, that fidelity comes through in Chaucer's refusal to mourn the present—that is, in his decision to fixate on the incursion of the future into the present, to not forget his encounter with *Il Filostrato*. Patterson writes of the "continual anxiety" that the Trojan story posed for "the medieval historical consciousness." At its most basic, Chaucer's refusal to forget his encounter with *Il Filostrato* represents a way of embracing that anxiety. Or, to put the matter somewhat differently, it represents another way of confronting the "anxiety of influence" that a text might have upon its reader. As Harold Bloom configures it, such anxiety stems from the daunting influence of a strong, ultimately inimitable precursor upon a belated poet—an influence that must then be countered by various strategies of misreading and rewriting. But the influence of *Il Filostrato* upon Chaucer suggests an alternative way of understanding anxiety, one hinted at in Patterson's description of cause as obscure and indecipherable. In *Inhibitions, Symptoms and Anxiety*, Freud raises the possibility that anxiety, rather than alerting the ego to some repressed content, may in fact have no determinate cause or object. Anxiety, Freud implies, has no essence: it is itself nothing, follows from nothing, and so precedes the economy of repression, of judgment and negation, that is constitutive of the ego. Anxiety is the affect one experiences when confronted by the sudden overproximity of a profoundly lost cause, the presentiment one feels upon finding oneself drawn into the ambit of something deeply felt yet utterly unknown—unknown because it arises from that which was cast out at the moment of the ego's emergence in the symbolic order. The power of anxiety is not that it alerts us to the threat of a danger we recognize but that it signals the paradoxical presence of a cause that, having no signifier, cannot be named. "It is in anxiety," writes Zupančič, "that the subject comes closest to the object (i.e., to the Real kernel of his *jouissance*), and . . . it is precisely this proximity of the object that lies at the origin of anxiety."[61] Rather, then, than designating the worry evoked by Bloom, the fear that one is not strong enough to measure up to the example set by a powerful precursor, anxiety points to the profound absence of the Other: to the fact that an apprehension of cause "dispossesses" the Other of its foundational lack. For Bloom, the anxiety of influence means that one must consciously struggle with the dead. Here, the anxiety of influence means that Chaucer was haunted, unconsciously, by a ghost: the ghost of cause. For Bloom, the anxiety of influence draws one inevitably into the past. For Chaucer, the anxiety of influence arose from an ironic encounter with the future: ironic because the process of symbolization/historicization had at last come around, in its recursive way, to touch upon cause in the guise of the new and noncomparable Thing. The source of anxiety may indeed be enigmatic, as Patterson suggests, but anxiety itself is never deceptive. What it signals is real.[62] To feel anxiety is to know that one is truly haunted by the ghost of a future that has no name, a lost cause that preoccupies the anxious subject because it has suddenly reoccupied the place from which it ought to be lacking.

Anxiety, then, is the affect most directly tied to the experience of being haunted—not by the return of the repressed, which, being yet another form of repression, is always misleading, but by the ghost of a *real* cause that precedes the very economy of repression. As Zupančič puts it, the feeling of anxiety "tells us nothing about the object" in and of itself; "it tells us something about the subject's 'window of fantasy' in the frame of which a certain object appears terrifying."[63] What this means in the particular case of Chaucer's encounter with *Il Filostrato* is that the experience of being haunted is then also caught up with the question of genre—specifically, with the question of whether *Il Filostrato* is a tragedy. That the ending of *Il Filostrato* exhibits certain characteristics of the *de casibus* tradition seems fairly evident. Monica McAlpine, for example, notes that while "it is an essential part of Chaucer's accomplishment [in *Troilus and Criseyde*] to have brought love and tragedy together," it is probable that "the combination, and the choice of the story of Troilus and Criseyde in particular, was sparked by the quasi-tragic rhetoric, in the *de casibus* mode, at the end of . . . *Il Filostrato*."[64] Henry Ansgar Kelly, meanwhile, more or less takes it for granted that while "Chaucer was doing something very original when he started to compose tragedies . . . he doubtless thought of himself as adding to a long list of such works, which included the *Filostrato* . . . the *De casibus*, and at least parts of the *De mulieribus claris*."[65] Confusing the situation, however, is the fact that the narrator of *Il Filostrato*, unlike his counterparts in the *Troilus* and the *Testament*, never refers to his work as a tragedy. This, I am inclined to argue, is no mere oversight. Rather, it is a tacit admission by the narrator that his story, despite "the germ of authentic tragedy" at its core, fails to perform, or else has little interest in performing, the basic work of tragedy, which is to inter the very Thing it has brought to light so that "the life of the, as yet unborn, national community" might take hold.[66] Whether it be *Antigone, Oedipus at Colonus, Romeo and Juliet, Othello*, or (as we have seen) the *Testament of Cresseid*, the point of tragedy is to establish the tomb, literal or figural, that will memorialize the foundational moment of the emerging community. Tragedy, to put it in the terms that I began to develop in the Introduction, and to which I shall return in the following chapter, marks the place of lack needed to institute, and also to perpetuate, the Other. Athens, Thebes, Verona, Venice, London: every polis, as the *Erkenwald*-poet clearly recognized, rests upon a foundational tomb.[67] But the *Filostrato* narrator, by his own admission, no longer has any concern for a polis that he can see only as empty and desolate. This, then, is the anxiety-producing quality of *Il Filostrato*: by undeadening Troilo, it denies medieval Europe its tomb.

Now whether Chaucer would have understood this to be a violation of "tragedy" in the generic sense is difficult to say. A long-standing critical tradition holds that the definition of tragedy with which Chaucer would have been familiar (and that he may well have helped to establish) is that summed up by the Monk of the *Canterbury Tales*:

Tragedie is to seyn a certeyn storie,
As olde bookes maken us memorie,

Of hym that stod in greet prosperitee,
And is yfallen out of heigh degree
Into myserie, and endeth wrecchedly.
(7.1973–77)

On the other hand, I see no reason not to accept Paul Strohm's sensible observation "that an awareness of tragedy might exist independently of the term," or even, I would go so far as to say, independently of any term at all.[68] Indeed, it is the very possibility that the idea of "authentic tragedy" (to borrow McAlpine's phrase) could persist without a signifier that allows us to think about the sadness of the *Troilus* narrator in a new way. The idea that tragedy aims to establish the polis by interring the Thing, usually in the form of a sacrificial hero who embodies the internal contradictions of the symbolic order, is of course not so far removed from the medieval conception of tragedy as the fall from prosperity to wretchedness. Both lament an incomprehensible (though not inexplicable) reversal of fortune, the exposure of human life to the mysterious workings of fate, the cyclical rise and fall of rulers and empires, the apparent necessity of civic regeneration through sacrificial violence. The difference is that, whereas the former conception presents us with the spectacle of a hero who actively embraces his or her fate, the latter simply registers the repetitive trauma of natural-historical cyclicality while remaining powerless to break free from it. *Il Filostrato*, then, is exemplary of medieval tragedy insofar as it remains an incomplete tragedy, stopping short of the interment that would guarantee the polis through the establishment of a memorial tomb. On the other hand, as a minor example of the *de casibus* tradition, *Il Filostrato* also brings us, as I am suggesting it did Chaucer, to the same endpoint as all tragedy: the point where the polis is forced to reorganize itself after a confrontation with the Thing-as-cause. The touch may be fleeting and somewhat awkward, but *Il Filostrato* does eventually come around to touching upon the very lost cause to which Chaucer would thereafter commit himself, producing the strange image of a foundational sacrifice capable of generating all of the affect associated with authentic tragedy but lacking the signifier to identify it as such. It is not just Troilo who remains unburied and unsettled at the end of *Il Filostrato*; it is a version of tragedy other than the medieval.

But what is that version, exactly? Problematically for Chaucer, it is a version that presents fidelity to a singular lost cause as itself inherently tragic. My touchstone here, as it has been throughout this chapter, is *Antigone*, a text that neither Chaucer nor Boccaccio could have known but that nonetheless uncannily resonates with the story of Troilus and Criseyde. In Lacan's reading of Sophocles' play, as Julia Lupton explains it, "Antigone suspends diachrony . . . by enshrining the irreparable loss of her brother in the barest outlines of a tomb (the pouring of dust on his corpse), a symbolic act that serves to dislodge human being from the temporal flux of both natural and historical change." "Antigone," Lupton later continues,

> fastens on her brother as the one immovable element in the world of *philôtes*, the pre-political rituals of reciprocity that encompass the bonds of kinship, friendship, and hospitality. She has defended those bonds in a more global manner up until this point; now she singles the brother out as the one person who cannot be exchanged for another, and in doing so she singles herself out, becoming in Lacan's description similarly "unshakeable" and "unyielding." She speaks for the irreplaceability of her brother, a stance that irrevocably isolates her from the polis, but she does so while also allowing . . . the total exchangeability of other elements in the world of intimate bonds, namely husbands and children.[69]

One could easily take this passage and substitute, for Antigone and her brother, Troilus and Criseyde, the *Filostrato* narrator and Filomena, even, I am claiming, Chaucer and the event of his encounter with *Il Filostrato*. In each case, we are dealing with a figure struggling to maintain fidelity to a radically singular commitment, a figure who rejects, for himself, the lure of infinite exchangeability promised by the economy of the symbolic order. In other words, we are dealing with three profoundly melancholic figures, figures who resist the compensations of mourning. But it is only Chaucer who bothers to explore, through the experience of the *Troilus* narrator, whether such a melancholic stance can be maintained indefinitely or if the pressure to symbolize the Thing is finally too great to be resisted.

IV

I have been arguing that Troilo's suspension between two deaths, like *Il Filostrato*'s generic indeterminacy, brought Chaucer into contact with the lost cause of late medieval Europe. Now I would like to consider how that argument might intersect with C.S. Lewis's famous (and famously contested) claim that Chaucer approached *Il Filostrato* "as a poet of courtly love" and that "the majority of his modifications are corrections of errors which Boccaccio had committed against the code of courtly love."[70] What interests me about this claim is not the basic question it raises—the question of whether such codes actually existed to be violated—but its basic insight: that Boccaccio's poem overturns the structural logic of sublimation, crystallized in the fantasy of courtly love.

I refer, of course, to the logic excavated by Lacan in *The Ethics of Psychoanalysis*. Like Lewis, Lacan has been criticized for basing his understanding of courtly love on faulty, if not outright fabricated, archival research.[71] Admittedly, this is not the best place to mount a vigorous defense of Lacan's eccentric methods, other than to point out that his performances can be read in different ways: as a travesty of scholarship, or as a sly challenge to the fantasy of a master, a display of fallibility meant to generate the level of dissatisfaction with the Other needed to produce new knowledge. Nevertheless, I feel it necessary at least to emphasize that Lacan had little interest in creating anything like a recognizable historical account (as his mockery of historical explanations for courtly love clearly indicates). His interest, rather, was in drawing a connection between two phenomena, anamorphosis and courtly love, that might be said to stand in an *extimate* relation to the different histories from which each emerged. Anamorphosis, in Lacan's idiosyncratic version of art history, is no mere anomaly, no simple parlor trick or cheap visual stunt. On the contrary, argues Lacan, anamorphosis manifests the true function of art, a function that representationalism, ordinarily regarded as a great breakthrough in the evolution of artistic technique, is meant to obscure. "I believe that the Baroque return to the play of forms, to all manner of devices, including anamorphosis, is an effort to restore the true meaning of artistic inquiry," says Lacan; "artists use the discovery of the property of lines to make something emerge that is precisely there where one has lost one's bearings or, strictly speaking, nowhere." He then continues: "At issue, in an analogical or anamorphic form, is the effort to point once again to the fact that what we seek in the illusion is something in which the illusion as such in some way transcends itself, destroys itself, by demonstrating that it is only there as a signifier."[72] What we seek in the illusion is not a faithful representation of reality but a highly orchestrated, thoroughly aestheticized encounter with the real. In Lacan's understanding of anamorphosis, as Sarah Kay explains it, "the coexistence of incompatible systems of perspective in the same painting shows up the constructedness, and consequent limitations, of its represented reality. By drawing attention to the shortfall in representation, the clash of perspectives points toward the disturbing, real 'Thing' behind it." Kay then underscores what remains, for Lacan, the salient point: "In the same way the supernatural qualities attributed to the courtly lady act as an anamorphosis in courtly love poetry, her sublime façade unmasks its own construction as a fantasy while at the same time pointing to the rigor of the inhuman 'Thing' beyond."[73] Like anamorphosis, then, courtly love is no mere aberration, no quaint anachronism or localizable practice. Rather, it brings to light the repressed truth of sex, and so reorients the history of love, by introducing "a highly refined way of making up for the absence of the sexual relationship by feigning that we are the ones who erect an obstacle thereto."[74]

It probably would do to say a word here about "the absence of the sexual relationship." When Lacan makes the apparently scandalous assertion that there is no such thing as a sexual relation, he is not suggesting that men and women don't have sex. He is claiming, in a manner that reflects his interest in set theory, that there is no relation, no common measure or symmetry, no proportion, between those subjects defined by masculine structure and those defined by feminine structure. Relations between the two sexes, rather than being direct, are always mediated by a third term, whether object or signifier (and here one need only call to mind the letters that Troilus and Criseyde send back and forth, or the interventions of Pandarus, or the brooch that, passing from Troilus to Criseyde to Diomede and then back to Troilus, serves as the final form of communication between the two lovers). Lacan's use of the terms *masculine* and *feminine* notwithstanding, these structures have little to do with a person's biological sex. There can be, and presumably have been, masculine-structured women and feminine-structured men. Far from serving as a blueprint for *biological* determinism, in fact, Lacan's formulas really map the two different ethical positions available to us as speaking subjects, the two sets of logical functions in which the subject must choose, in a primal moment of decision, to inscribe itself. On one side is the set of all men, each and every one of whom, Lacan maintains, is "completely defined by the phallic function," his desire strictly limited by the cut of symbolic castration—that is, by *le nom/non du père*, the Father's name or "No," as representative of the imposition of symbolic order. "To write oneself as 'man,'" Reinhard explains, "is to enter into a social contract where access to unmediated *jouissance* . . . is sacrificed for the sake of the symbolic substitutions and displacements of culture and the remnants of *jouissance* that it promises."[75] Yet if the set of all men is bounded by the phallic function, it is only because there exists "at least one man who is not subject to the phallic function." In other words, if the set of all men is whole, bounded, it is only because of the belief, held by all those defined by masculine structure, that there exists an exception to the rule of symbolic castration: a position occupied, for example, by the notorious father of the primal horde or the figure of the sovereign in political theology. For men, then, there is no possibility of enjoying a woman directly, a privilege reserved for the primal father alone. "Ordinary masculine subjects," as Bruce Fink puts it, "must resign themselves to getting off on their partner, object (a)."[76]

On the other side of the equation are those subjects defined by feminine structure, and here things get a bit more complicated. For those subjects who inscribe themselves in the set of women, there is no exception to the phallic function. Just as all men are "under the universal thrall of the phallus as signifier," having undergone the cut of symbolic castration, so too there is not one woman who is not subject to the phallic function. But whereas the set of all men is bounded by an exception to that set, the fantasy of a figure who still has access to *jouissance*, the set of women remains, by stark contrast, open and un-bounded. As Reinhard puts it: "A man belongs to and is included in the subset of humanity called 'all men,' a set that constitutes a unified group, guaranteed by the transcendental exceptionality of the primal Father. A woman, however, belongs to the subset of women without being included in it, insofar as that subset has no border that would determine membership and delimit inside from outside." Women may be "no less irrecusably marked by the phallus" than are men; but un-like men, "the terms of their reprieve are not given by a transcendental sovereign who represents the possibility of eventual satisfaction."[77] In-deed women, because they have not sacrificed all of their *jouissance* to the fantasy of a sovereign whose place they might someday occupy, are able to hold a certain amount of *jouissance* in reserve. They may elect to take, as their partner, the phallus as the signifier of contingent, ac-culturated desire. But they also have the option of experiencing, as do Lacan's favorite examples of those with feminine structure, the medi-eval mystics, another *jouissance* not subject to the depredations of the phallic function.

With this in mind, let us return to the topic of courtly love. The genius of courtly love, Lacan seems to imply, is that it allows the mas-culine subject to maintain two illusions at once. On the one hand, the presence of the Lady makes it seem as though genuine *jouissance* might still be possible, because the Thing isn't completely lacking—that is, rendered inaccessible by the death of the primal father. On the contrary, a man might still be able to experience true enjoyment if only there weren't so many obstacles—all those jealous rivals, endless deferrals, cruel demands, and, finally, the inaccessibility of the Lady herself—standing in the way. This is the wink-wink side of courtly love, the part that allows us to perform the "fundamentally perverse" nature of human sexuality: to playfully acknowledge the profound unnatural-ness of sexuality, the way that sexuality "swerves from any teleologi-cal orientation provided by instinctual endowment" into the realm of symbol, metaphor, and displacement.[78] On the other hand, that performance is possible only because the presence of the Lady also relieves the masculine subject of having to discover that the Other has not, in fact, placed the Thing safely off limits—that, on the contrary, the Thing has already been encountered in the very impasses that the rituals of courtly love were designed to occlude. Ultimately an extension of the pleasure principle, courtly love works precisely by substituting something moderately unpleasant, the experience of deferral and frustration, for an encounter with something distinctly unpleasurable: the conflation of the good object, the Thing, with the bad object, the Thing as traumatically absent from the place of lack temporarily occupied by the courtly Lady. In short, it provides a way of *not* having a sexual relation, of performing, while at the same time evading a direct confrontation with, the lack of the Other manifest in the impossibility of the sexual relation. Endless foreplay without the inevitable disappointment of what follows: that, for Lacan, is the essence of courtly love.

What I want to suggest, then, is that Lewis discerned how *Il Filostrato*, rather than fulfilling the role of sublimation performed by courtly love—allowing one to carry on as though the sexual relation were prohibited, and thus potentially attainable, and not structurally impossible—instead abandons that role. Doing exactly the opposite of what courtly love was intended to do, *Il Filostrato* works so hard to preserve loss that it ends up exposing not lack as such, not the prohibition of the Thing that constitutes the symbolic order, but the lack of lack: the lack even of the lack (of the Thing) that would keep us in desire. When Lewis claimed that *Il Filostrato* committed errors against the code of courtly love, errors that Chaucer then set out to correct, he was picking up on this melancholic dimension of Boccaccio's poem: its transformation of lack into loss. "What man demands," according to Lacan, "what he cannot help but demand, is to be deprived of something real."[79] In other words, what man really demands is to *not* have to encounter the Thing—a demand met, as it were, by the orchestrations of courtly love. Going beyond Lewis, then, one could say that *Il Filostrato* does not simply transgress against the codes of courtly love; it discloses how transgression, rather then providing access to *jouissance*, merely reveals the absence of the Thing from the place of lack—a situation then remedied only by melancholic gestures of disavowal. Throwing off the conventions of courtly love, *Il Filostrato* ends up going too far in the other direction, hastening, rather than deferring, an encounter with the Thing. The poem's "error," as Lewis called it, the error that Chaucer set out to correct, is that it doesn't meet man's demand to be deprived of something real.

This complicated dynamic of sublimation, transgression, and disappointment—the dynamic that Lacan associates with courtly love—is at issue in two of *Il Filostrato*'s pivotal scenes: Troilo's first encounter with Criseida in the temple of Pallas Athena, and the so-called bedroom scene. Troilo's first sight of Criseida, wearing "a white veil under a black habit" and "holding her mantle before her face," is pleasing to him not only because of how she looks but because of a certain act: the way she turns away in a "somewhat disdainful" manner "as if to say, 'No one may stand here'" (1.28). These imagined words might be interpreted in two ways. Their obvious sense is that no one may approach Criseida, either because she is too formidable or because she is off limits. In this way, an otherwise innocuous act is made to promote the fantasy that the Thing in whose place the courtly Lady stands is merely prohibited and might therefore still be possessed. In other words, the prohibition against approaching the Lady holds out the possibility that transgression is still possible. It is "as if" Criseida were unapproachable—that is the fantasy. At the same time, however, Criseida's words can be taken literally: no one may truly stand in the place of the Thing. Where the first way of reading Criseida's gesture holds out the promise of enjoyment, this second way just as quickly snatches it back, reminding us that the Thing is not merely prohibited but utterly impossible, not merely forbidden but fundamentally lacking. The words imagined in the place of Criseida's act thus end up unraveling the very fantasy that courtly love is meant to perpetuate. Rather than serving as an extension of the pleasure principle, allowing desire to continue, they only point to the revelation that enjoyment is impossible. Where is the pleasure in that?

The scene is subtly different in Chaucer's version. Where Boccaccio's Criseida acts as if to say "No one may stand here," Chaucer's Criseyde lets fall "Hire look a lite aside in swich manere, / Ascaunces,

'What, may I nat stonden here?'" (1.291–92). On the one hand, this imagined question registers not only the arbitrariness but also the awkwardness of Criseyde's impending elevation to the position of courtly Lady. Far from making her seem intimidating, in fact, Criseyde's tentativeness, signaled by Troilus's perception of her as asking rather than commanding, already suggests that she will not be able to fulfill the Lady's prohibitory role. Yet paradoxically that same tentativeness signals just how much Criseyde *does* belong in that role. Chaucer draws our attention to this fact by changing a significant detail of the scene. In *Il Filostrato*, Criseida acts; in Chaucer's version, Criseyde lets fall a look. Why should a look make all the difference? Like other iterations of what Mladen Dolar calls "the myth of the first encounter, 'the first sight,'" Criseyde's fallen look constitutes, for Troilus, a moment in which he "recognizes what has 'always already' been there, since the beginning of time, and [his] whole previous existence retroactively acquires the sense of leading just to this moment." At such a moment, writes Dolar,

> there is an exchange of the gaze, *the Real has returned the gaze*, even if the other person didn't respond, or was unaffected by it, or even unaware of it. The lack of sense of a contingent fate, the haphazard string of events was in that moment suddenly filled by the gaze, that Lacanian paramount evocation of what he called the object *a*. For once one saw instead of just looking. . . . If the gaze comes to fill the lack of sense in that senseless fortune, it also creates it by filling it, for it is only looking backward that one sees the lack, and only as a lack destined to be filled. Life didn't "make sense" before, but now, suddenly, it does.[80]

What Troilus detects in Criseyde's look, then, is not really a look at all, in the sense of being directed at someone specific, but a gaze that, turning downward, taking in no one in particular, materializes the object he lacks. It is Criseyde's fleeting gaze, inscrutable and open-ended, directed away from the viewer and yet asking to be read, that moves her into the position of the courtly Lady, because it is that gaze alone that makes Troilus a desiring subject (1.295–96). Seeming to

possess the object that Troilus lacks, Criseyde manages, without consciously knowing it, to deprive him of something real.

Another way of putting this is to say that Criseyde's look manifests, while also helping to mediate, the lack of any sexual relation, any
common measure or symmetry, between her and Troilus. Broadly, that
lack is of a piece with the overall lack of relation, evident in a persistent
pattern of class differences and imbalances of power, that dogs the
lovers throughout the poem.[81] Here it is felt, for example, in the odd
little detail, added by Chaucer, that has Troilus "On this lady, and now
on that, lokynge, / Where so she were of the town or of withoute" as he
makes his way through the temple (1.269–70)—an image that may be
intended to evoke nothing more than the competing claims of endog-
amy and exogamy but that cannot help bringing to mind the "cleavage
between town and country" that Marx calls the first great division of
civilization, the first lack, as it were, of any social relation.[82] My argument here, however, is that there exists a crucial difference between
the lack of relation manifest in social antagonism and the lack of the
sexual relation as it gets orchestrated in courtly love. Strictly speaking, antagonism is what defines the situation as Troilus understands it.
War, struggle, aggression, treachery—these are what define everyday
life in Troy. But the absence of the sexual relation, which Lacan locates not in the symbolic order but in the real, is something truly new,
at once in the situation that Troilus knows but not of it.[83] It therefore
retains the power to transform him, allowing him not only to step out
of the situation but also, perhaps, to transform it.

Once again, Chaucer makes us feel as much by adding what may
be the most significant detail of all: Troilus's lack of experience with
love. For Boccaccio's Troilo, who has been in love before, Criseida
represents yet another substitution in a chain. Troilus, by contrast, has
never loved, a state of affairs that allows his encounter with Criseyde
to register as an event: the moment that "converts" Troilus to genuine
subjectivity, a subjectivity of fidelity. The ability of Criseyde's gaze to
penetrate Troilus may be a commonplace, but here it assumes an added
force by being tied to the fantasy of recognition mentioned above: the
fantasy in which one is recognized by, and recognizes oneself in, the
other's gaze. Troilus, by "subjectivizing" Criseyde's gaze, by allowing it

to penetrate deep within him, elevates Criseyde to the singular position of the Thing. In that, he arrests the movement of the symbolic order, taking her out of the cycle of substitution. That moment of arrest is an event: a singular moment in which Troilus is seized and broken by his encounter with Criseyde, and to which he thereafter pledges his fidelity. The irony, however, is that in pledging that fidelity Troilus destroys the situation, since his recognition of himself in and as cause spells the undoing, the overturning, of that situation from within. By subjectivizing cause, the prehistory of the present in which Chaucer is writing, Troilus hastens the introduction of the future within the situation. In Troilus's recognition of himself in the gaze, the death of the past, the death that, for Chaucer, already will have been, is anticipated within the very situation it will undo.

Just as important, though, Troilus's lack of experience with love also allows us to read that moment as an allegory of Chaucer's encounter with *Il Filostrato*—that is, as an allegory of Chaucer's own event. It is notable, for example, that in *Il Filostrato* Troilo looks over the women in the temple much as the narrator did "old books" when searching for a suitable counterpart. Just as the narrator conjured Troilo from out of the historiographic tradition, so too does Troilo single out Criseida from a group of women. The one's approach to texts is echoed in the other's selection of a lover. The same is true of Chaucer as well, but with a difference. Rather than acting as a conjurer of the dead, Chaucer is, like Troilus, suddenly haunted by something arbitrary and unexpected, something truly "new and non-comparable," as Freud says of the Thing. For both, the moment marks an event: a sudden disruption of the situation that, being impossible to forget, marks the new point from which each one has no choice but to proceed.

The differences between Boccaccio's version of courtly love and Chaucer's become even more pronounced, and accordingly more instructive, when one compares their treatments of the bedroom scene. Most readers note the rawness of the scene in *Il Filostrato*: the haste with which it happens, its frank carnality. The brevity of the scene, in particular, is striking, especially when compared to its analogue in *Troilus and Criseyde*. In *Il Filostrato*, the whole scene, from secret meeting to undressing to consummation to pillow talk to parting, adds up to perhaps 32 stanzas. In *Troilus and Criseyde*, it has been expanded to 141. E. Talbot Donaldson famously argued that the multiple endings of *Troilus and Criseyde* are intended to help the narrator avoid, for as long as possible, the inevitable conclusion of his story.[84] The amplification in this scene serves a similar purpose; for it makes it seem as though the narrator has taken it upon himself to defer an encounter with the Thing for as long as possible. Or, to put the matter somewhat differently, it makes it seem as though the narrator were trying to defer, indefinitely, an encounter with what happens in *Il Filostrato*. In the latter, after Troilo and Criseida have undressed and gotten into bed, what we encounter is something "impossible": "Long would it be to recount the joy and impossible to tell the delight which they took together when they came into [the bedroom]"; "O sweet night, and much desired, what were you to the two happy lovers! If the knowledge were given to me that all the poets have had, it could not be described by me" (3.31, 33). Perhaps this is why the narrator immediately tries to disavow that impossible encounter, first by forging imaginary communities, appealing to his readers to imagine the bliss enjoyed by the lovers—to fill in the absence by imagining another *jouissance*—then by going the next step and imagining a union between Troilo and Criseida, repeatedly figured in the invocations of "they." Troilo and Criseida speak the same, express the same emotions, experience the same feelings. They are one. Again, this is a move designed not simply to disavow lack but to turn loss itself into a possession—to make an unobtainable (impossible) object appear as if it could be recovered, thereby maintaining the fantasy that it was once possessed. Quite literally, the poem transforms the object of contemplation, once hidden behind a veil, into an object that can be embraced. The narrator of the poem only ever got to look at Filomena; Troilo fulfills the impossible fantasy of getting to possess her.

Chaucer seems to have picked up on this resort to fantasy, to judge by how thoroughly he restores an atmosphere of lack, of difference, to the scene. Unlike their Boccaccian counterparts, Troilus and Criseyde have different voices, express different emotions. Rather than describing them in terms of the one, the *Troilus* narrator refers to them as "thise ilke tweye" or "hem bothe two"—as two who are the same but who remain two nevertheless. In *Il Filostrato*, Troilo and Criseida "gazed at one another with such desire that they did not turn their eyes from each other, and the one said to the other, 'My love, ah! Can it be that I am with you?' 'Yes, heart of my body, thanks be to God,' frequently replied the other. And very often clasping each other closely, they kissed together sweetly" (3.35). The voices of the lovers, like their actions, are interchangeable, never rising above the level of specularity. In *Troilus and Criseyde*, by contrast, "these ilke two," at once "same" and different, may reflect one another, but they are far from interchangeable:

> And Lord! So he gan goodly on hire se
> That nevere his look ne bleynte from hire face,
> And seyde, "O deere herte, may it be
> That it be soth, that ye ben in this place?"
> "Yee, herte myn, God thank I of his grace,"
> Quod tho Criseyde, and therwithal hym kiste,
> That where his spirit was, for joie he nyste.
>
> (3.1345–51)

Troilus says one thing, Criseyde says another (however complementary); Troilus gazes intently upon Criseyde's face, Criseyde kisses Troilus. Each word, each gesture, though similar, is clearly distinct. This same pattern is then continued, with a slight variation, one stanza later, when Troilus takes Criseyde fast in his arms

> And wel a thousand tymes gan he syke—
> Naught swiche sorwfull sikes as men make
> For wo, or elles when that folk ben sike,
> But esy sykes, swiche as ben to like,
> That shewed his affeccioun withinne;
> Of swiche sikes koude he nought bilynne.
>
> (3.1359–65)

Here the sighs are all Troilus's, making him the agent and Criseyde, who passively receives the sighs while performing no action herself, the object. This introduction of difference (however conventionally Aristo-telian it may be) is itself suggestively different from the corresponding stanza in *Il Filostrato*, where we are told that Troilo "kissed [Criseida's eyes] and kissed them yet again, and Criseida kissed his also; then he kissed all her face and breast, and never an hour passed without a thou-sand sighs, not those grieving ones by which one loses color but those devout ones by which was shown the affection which lay in their breast; and after this their delight was renewed" (3.37). Here the two lovers perform the same act, kissing one another's eyes, while "a thousand sighs," simultaneously belonging to neither and both of them, fill the air in a testament to their mutual, and vaguely anonymous, devotion.

Similarity, difference: Boccaccio's and Chaucer's heterogeneous treatments of the bedroom scene ultimately come down to divergent understandings of the way that love, to paraphrase Lacan's gnomic proposition, makes up for the lack of the sexual relation. A love that stays rooted in the imaginary, unable to escape the lure of specular identification, makes up for the lack of the sexual relation by denying it, that is, by pretending that no such lack exists and that the One is still possible. If there is no lack, there is no difference; and so, as hap-pens in *Il Filostrato*, the difference between lovers is transcended at the level of fantasy. But there is another, more radical, way of understand-ing how love makes up for the lack of the sexual relation: namely, as a way of embracing lack, the radical ground of difference, as the Same that two might share between them. Rather than insisting upon a mir-ror likeness, this type of love works by acknowledging that the Thing one isolates in the other is one's own Thing as well: that what joins two lovers is not specularity, but the self-estrangement experienced by each partner as the bearer of the other's secret. The love that makes up for the lack of the sexual relation, in other words, has the potential to become a form of neighbor love—one based, as Reinhard puts it, not on a Pauline conception of universalization, but "on structural differ-ence, invoking the recollection of one's own strangeness rather than an imaginary expansion of the category of self."[85] It is no coincidence that Lacan cites, as one of the "series of motifs" he finds in courtly love, the moment in his poems when "the extraordinary Guillaume de Poitiers calls the object of his aspirations *Bon vezi*, which means

'Good neighbor.'" After dismissing those "historians" who, despite having "abandoned themselves to all kinds of conjectures," had proved "unable to come up with anything better than the name of a Lady . . . whose estates were close to Guillaume's"—in other words, after dismissing those naive enough to believe that "courtly love" was an actual historical phenomenon and not a fantasy meant to compensate for the impossibility of the sexual relation—Lacan goes on to specify the following: "What is for us much more important than the reference to the neighbor, who is supposedly the Lady whom Guillaume de Poitiers occasionally played naughty games with, is the relationship between the expression just referred to [i.e., *Bon vezi*] and the one Freud uses in connection with the first establishment of the Thing, with its psychological genesis, namely, the *Nebenmensch*."[86] Courtly love is like neighbor love, Lacan seems to suggest, because it allows one to approach one's own most intimate neighbor—*jouissance*, the supreme Good that one cannot bear, the Thing at once internal to the masculine subject and also prohibited to him—through the mediating figure of the physical neighbor. Who that neighbor happens to be is incidental. What matters is that courtly love, as one of the first forms of sublimation, allows one to bring the arbitrarily proximate neighbor to the place of the drive—that is, the unique place of what was never sacrificed to the exchange economy of symbolic order—and so to raise an everyday object to the "dignity of the Thing."[87]

Yet courtly love is at the same time not neighbor love. Indeed, it may even represent an especially devious way of avoiding the *jouissance* that the imperative to neighbor love asks us to take up. Note how, in the passage from Lacan quoted above, the neighbor of courtly love is construed as the Good Neighbor, the neighbor who protects the desiring subject from having to assume the full weight of *jouissance* by cultivating the illusion that she, the neighbor, has *jouissance* fully in her possession—that she will limit our access to enjoyment (and enjoyment's access to us). That version of the neighbor can also be found in *Il Filostrato*, but in an ingeniously oblique, one might even say anamorphic, form. Earlier I argued that the *Filostrato* unmasked the way that its source texts in the tradition of medieval Trojan historiography "bet on Father." It turns out, however, that the *Filostrato* narrator also bets on Father; he just happens to do so in the form of the Lady of courtly love, who in this case goes by the name of Filomena. Where the poem makes Criseida available, both to Troilo and to the reader, its framing narrative insists on Filomena's continued absence, and on the power of that absence to determine how much, or even whether, the narrator will experience pleasure. By "betting on" Filomena, the narrator is thus able to disavow the *jouissance* that one actually encounters in his text, the *jouissance* unleashed by the breakdown of sublimation otherwise orchestrated by the conventions of courtly love. Retaining the vaguely cruel, inaccessible, and probably fictional Filomena as his own Good Neighbor, the narrator turns the rest of *Il Filostrato* into the bad neighbor: the neighbor that, far from playing the "naughty games" meant to keep us at the proper distance from *jouissance*, forces us to confront the overproximity of an enjoyment from which we would just as soon flee.

One way Chaucer assumes responsibility for that enjoyment, the enjoyment of the neighboring text, is by allowing Troilus and Criseyde to experience a sort of neighbor love, one made possible by the controlling rituals of courtly love even as it gestures to a realm of *jouissance* beyond them. "To speak of love is itself a *jouissance*," contends Lacan, and in Chaucer's amplification of his source material we begin to get a sense of how this might be.[88] When critics refer to the frank carnality of the bedroom scene in *Il Filostrato*, what they really note is its conspicuous absence of love. What the scene gives us instead is a glimpse of the deficiency, the sheer disappointment, of what Lacan terms "phallic *jouissance*," a deficiency counteracted by the narrator's injunction to sacrifice that *jouissance* in exchange for a *jouissance*—"the Other *jouissance*"—so satisfying, it can only be imagined.[89] In other words, all we experience is an impossibility, the impossibility of the sexual relation, that we are then asked to disavow. Chaucer, by contrast, allows Troilus and Criseyde ample time to speak of love before they must finally give themselves over to the impossibility of the sexual relation. By doing so, he does more than simply call on us to imagine another *jouissance*. He actually manages the far more elusive task of allowing us to experience—or, at the very least, to experience two lovers experiencing—a *jouissance* that, while tied to speaking, nonetheless remains ineffable: a thing not spoken, but rather spoken of. Simply put, Chaucer makes it possible for Troilus and Criseyde to love, not as men, structurally speaking, but as women—that is, as subjects capable of enjoying *jouissance*, rather than having to refer it elsewhere.

There remains, however, one figure cut off from this other *jouissance*, and that is the narrator himself. "Of hire delit or joie soon the lest / Were impossible for my wit to seye," he confesses;

> But juggeth ye that han ben at the feste
> Of swich gladnesse, if that hem liste pleye!
> I kan namore, but thus thise ilke tweye
> That nyght, bitwixen drede and sikernesse,
> Felten in love the grete worthynesse.
>
> (3.1310–16)

Although he is able to transcribe the experiences of his characters, the narrator somehow stands at an even greater remove from their enjoyment than does his counterpart in *Il Filostrato*. When the latter calls on his readers to imagine what was otherwise impossible to describe— "Let him think of it who was ever as much advanced by the grace of love as these were, and he will know in part their delight" (3.33)—he does so in a familiar manner that suggests his own knowledge of the lovers' bliss. The *Troilus* narrator, by changing "him" to "ye," and so precluding himself from possible inclusion in the group, makes it clear that the lovers experienced something that he himself will not even try to imagine. Resisting the temptation to sacrifice the only *jouissance* available to him, and so make matters even worse than they already are, he simply affirms the lack of relation, the constitutive difference, between himself as a resolutely masculine subject and a pair of long-dead lovers whom he has only ever encountered through the mediating presence of a text.

V

My argument has been that Chaucer's encounter with *Il Filostrato* revealed the lack of lack that the sublimating logic of courtly love was ordinarily used to conceal. What makes that revelation in *Il Filostrato* additionally significant is that it happens, not simply at a particular historical juncture, a particular moment in lived time, but at a moment defined in part by a rupture in historiography. To demonstrate as much, I want to return, momentarily, to the matter of identification. I argued above that, even as it asserts a radical equivalency between the pre-Christian Troilo and its narrator, *Il Filostrato* also manages to disavow any correspondence with the historiographic tradition on which it neighbors. This odd juxtaposition—an equivalency that denies correspondence—is crucial, I want to suggest, because it both captures and problematizes a Renaissance historical consciousness in which, to paraphrase A. C. Spearing, the concept of a divinely ordained human nature already present within medieval Christianity was expanded and strengthened to where even the fundamental opposition between Christian and pagan might be overcome, or at least alleviated.[90] Spearing seems to regard the kind of universalizing equivalency I have been describing in *Il Filostrato* as a natural outgrowth of medieval Christianity, and he is undoubtedly correct from a purely linear point of view. But what would it have meant for Chaucer to encounter this level of "historical human universality" too early, as it were: a full century before his fellow countrymen? Surely such noncorrespondent equivalency would have represented for Chaucer, not an extension of the Christocentric symbolic order he knew, but a kind of rupture with that order: a disturbance in the present brought on by a forward-looking identification with a dead figure from the pre-Christian past.

It is that act of "looking" that I want to focus on here. Much of the best work done on *Troilus and Criseyde* has been concerned to show the poem's interest in understanding or processing an essentially alien past.[91] But such an account tells only half the story. If *Troilus and Criseyde* turns to the past, it does so principally as a reaction to the future: the future that is always, and more profoundly so than the past, the other to the present, the revelation that the present can never achieve totality.[92] Nowhere, in fact, is *Troilus and Criseyde* more affirmative of the "medieval," the time in the middle, than when looking ahead to the future.

The late medieval attitude toward the future tended to be, at best, ambivalent. It was not that people dreaded the future; as A. J. Gurevich observes, even a "fear of the Last Judgment mingled and blended with hopes of salvation and attaining the kingdom of heaven."[93] It was just that the future had already been sealed. The world, calculated to be in its sixth age and final age, had grown old; the final catastrophe was imminent. What was there to do, then, other than to follow the course of history to its predetermined end? One detects a slight hint of such ambivalence in the alliteration, pitched somewhere between weariness and contempt, that Chaucer deploys to show *C*alkas *k*nowing by "*c*alkulynge" that "Troie moste ben fordo" and so immediately *c*asting (i.e., plotting) to steal off to the Greek camp, leaving his fellow Trojans to their unhappy fate (1.71–84). Having been granted a vision of the imminent catastrophe that awaits Troy, Calkas simply turns his back on a present he knows is already in ruins. The same ambivalence is also felt, and more powerfully so, in the implications of a detail that Chaucer adds to his source material. In book 3, during their first night together, Criseyde gives Troilus a brooch made of "gold and asure, / In which a ruby set was lik an herte" (3.1370–71). Although this may or may not be the same brooch that Troilus will give to Criseyde on the morning of her departure from Troy, the brooch that will later turn up on Diomede's captured tunic, providing Troilus with the ocular proof that he has been supplanted in Criseyde's heart and that his world has come undone, the coincidence is in and of itself significant. For what it means is that the catastrophe held in store by the future is not just imminent but also immanent, already present even at the moment of the lovers' greatest bliss. They quite literally hold the future in their hands and don't realize it.

In a sense, then, Chaucer has turned the scene in which Troilus and Criseyde not only consummate their love but pledge their *trouthe* to one another into an allegory of his own uneasy relation both with the future and with the "impossible present" to which he struggles to maintain fidelity.[94] What remains most striking about the particular future that Chaucer encountered in *Il Filostrato*, however, is that it manifests itself in the sort of universalism without lack evoked by Spearing, above: a universalism in which not only temporal distance but also cultural difference is collapsed. Four centuries' worth of what James Simpson calls "very deep-set scholarly commitments . . . to the notion of a static Middle Ages" has convinced even literary historians that the passage from medieval to early modern was necessarily a story of progress. Turning that logic on its head, Simpson demonstrates that, on the contrary, the transition from medieval to early modern can be interpreted as "a narrative of diminishing liberties": the gradual decline from "a culture of jurisdictional heterogeneity" that allowed for diverse forms of expression to one of "institutional simplifications and centralizations" that aggressively imposed an ideal of unity and conformity.[95] It may be a lot to claim about the love of two fictional characters that it somehow captures the cultural shift from heterogeneity to universalism. And yet it seems clear, from a side-by-side comparison of the *Filostrato* and the *Troilus*, that Chaucer seizes every opportunity to counter the specular universalism at work in his source text by replacing it with the sort of heterogeneity constituted, for example, in the lack of the sexual relation. If there is a universalism to be found in *Troilus and Criseyde*, it is one based not on a regime of unification but on the radical proposition that what we share is not just difference but self-difference: the kind of internal heterogeneity brought on by the sudden realization that one can be deracinated even from one's situation in history, thrown out of time by the untimely appearance of the future.

For Chaucer, I want to suggest, returning to the trope of the neighboring text, this was a temporal issue that emerged spatially, through an apprehension of the gaze. Stated baldly, the gaze implied by Boccaccio's poem is not there to validate the symbolic order of which Chaucer was a part.[96] The poem's gaze goes elsewhere: back to Troy, back to Troilus—yet in such a futuristic way that it ends up disrupting the writing of their histories as a means of defining the medieval present. That Chaucer understood the power of this gaze and associated it, on some level, with the work of Boccaccio can be demonstrated by comparing a scene in Chaucer's *Knight's Tale*, written about the same time as *Troilus and Criseyde*, with its analogue in Boccaccio's *Teseida*. In Boccaccio's version of the story, the young knights Palemone and Arcita, imprisoned in Theseus's palace, catch a glimpse of Emilia sitting one morning in an adjacent garden, singing to herself and making a garland of flowers. Since the details of the scene are instructive, I wish to quote it at some length:

As [the two knights] both with rapt attention delighted their eyes and ears alike by keeping them fixed on her alone—marveling greatly at her and lamenting to themselves the time that had passed by in vain when they had not seen her—Arcita said: "Palemone, do you not behold what I see within those fair celestial eyes?"

"What is it?" Palemone then asked in reply. Arcita said: "If I am not mistaken, I can see within them the god who once wounded Phaeton's father by means of Daphne, and in his hand he holds two gilded arrows. And already he is setting one of them against the bowstring and fixing his gaze on none but me. It may be that I am angering him by gazing at this woman who gives me such delight."

"Indeed," Palemone then answered, "I can see him, but it may be that he has shot one of them, for he has no more than one in his hand now." Arcita said: "Yes, he has given me such a wound that I shall be racked with pain unless the goddess comes to my aid." Then Palemone cried out in utter dismay: "Alas, the other one has struck me!"

At the sound of that "alas" the young girl quickly turned to her left and her eyes flew straight away nowhere else but to that little window—and that made the white on her cheeks grow red with shame, for she did not know who these men could be. Then, regaining confidence, she rose to her feet with the flowers she had gathered and made ready to leave.

But as she went she was not unmindful of that "alas," and although she was a maiden as yet unready for love's fulfillment, she was nonetheless aware of what it implied. (3.15–19)[97]

Now compare this to the same scene in the *Knight's Tale* (1.198–328). Not only does the emphasis shift, in Chaucer's version, to the growing enmity between the counterparts Palamon and Arcite, but there also can be found no comparable act of looking back, no gesture of recognition or acknowledgment, on the part of Emelye. Whereas *Il Teseida* happily promotes the fantasy of an (O)ther that looks back at the smitten subject—an (O)ther that rewards the subject's desire with the gift of recognition—the *Knight's Tale* studiously refuses to do so until the bitter end, and then only as part of a larger fantasy of concord and reconciliation promoted by Theseus. In the *Knight's Tale*, there is something—a desire, a gaze—in the various avatars of the Other (gods, pagan rituals, the Lady) that goes beyond the tale's putative subjects (and its teller). As Arcite dies, says the tale, "Dusked his eyen two, and failled breeth, / But on his lady yet caste he his ye; / His laste word was 'Mercy, Emelye!'" (1.1948–50). Whether that mercy was ever forthcoming, or even available, the tale declines to tell us outright. All we get is the subject's fervent appeal.

I have made this short detour through the *Knight's Tale* not simply to suggest the apparent asymmetry between the texts of Chaucer and Boccaccio but also to illustrate, by way of that asymmetry, yet another aspect of the "ex-citement" Chaucer must have felt upon encountering *Il Filostrato*. In *The Four Fundamental Concepts of Psychoanalysis*, Lacan recounts the story of Petit-Jean, a young boy who taunted Lacan by pointing to an empty sardine can bobbing on the sea and demanding, "Do you see that can? Do you? Well, it doesn't see you!"[98] In similar fashion, the gaze at work in *Il Filostrato* directs itself *away* from the situation Chaucer knew, toward some new and indeterminate horizon. The very opposite of comfortingly panoptical, the gaze that Chaucer encountered in *Il Filostrato* was one that, to paraphrase Joan Copjec, didn't care about what or where he was, that didn't pry or keep tabs on his whereabouts, that took no note of all his steps and missteps. It was the gaze, not *of* the Other, but *in* the Other: the inscrutable gaze that withholds the recognition on which subjectivity depends. The result was an instance in which one bid for recognition from the other neutralized another bid. For in looking to a pagan other for subjective ratification, the ostensibly Christian narrator of *Il Filostrato* extended the project of universalization to the point where it turned away from Chaucer: the point where there emerged, in the place of the gaze, an intimation of the Other's lack. *Il Filostrato*, that is to say, could only have described for Chaucer an ironic circle: a series in which the narrator's backward turn to the pagan other became, for Chaucer, a gaze intrinsic to the Other that, looking beyond him, to the future, left him stranded in a fractured present.

As the comparison between the *Knight's Tale* and *Il Teseida* suggests, however, it was precisely at this point of the gaze, this point where the *Filostrato* narrator's desire to identify with Troilo implies a lack of identification between the narrator and Chaucer, that Chaucer might have seen most clearly, as it were, not only the narrator's possible blind spot but his own position as a writer. Throughout this chapter, I have sought to address the question of why Chaucer did something to *Il Filostrato* by showing the various ways in which he would have been "ex-cited" by the narrator's identification with Troilo. The final twist to this analysis is that Chaucer would probably have regarded that same identification as fundamentally impossible. There is, so far as we know, but one place in the Chaucerian oeuvre where Chaucer comments *in propria persona* on the pre-Christian other. This is in part 2 of the *Treatise on the Astrolabe*, where Chaucer, writing on the matter of astral determinism—that is, on the matter of predicting the future—notes in passing that "natheles these ben observaunces of judicial matere and rytes of payens, in whiche my spirit hath no feith, ne knowing of her *horoscopum*" (2.4.57–60). Admittedly, these words, while having the force of rejection, carry surprisingly little in the way of outright condemnation. Chaucer does not seem to be recoiling in horror so much as acknowledging the simple fact of difference between his own "feith" and "knowing" and those that inform the "rytes of payens." For all its ecumenicalism, however, Chaucer's attitude here is directly in line, philosophically, with the distancing techniques he adopts in *Troilus and Criseyde*. Morton Bloomfield has put the matter this way: "We may call certain aspects of Chaucerian distance religious. Troilus, Pandarus, and Criseyde are pagans who lived 'while men loved the lawe of kinde' (*Book of the Duchess*, l.56)—under natural law. The great barrier of God's revelation at Sinai and in Christ separates Chaucer and us from them."[99] Chaucer, as a self-identifying subject of the New Law, apparently regarded himself as fundamentally estranged from the pagan other—cut off from them, as they were from him, by the twin events of dispensation and grace. How, then, would Chaucer have been likely to view an act of identification such as that between the narrator of *Il Filostrato* and Troilo? He could only have viewed it, from within the confines of the law, and of the New Law in particular, not as foolish or heretical, but as an exercise in the impossible: an attempt by one of his contemporaries to transgress, if not collapse, the law's supposedly inviolate barrier.

This would have confronted Chaucer with a paradox. For regardless of what he might have thought about it, the fact remained that the identification between the narrator and Troilo had already been achieved—achieved as "successfully" as is any imaginary identification. That any direct relation between the two would be impossible once the "great barrier" of the Law had been imposed was now beside the point; the fantasy of relation had already introduced the possibility of the impossible. What is ironic about this introduction of the impossible, however, is that it remains tied to a process of comparison and analogy—in short, a symbolic process—that fails. For the narrator is not, in the end, like Troilo at all. Troilo dies; the narrator lives. Troilo has no power; the narrator has more power than he is willing to admit. The narrator may want to insist that he and Troilo share a common "myth," that the "material contents" of their stories overlap.[100] Yet that insistence only ends up revealing the otherwise obscure truth content not only of the Troilus and Criseyde story but of the entire medieval tradition of Trojan historiography: natural-historical succession generates, in its figures of displacement and suffering, the "new and non-comparable" Thing with which no identification is possible. Natural-historical succession, the very engine of *translatio imperii*, creates the lack of relation that precludes the cohesion of a transhistorical Other.

In the *Filostrato*, that lack of relation is most evident, at the formal level, in the absence of the narrator's mistress, Filomena, to whom the poem is addressed. So far as we know, the narrator and Filomena never relate to one another directly; their entire relationship is mediated by a text—a text explicitly presented as an allegory of that nonrelation. Chaucer, I am arguing, saw in that lack of relation an uncanny reflection of his own lack of relation, as a reader, with the poem *Il Filostrato*. The "story" of the *Filostrato* narrator's nonrelation with his mistress, that is, corresponds to the "story" of Chaucer's encounter with Boccaccio's text. More urgently, perhaps, the analogy between the *Filostrato* narrator and Troilo also forced Chaucer to grapple with the lack of relation between his own present and a pre-Christian past that emerged, through his encounter with *Il Filostrato*, in the place of what I earlier termed the "future." The very assertion of an equivalence between Boccaccio's narrator and Troilo—between someone who was evidently one of Chaucer's rough contemporaries and a dead figure from the pagan past—imagines a kind of transhistoricism about which Chaucer, if Lee Patterson's reading of the *Knight's Tale* is correct, appears to have been distinctly skeptical.[101] Just as the *Filostrato* narrator presents his text as mediating the lack of any direct relationship with his absent mistress, so "old stories" are thought to collapse the distance between past and present. In the writing of *Il Filostrato*, the rupture between a pre-Christian past and a Trecento present can be crossed, if only at the level of specularity. Not only can one conjure the long dead; one can make them serve the needs of the living. On the surface, at least, that act of conjuring appears to force a transhistorical analogy, a substitution that collapses time, extending a particular order of counting across the ages. Yet in forcing such a collapse, the *Filostrato* narrator's identification with Troilo creates just the opposite effect. Rather than extending the symbolic order of substitution and infinite exchange, it manifests the real lack of relation that precludes the totalization of the Other. Perhaps that is why the *Troilus* narrator's apostrophe to his poem—"Go, litel bok, go, litel myn tragedye . . . / And kis the steppes where as thow seest pace / Virgile, Ovide, Omer, Lucan, and Stace" (5.1786–92)—sounds uncannily like the *Filostrato* narrator's to his: "My piteous song . . . [w]e have come to the port which we were seeking. . . . I judge, therefore, that the anchors are to be cast here and an end made to the journey. . . . Then you, somewhat rested, will betake yourself to the noble lady of my thoughts. O happy you who will see her which I, sorrowing wretch, cannot do! And when with joy you have been received in her hands, humbly commend me to her high worth, which alone can give me salvation" (9.1–5). Both texts are sent to destinations they have no hope of reaching, imaginary halls where they will never be received.[102]

Wherever he would have turned, then, in his encounter with *Il Filostrato*, Chaucer would have come up against a series of nonrelations: between the narrator and his absent mistress, between the narrator and Troilo, and, finally, between the narrator and him. Again, though, it is this final nonrelation that I believe would have affected Chaucer most immediately, since it came in response to an identification—the *Filostrato* narrator's undeadening identification with Troilo—that denied the medieval present its foundational lack.

It is thus that we return, in the most dramatic way possible, to the importance of David Wallace's claim that Chaucer would have encountered *Il Filostrato* "within a familiar international nexus of capital, mercantile activity, and warfare." There can be no denying, I think, the basic truth of what Wallace says: Chaucer would almost certainly have approached *Il Filostrato* as a contemporary work, just as, had he met Boccaccio (which seems unlikely), they would have understood one another as subjects to and of the same symbolic order. But though the nexus itself might have been a familiar one, the presence of *Il Filostrato* within that nexus would have pointed at something else, something other. *Il Filostrato* was, for Chaucer, a neighboring text. And like all encounters with the neighbor, it was Chaucer's mundane encounter with *Il Filostrato*—his unremarkable, everyday act of reading—that forced him to confront the fact that neither the whole Other of the imaginary nor the lacking Øther of the symbolic order exists, except as fantasy. The only question that remained was, what, if anything, was he expected to do about it?

CHAPTER 3

Troilus and Criseyde
between Two Deaths

I

Say this much for the living in the Middle Ages: they cared a lot about the dead. Where the dead of the contemporary West have been, in the words of one observer, "banished from our society," the medieval dead constituted what some historians have begun to call a distinct "'age group,' with rights and responsibilities *vis-à-vis* their 'younger' living contemporaries."[1] The medieval dead, so many of whom were obliged to spend an intermediate period of atonement in purgatory, made numerous demands upon the living, which the living, who would one day number among the dead, felt duty-bound to fulfill. Masses, prayers, almsgiving, indulgences: all were thought to ease the sufferings of the dead in purgatory, and all were offered up, either in person or by proxy, from the dead person's friends, descendants, or associates. The living expected something in return for their troubles, of course. "Reciprocity, exchange and mutual gift-giving between the living and the dead" were the order of the day, with "the saints in heaven" interceding on behalf of the living "as the living interceded for the dead in Purgatory."[2] Nor were relations between the living and the dead without their "generational" tensions. Indeed, some historians have begun "to speak of an unbearable weight of obligation," an "over-burdening of the living by the dead" that would help fuel the Reformation.[3] And Jean-Claude Schmitt, writing on the practice of "liturgical remembrance," notes that the "word 'remembrance' is in fact misleading" in this case, since the goal of such *memoria* was ultimately "to enable the living to forget the deceased" and move on with their own lives.[4] No doubt, then, relations between the living and the dead were undergoing a significant change. But even when we take into account such evidence of ambivalence and growing resentment, it remains striking how much of the day-to-day practice of late medieval Christianity amounted, in the words of A. N. Galpern, to "a cult of the living in the service of the dead."[5]

If this emphasis on reciprocity, rights, and mutual obligation sounds familiar, it is because we have already come across it in accounts of medieval neighborliness. Indeed, the evidence seems to suggest that the same ideal of neighborliness that governed relations among the living also governed those between the living and the dead. As with one's living neighbors, one would have preferred that the dead maintain a "quiet self-sufficiency" and abstain "from behaviour liable to cause injury or provoke disquiet."[6] Thus, as Schmitt points out, the ultimate aim of "liturgical remembrance" was less to help the dead than to make it easier for those who survived them to carry on with their own lives. But by the same token, if the living failed to hold up their end of the bargain and neglected to fulfill their obligations to the dead in the same way they were expected to fulfill their obligations to their neighbors, then the dead were not above returning long enough to remind them of their duties. Yet even such ghostly visitations, disturbing as they could be, held the potential to strengthen social ties. As Schmitt puts it: "The apparition flowed within the framework of earlier relationships, between people whom the death of a relative had once again brought close: affective relationships; social relationships of friendship or neighborhood, of a common community of inhabitants; and above all, relationships of natural and/or spiritual kinship."[7] Note how, in Schmitt's roll call of social relations, no great distinction is made between affective, kinship, and communitarian bonds. The three categories were essentially interchangeable, each one operating, at least where the dead were concerned, according to the principle of reciprocity that defined the ideal of neighborliness. And note as well that the dead, far from being relegated to the past or regarded simply as precursors, enjoyed the same sort of incessant contemporaneity (to paraphrase Kenneth Reinhard) as any other neighbor.[8] If medieval European society can indeed be described as "a cult of the living in the service of the dead," then it was a cult that borrowed the values and practices of the even more ubiquitous cult of the neighbor.

One place where that cult, the cult of the neighboring dead, appears to have particularly flourished was at the court of Richard II. Richard himself had something of a mania for tomb building, as John Bowers's work on *Pearl* so amply demonstrates.[9] In addition to the marble sepulchers that he commissioned for himself and Queen Anne (the "most expensive of all fourteenth-century royal tombs"), Richard had tombs or monuments built for Edward III, Edward the Black Prince, his mother, Princess Joan, his brother Edward, and his mother-in-law, Elizabeth of Pomerania.[10] The king also took the unprecedented step of securing space in Westminster Abbey for the interment of various chamber knights, ecclesiastical courtiers, friends, and even favorite servants—an honor usually reserved for members of the royal family or for abbey residents.[11] Then there was the matter of Richard's extravagant mourning for his dead queen, Anne of Bohemia. It is well known, for example, that the grief-stricken Richard, as if trying to create a kind of secondary tomb, a memorial ruin, "ordered his Clerk of the Works to pull down the royal residence where [Anne] had died at Sheen." But perhaps less well known, according to Bowers, is that Richard subsequently had "the first funeral effigy ever produced for a queen of England . . . carved in London and transported to Sheen." Or that "Richard was so infuriated by the Earl of Arundel's late arrival for [Anne's] funeral that he struck him to the ground, committing sacrilege by polluting Westminster Abbey with human blood." Or that "for all the remaining years of his life, Richard II avoided entering any place where he knew that Anne had been."[12] Such anecdotes might lead one to conclude that Ricardian court life (or at least the king himself) was profoundly melancholic, characterized by a refusal to mourn completely, to separate fully from the dead. But how much separation from the dead could there, or should there, be when one remained bound to the dead by the same networks of reciprocity and obligation that bound one to one's still-living neighbors? Richard's behavior may strike us as bizarre, if not a little unhinged. But perhaps we should recognize it as an especially intense example of social obligation, neighborliness taken to an extreme degree.

This is where I intend to situate Chaucer's *Troilus and Criseyde*: among the tombs and ruins and monuments, the masses and *memoria*, of the Ricardian court. We have long been accustomed to thinking of *Troilus and Criseyde* as a love story, a story of two, and have titled it accordingly. And of course the poem is that, up to a point. But the fact that Chaucer himself refers, in his Retractions to the *Canterbury Tales*, to "the book of Troilus" hints at yet another way of approaching the text. Granted, Chaucer mentions several other "books" in his Retractions as well: "the book . . . of Fame"; "the book of the XXV Ladies"; "the book of the Duchesse"; "the book of Seint Valentynes day of the Parlement of Briddes"; the lost "book of the Leoun"; "othere bookes of legendes of seints, and omelies, and moralitee, and devocioun"; and, enticingly, "many another book, if they were in my remembrance" (10.1085–87). This seems to suggest that Chaucer intended *book* primarily to mean an independent story, if not simply a collection of leaves. Note, however, that all of the known "books" besides *Troilus and Criseyde* that Chaucer lists—*The Book of the Duchess*, *The Parliament of Fowls*, *The House of Fame*, *The Legend of Good Women*, saints' lives, such as the Second Nun's tale of Saint Cecilia—are commemorative in some way.[13] They recount dreams, recall past lives, remember the dead. Like the Retractions in which their author calls them to mind, Chaucer's "books" assume the added meaning—or, at the very least, the shading—of a written act of remembrance, an accounting. Chaucer's "book of Troilus" may thus be read, in these terms, not only as Troilus's story, the record of his fortunes in love, but as his commemoration. This is the memorial of Troilus's life; yet in order to be such, it must also be the memorial of his death, the site where his death is resymbolized in the wake of *Il Filostrato*'s neglect. The "book of Troilus," as Chaucer entitles it, is the book as final resting place, the book as tomb.[14]

This would not be the first time that Chaucer revived a character only in order to restage that character's death. He had done more or less the same thing in *The Book of the Duchess*, a poem in which, as Steve Ellis argues, "Blanche is brought back to life in [the man in black's] memory only to 'die' again," making the work not only a commemoration of Blanche's life but also, as Ellis puts it, "a reenactment of Blanche's death."[15] But the fact that *Troilus and Criseyde* ends as it does, completing the work of *Il Filostrato* by directing Troilus to his symbolic death, suggests that, in this case, Chaucer seized upon the strategy employed in *The Book of the Duchess*, simultaneously enshrining a character and dramatizing the finality of that character's death, not only as a mode of commemoration but also as a particular way of understanding what it means to love one's neighbor. We have seen that the living in the Middle Ages were bound to the dead by the same networks of obligation and reciprocity that connected the living to one another. But if that were the case, then what would reciprocity between Chaucer and Troilus look like? What would Chaucer owe to Troilus, and vice versa? Schmitt writes that "the dead returned at different times after the prayers and masses from which they benefited directly, in order to attest to the efficacy of those suffrages, to ask the living for an additional effort, and to thank them for their help before disappearing forever."[16] "The success of ghost tales . . ." he continues, "derived from the fact that they always placed two people in a relationship—a dead person and a living person, united beyond death—and most often many other people as well."[17] I want to propose that we think of Troilus as being like one of those medieval ghosts— except that Troilus, being neither a Christian nor a virtuous pagan, not only does not know how to ask for help but may not even realize that he needs help in the first place.[18] It fell to Chaucer, then, to take Troilus's part, a situation that in effect required him to make a choice about the demands of neighbor love. And that choice, as the narrative arc of *Troilus and Criseyde* makes clear, was a stark one: within the reciprocal economy that governed relations between the living and the dead, Troilus was obligated to die, while Chaucer was obligated to provide Troilus with the symbolic death still owed him, as a neighbor.

To be sure, *Troilus and Criseyde* is broadly concerned with death in a way that Boccaccio's *Il Filostrato*, its principal source text, is not.

Death is forever skulking about the edges of Chaucer's narrative, making its presence felt, for example, in our early knowledge that Criseyde
will forsake Troilus "ere she deyde" (1.56), in Calkas's prediction "that
Troye sholde / Destroyed ben, ye, wolde whoso nolde" (1.76–77), and
in the narrator's uncanny evocation of the death drive after the Trojan
parliament decides to trade Criseyde for Antenor:

> O Juvenal, lord, trewe is thy sentence,
> That litel wyten folk what is to yerne,
> That they ne fynde in hire desir offence;
> For cloude of errour let hem to discerne
> What best is. And lo, here ensample as yerne:
> This folk desiren now deliveraunce
> Of Antenor, that brought hem to meschance.
>   (4.197–203)[19]

The characters themselves, meanwhile, invoke death so often, both
directly and in passing, that it becomes a kind of leitmotif. As Barry
Windeatt points out, "Chaucer associates some of the most important
emotional transitions and experiences for the poem's characters"—
including the pivotal moment when Troilus falls in love—"with death
and dying."[20] Yet even when we take into account death's overall presence in the poem, it is remarkable how many of the characters' (and
the narrator's) references to death are to Troilus's death, or at least the
prospect of Troilus's death, in particular. A representative selection
might include the following: the moment, alluded to just now, when
Troilus is so smitten at his first sight of Criseyde "that sodeynly hym
thoughte he felte dyen, / Right with hire look, the spirit in his herte"
(1.306–7); the end of the so-called *Canticus Troili*, when Troilus, contemplating love in the Petrarchan manner, asks, "Allas, what is this
wondre maladie? / For hote of cold, for colde of hote, I dye" (1.419–
20); the moment when Troilus, convinced that his love for Criseyde
is doomed, concludes that "God wolde I were aryved in the port /
Of deth, to which my sorwe wol me lede," before bursting out with "O
mercy, dere herte, and help me from / The deth, for I, whil that my
lyf may laste, / More than myself wol love yow to my laste" (1.526–27,

535–37); and certain points in the extended sequence following Pandarus's first arrival in Troilus's room, as when a distraught Troilus asks:

> What cas . . . or what aventure
> Hath gided the to sen me langwisshing,
> That am refus of every creature?
> But for love of God, at my preyinge,
> Go hennes awey; for certes my deyinge
> Wol the disese, and I mot nedes deye;
> Therfore go wey, ther is na more to seye.
> . . . .
> Ther is another thing I take of hede
> Wel more than aught the Grekes han yet
>   wrought,
> Which cause is of my deth, for sorowe and
>   thought.
>   (1.568–79)

or when Troilus explains that

> Love, ayeines the which whoso defendeth
> Hymselven most, hym alderlest avaylleth,
> With disespeyr so sorwfulli me offendeth,
> That streight unto the deth myn herte sailleth.
> Therto desir so brennyngly me assailleth,
> That to ben slayn it were a gretter joie
> To me then kynge of Grece ben and Troye.
>   (1.603–9)

or when, in response to Pandarus's counsel, Troilus

> No worde seyde,
> But longe he ley as stylle as he ded were;
> And after this with sikynge he abreyde,
> And to Pandarus vois he lente his ere,
> And up his eighen cast he, that in feere

Was Pandarus, lest in frenesie
He sholde falle, or elles soone dye.
(1.722–28)

or when Troilus says, in a withering response to his friend's "prover-
bes," "Nor other cure kanstow non for me; / Ek I nyl nat ben cured; I
wol deye. / What knowe I of the queene Nyobe?" (1.757–59). And this
is all in book 1, mind you. In book 2, Pandarus asks of the anxious
Troilus, albeit teasingly, "Who is in his bed so soone / Iburied thus?"
(2.1310–11), while the book itself ends with Troilus thinking, "O Lord,
right now renneth my sort, / Fully to deye, or han anon comfort!"
(2.1754–55). Meanwhile, in book 4, after the Trojans have made their
fateful decision to exchange Criseyde for Antenor, we are given two
indelible images of Troilus: one in which, like a man preparing a living
tomb, he shuts every door "and window ek" before sitting down on the
side of his bed "ful like a ded ymage, pale and wan"; and another, as
the book draws to a close, in which "the day gan rise, and Troilus hym
cladde, / And rewfullich his lady gan byholde, / As he that felte dethes
cares colde" (4.1690–92). Then there is the special matter of book 5, in
which all of the poem's intimations and foreshadowings finally come
to pass in Troilus's actual death. But of that I will have more to say as
the chapter unfolds.

One might well protest that all of this morbidity merely reflects
the conventions of lovesickness, a common topos of courtly literature.[21] What such an argument must fail to register in this particular
instance, however, is the extent to which *Troilus and Criseyde* exploits
that conventional language in a unique way, as a kind of marker. It is
not only that the poem's fixation on death goes well beyond generic
or even intertextual expectations.[22] It is that Troilus, though he may
express his lovesickness in conventional terms, is not just any conventional courtly lover. He is, on the contrary, "the king Priamus sone
of Troye" (1.2); his very name, *Troilus*, "contains both the beginning
and the end of Troy."[23] Troilus, with all of his being, was meant to be
both the life and death of the city whose very name existed, as a diminutive, in his own: a city on whose destruction was predicated the
subsequent rise of London as a self-styled "New Troy." More, then,

than a conventional attribute of the courtly lover, Troilus's abiding association with death in Chaucer's poem underscores the uncomfortable fact that, as the embodiment of both the beginning and the end of an always-already ruined city, he really *is* dead, or least *should* be dead, and that precisely the unsettling thing about him is that he keeps being brought back to life, retroactively, by the workings of what Žižek terms symbolization/historicization—the process, in short, of writing about his tragic death.

That process, as Žižek explains it, "implies an empty place, a non-historical kernel around which the symbolic network is articulated." What separates "human *history* . . . from animal *evolution*" is that the former references "this *non-historical* place, a place which cannot be symbolized, although it is retroactively produced by the symbolization itself: as soon as 'brute,' pre-symbolic reality is symbolized/historicized, it 'secretes,' it isolates the empty, 'indigestible' place of the Thing."[24] Žižek's argument here remains firmly tied to the Pauline logic of Lacan's *Ethics of Psychoanalysis*: "Is the Law the Thing? Certainly not. Yet I can only know of the Thing by means of the Law. In effect, I would not have had the idea to covet it if the Law hadn't said: 'Thou shalt not covet it.' But the Thing finds a way by producing in me all kinds of covetousness, thanks to the commandment, for without the Law the Thing is dead."[25] The Thing, as Lacan understands it, emerges as such only upon the advent of the symbolic order. It is not as though there had once been *a* Thing and the Law came along to take it from us. Prohibition—the negative injunction "Thou shalt not"—retroactively confers upon the Thing its unique status. The Thing is "alive," charged with *jouissance*, only because it has been placed off limits; it has not been placed off limits because it was once charged with *jouissance*. At the same time, however, the prohibition of the Thing also holds out the possibility that it might one day be recovered—and that we might therefore still experience *jouissance*. To have the fantasy of transgression, one must first have the law. In this way, then, the simultaneous naming and prohibition of the Thing institutes the economy of desire—the whole symbolic order of compensatory objects—while also designating that which remains outside of that economy, no longer subject to exchange. It is the workings of the symbolic order, in other words, that retroactively isolate the lacking object on which the substitutional economy of desire is based.

But what if that lacking object were itself lacking? What if the Thing were missing, so to speak, from its place of exile outside of the symbolic order? This is the more radical way of understanding what Žižek means by the "empty place" of the Thing: as the lack even of lack. The lack of the Thing at least holds out the promise that it might be discovered somewhere else, like a library book temporarily missing from its spot on the shelf. The lack of lack reveals instead that the Thing is, paradoxically, too present: missing from the place of lack. If lack, instituted by prohibition, lies at the heart of the symbolic order, then one can see how the lack of lack would threaten that order. Lack and desire go hand in hand; to suffer the one is to be subject to the other. The lack of lack, by contrast, rather than instigating desire, instead confronts us with the specter of something utterly Other to the logic of desire, immune to substitution, beyond sacrifice. In short, as the image (intended, in Lacan as in Paul, to invoke the Tenth Commandment) of the subject coveting the Thing suggests, the lack of lack confronts us with drive—specifically, the death drive. I covet my neighbor's Thing in the same way I covet his wife or his maidservant or his house. Ultimately, the thing I desire most is to deprive my neighbor of his Thing. That is how I experience the *jouissance* I cannot otherwise bear: by fantasizing about the ways in which I might deprive my neighbor of his. Mutability may indeed be the abiding obsession of *Troilus and Criseyde*, but mutability is still on the side of desire, still on the side of substitution and exchange. To apprehend the sudden proximity of the Thing is to catch a glimpse, fleeting and anamorphic, of the "complete annihilation" of the symbolic universe.

If it is indeed the case, then, as Lee Patterson has argued, that by finally rejecting "the dominion of the transcendent mind," *Troilus and Criseyde* "admits that there is no immunity from historicity," then by the same token the poem must also admit that there is no escape from the empty space—the site of the nonhistorical, nonsymbolizable Thing—opened up by that same historicity, that same immersion of the subject in the process of symbolization/historicization.[26] In time, the law will generate its own internal limit, its own point of failure.

Following this logic, one strand of my argument in this chapter is that *Troilus and Criseyde* is finally less concerned with exploring the nature of history as such—with understanding history as a force or a process, a sequence of events tied to the clash of material interests—than with symbolically accounting for that which it itself, as a work of both historicization and symbolization, uncovers: the *extimate* Thing at the heart of the symbolic order.

    Troilus and Criseyde has a name for that nonhistorical place, that Thing. It calls it *Troy.* To say, however, that *Troilus and Criseyde* produces Troy as something nonhistorical is not to suggest that the poem is therefore indifferent either to the past or, more crucially, to its own historical moment.[27] On the contrary, it is fair to say that, on some level, the poem's interest in its own historical moment's founding myth translates into an interest in that moment as such: in how that moment conceived of its own historical position. Yet at the same time the very fact that the poem's "principal subject" turns out to be Troy, the mythical, foreclosed origin of the medieval West, automatically complicates its vision not only of what history is, what constitutes its workings, but of the untimely ways in which the present can reanimate the past.[28] To claim that the poem is interested in *Troy* is not the same thing as claiming that it is interested in antiquity or even history. It is to claim, rather, that the poem is interested in, even fascinated by, the "nonhistorical kernel" produced retroactively by the process of historicization itself. What fascinates the poem, in other words, is not Troy so much as the "matter" of Troy: the dead matter around which the poem, and the culture that produced it, articulate themselves. And the way it finds to approach that dead matter is through the displaced figure of Troilus, missing from the place where he ought to be lacking, suspended in the space between two deaths.

    One hates to be reductive. Nevertheless, the fact remains that, with the possible exception of book 3, Troilus exists in something of a continuous deathlike state—hovering "bitwixen hope and drede" (5.1207), doomed, as he puts it, to "evere dye and nevere fulli sterve" (4.280)—until the end of book 5, when he discovers, on the collar of a "cote-armure" taken from Diomede, "a broch that he Criseyde yaf that morwe / That she from Troie moste nedes twynne, / In remembrance of hym and of his sorwe" (5.1651, 1660–63). Although there have been other indications, most notably the *Litera Criseydis*, that Criseyde will not be returning to Troilus (or, for that matter, to Troy), the brooch is of particular significance because it indicates not only that Troilus has lost Criseyde but that the hour of his fate is at hand—and that his fate is to be supplanted. "Al is lost that he hath ben aboute" (5.1645), says the narrator of Troilus, an observation that assumes its full significance only when we recall Troilus's association with the lost city of Troy. For that is what Troilus has always been about: the fate of Troy. From the narrator's perspective, the thing that Troilus is finally "about," the thing he finally stands for, is Troy, and Troy has always been lost. The only problem is that Troilus, being suspended between two deaths, doesn't know it. Thus the importance of the brooch. Where once the brooch had been a token of Troilus's devotion to Criseyde, now it has become a kind of stage property, in the sense that Walter Benjamin has given the term: an object that reflects, and indeed shares, Troilus's disastrous fate.[29] For like the brooch, which returns, as if from a temporary exile, to the place whence it came, Troilus is immediately aware not only that he has been displaced but also that he is profoundly out of place. It is the return of the brooch that lets Troilus know, once and for all, that his fate is to return to the place from which he has gone missing, the place of loss and destruction that he has always "ben aboute."

How else to explain Troilus's extreme reaction to the appearance of the brooch—that is, to the materialization of his fate? In *Il Filostrato*, Troilo's initial reaction upon seeing the brooch is one of sorrow, of course, but that feeling quickly turns to a longing for revenge at any cost. Indeed, his last words in the poem are a kind of prayer for vengeance. "Mandimi Dio Diomedes davanti / la prima volta ch'io esco alla battaglia" [May God send Diomede in front the first time that I go to battle], he says.

> [Q]uesto disio tra li miei guai cotanti,
> sí ch'io provar gli faccia come taglia
> la spada mia, e lui morir con pianti
> nel campo faccia, e poi non me ne caglia

che mi s'uccida, sol ch'io muoia, e lui
misero truovi nelli regni bui.

(8.21)

[This I desire among my great woes so that I may make him test
how my sword cuts and may make him die with lamentations in
the field, and then it does not matter to me that someone may kill
me, if only I may die and find him in misery in the dark kingdom.]

In *Troilus and Criseyde*, by contrast, Troilus may still crave revenge
against Diomede, but it is not his ultimate desire, as it is here. On
the contrary, where his counterpart in *Il Filostrato* seems merely indifferent to his fate, claiming that "it does not matter" to him whether
he dies so long as he gains revenge, Chaucer's Troilus clearly admits
that it is not Diomede's death he longs for so much as his own. "And
certeynly, withouten moore speche," he tells Pandarus,

From hennesforth, as ferforth as I may,
Myn oewen deth in armes wol I seche;
I recche nat how soone be the day!
But trewely, Criseyde, swete may,
Whom I have ay with al my myght yserved,
That ye thus doon, I have it nat deserved.

(5.1716–22)

Although the differences here may seem subtle, the fact remains that,
in *Troilus and Criseyde*, Troilus's final speech has been rearranged
so as to emphasize his ultimate desire, not for revenge, but for self-
destruction—for death. Such a move can hardly be coincidental. On
the contrary, Troilus has at last come to recognize what the poem itself
has known all along, although it has been loath to say so outright: his
function is to die.

But as the aftermath of that death—arguably the climax of the
poem—makes clear, Troilus's cannot be just any death. Rather, it must
be, as it arguably was in Benoît's *Roman de Troie*, and arguably was not
in Boccaccio's *Il Filostrato*, a death that means something, that does

not simply allow Troilus to die without his death being adequately symbolized. At the same time, however, it is obviously not enough, within the explicitly Christian framework articulated at poem's end, to have that death be for the sake of Troy alone, as it was in the *Roman*. The reason for this, as we have already seen, is that Troilus's "proper" memorialization is not just individual, restricted to Troilus himself. In the previous chapter, I noted the homology between *Troy* and *Troilus*, just as I noted how, in the Trojan myth, the fate of the city was tied to that of its (second) favorite son. When Troilus died, so the medieval version of the legend had it, the city would fall. In symbolically interring Troilus, then, Chaucer's poem attempts much more than the "burial" of a dead character. It tries to seal within itself, as in a tomb, the figuration of a temporal and conceptual rupture—what Freud might have meant by a "disturbance of memory."[30] Troilo, the embodiment of that disturbance, had confronted Chaucer with a displaced figure, a temporal exile whose absence from his "proper grave" disrupted the process of ordered succession: those lineal inheritances, carried through linear time, that constitute the symbolic order.[31] Yet that temporal disruption had also forced Chaucer to confront the impasse produced by the moral imperative to love one's neighbor as oneself. After all, if Chaucer were truly to love Troilus as *himself*, he would have to treat him as a sort of contemporary, one of the neighboring dead. Indeed, one might go so far as to say that were Chaucer to take the injunction literally, he would be obliged to keep Troilus "alive," as it were, by preserving his insistent contemporaneity. But of course that would also mean Chaucer having to embrace the very destruction of the symbolic order by taking on the Thing in all of its paradoxical overproximity—that is, in its radical absence from the place of foundational lack. At the very least, he would have to accept that what he and Troilus had in common—the reason why he could love this particular neighbor as himself—was their mutual displacement. For just as Troilus had recovered the brooch that signified, by its simple material presence, that he had been supplanted and that the future was upon him, so Chaucer had encountered, in *Il Filostrato*, the materialization of a future immanent within, and thus already at work dislodging, his own present moment. In order, then, to complete its work of mourning Troilus, of releasing him from his destabilizing suspension between two deaths, *Troilus and Criseyde* has little choice but to devise a way of memorializing him without, at the same time, violating the terms of its own, Christocentric symbolic order.

And this is precisely what the poem attempts to do, however awkwardly, at the end of book 5, first by granting Troilus's "lighte goost" its apotheosis to the "eighthe spere," then by having the dead Troilus laugh in contempt at "al oure werk that foloweth so / The blynde lust, the which that may nat laste," and finally by asserting the primacy of Christianity over the "olde" world of the pagans (5.1809, 1823–24, 1842–55). In her *Afterlives of the Saints*, Julia Lupton notes that symbolic (as opposed to biological) death has to do with "proper" memorialization—with the socially acceptable, ritualistic interment of the dead in the "cemetery of memory." But Lupton goes on to draw an important distinction between symbolic death as figured in classical tragedy, on the one hand, and in Christian hagiography, on the other. "In the Greek drama," she writes, "the refusal of burial disastrously interferes with divine communication," whereas, "in the Christian scene . . . the exposed, battered, and truncated cadaver of the saint triggers God's further revelations." She then goes on:

> Both the tragic and the hagiographic narratives maintain the status of the corpse as refuse, as fundamentally undisposable debris, which, like the interminable half-life of radioactive waste, returns with uncanny persistence and disturbing effects to haunt the order that has foreclosed it. In the Greek drama, however, the insistence on the corpse as detritus flags the continuing scandal of its sacrilegious degradation, whereas in the *Golden Legend*, the unsinkable character of the floating corpse [of St Vincent] is precisely the means and sign of its sublimation.[32]

What we encounter in *Troilus and Criseyde*, I would argue, is a partial reconciliation of the classical/tragic and hagiographic/comedic modes of symbolic death: a reconciliation at once centered on and enacted upon the figure of Troilus. The problem facing Chaucer, as I understand it, is that the revived Troilus occupies the privileged position between two deaths ordinarily reserved, in hagiography, for the saint.[33] That position, as the saints' lives make abundantly clear, is invariably a threat to the state, a sign of Rome's typological supersession. And what makes it a threat is the fact that, far from disrupting the process of divine communication, as it would in a classical tragedy like *Antigone*, the saintly suspension between two deaths serves instead as a direct message from God, a sign of his miraculous intervention in earthly life. Ironically, then, for *Troilus and Criseyde* to "get medieval" (as it were) on its eponymous hero, it first needs to get a little pagan, restoring Troilus to his classical function lest he continue, like a saint, to disrupt the workings of the symbolic order. Accordingly, the approach taken by the poem is to compromise by transforming Troilus's classical death into something both more and less like the death of a saint, a death that opens up the lines of communication between heaven and earth without, at the same time, allowing Troilus's unburied corpse to flag "the continuing scandal of its sacrilegious degradation." Thus, as he looks down from the heavens and laughs, Troilus, the embodiment of a pagan world that had returned "with uncanny persistence and disturbing effects to haunt the order that [had] foreclosed it," becomes instead a sign of that order's own self-meaning, its own, self-proclaimed divine purpose. Denied the saintly privilege of sublime indestructibility, the symbolically dead Troilus is instead rendered, like the doubling opposite of St Vincent's floating corpse, one of God's revelations: a pagan who offers, with his last breath, a lesson in *contemptus mundi*.

The basic "work" taken up by *Troilus and Criseyde* was thus to address, through its reinterment of Troilus, a profound disturbance in the symbolic order, a disturbance with temporal no less than cultural implications. Yet even as the poem goes about pursuing that larger task, responding to a Florentine text, contemplating the fate of a universalizing symbolic order, it also turns its attention to the effects of temporal disruption upon the city in which it was composed. We recall that many of Chaucer's contemporaries, including Richard II, traced the founding of London to a legendary Trojan diaspora. For them, London was "New Troy": the rightful inheritor of the lost city's ancient grandeur, the occupant of its canceled ground. For Troilus to

be suspended between two deaths meant, then, that Troy was temporarily out of place, out of time, out of history. And so interring him
meant interring more than any one figure or body; it meant interring,
at the levels of signification and association, the ancient city whose
place had been taken over by London as "New Troy."

Understood this way, Troilus's symbolic interment starts to seem
not only like an answer to the desire in a neighboring text but also
like a sly, ironic commentary on the desire for Troy among Chaucer's
London neighbors. This is an elaborate commentary, to say the least.
On the one hand, Chaucer seems intent on dismantling the merely
imaginary (that is, specular) identification between Ricardian London
and the lost city of Troy. Such identificatory gestures always assume
that there exists a past to be recovered, recuperated, resurrected, remembered. More suspect still, they assume that there exists a place
of mastery that one might yet occupy, provided one can move into
the symbolic position vacated by one's dead precursor. One way *Troilus and Criseyde* counteracts that will to specularity is by introducing
certain small details, as "when Pandarus swears 'by stokkes and by
stones' (3.589)," or when "the narrator refers to 'hire olde usage' (1.150)
instead of Boccaccio's 'modi usanti' ('usual customs,' 1.17) and 'hir observaunces olde' (1.160) instead of 'li consueti onori' ('customary devotions,' 1.18)," that stress the *past-ness*, the *remoteness*, of Troy.[34] Yet
just when the poem seems in danger of succumbing to the very lure
it seeks to criticize, buying into the fantasy of mere loss, the narrator
will invoke a detail of "Trojan" life uncannily reminiscent of Ricardian
London: a place of war, parliamentary debate, political squabbling,
shortsightedness, human frailty, and, ultimately, death. (One thinks
especially of "the headlong and ill-advised Trojan parliament" in
which Criseyde is traded for Antenor.)[35] Counterintuitive as it may
seem, then, Chaucer's poem sets out to inter Troilus, the "Little Troy,"
not in order to reiterate the loss of Troy but rather to deny Ricardian
London the consoling fantasy of loss that had distorted *Il Filostrato*:
the fantasy wherein "what cannot be lost because it has never been
possessed appears as lost, and what could never be possessed because it
had never perhaps existed may be appropriated insofar as it is lost." At
once counteracting and radicalizing the stratagem of the melancholic,

Troilus and Criseyde insists that Troy is not simply absent—and so also, perhaps, recoverable—but all too impossible: woven so deeply into the fabric of everyday life as to preclude the coherence of the Other.

The focus of *Troilus and Criseyde*, in other words, is not on loss but on lack: the lack not simply *in* but *of* the Other that the fantasy of loss is meant to conceal. Chaucer, it seems, saw in his English contemporaries the same thing that had caught his attention in *Il Filostrato*: namely, that their desire for Troy amounted to an elaborate disavowal of the real of Troy. Rooted in the "sovereign fantasy" (to adapt Patricia Ingham's term) that *jouissance* is at once prohibited and recuperable, the desire for Troy among the English elite of the fourteenth century expressed a desire to move into the place of the sovereign while at the same time making it possible to evade the *jouissance* actually immanent in the antagonisms of Ricardian society. No doubt some of those desires for Troy were utopic. Some of them may even have been ironic and self-knowing. But even if they were, what difference would it make? The very fact that some of Chaucer's most influential London neighbors looked to Troy for civic aggrandizement meant that a universalizing symbolic order was *already* incomplete, *already* lacking—already as "dead," if we take *dead* to mean nonexistent, as Troy itself. Ultimately, then, Chaucer's efforts both to provide Troilus with the achievement of his symbolic destiny and to figuratively inter him seem designed, not only to commemorate Troilus, but also, to paraphrase Jean-Claude Schmitt, to help the living forget him and move on.[36] This may make it sound as though Chaucer were acting in a way that we have come to regard, in the wake of Derrida, as unethical: forgetting the dead, leaving the dead behind. But as I have been arguing all along, Chaucer's insistence on removing Troilus from between two deaths was deeply ethical, insofar as it signaled his fidelity to his encounter with the neighboring text. The interment of Troilus is Chaucer's direct response to the Thing, his affirmation of the lack both in and of the Other that some of his friends and associates seemed all too eager (if perhaps also playfully) to betray.

By interring the pagan other, then, Chaucer was striving to maintain fidelity to a ruined present, an impossible Other. There is little reason to believe, however, that he felt entirely comfortable doing so.

In fact, there is every reason to believe that he knew only too well how pathetic, how *tragic*, it is to work on behalf of an Other that does not exist, as we shall now see.

II

Troilus's first glimpse of Criseyde inspires a moment of wonder and prompts a question: "O mercy God . . . wher hastow woned, / That are so feyr and goodly to devise?" (1.276–77). *Devise* can mean, as it evidently does here, "to inspect, examine, look upon, or observe" (*MED*). But it also means "to form, fashion, shape, or construct," "to describe, discuss, explain, or interpret," and, by extrapolation, "to set off or separate" (*MED*). From the first time he sees her, then, Troilus can be said to think of Criseyde, not only as someone lovely to behold, but as a fascinating object to be shaped, described, interpreted, set off from those around it. Criseyde, that is to say, finds herself being "devised," fashioned into a thing apart, from the very moment Troilus first lays eyes on her.

And not just Troilus, but Pandarus and the narrator as well. *Devise* in its noun form primarily means "a plan or design, a literary composition, an artistic design, or a work of art" (*MED*). It is this sense of *devise* that Elizabeth Scala emphasizes in her reading of Chaucer's other translation of Boccaccio in the 1380s, the *Knight's Tale*. "The end of much of [the Knight's] 'devising,'" observes Scala, is "order." And yet, she argues, "the order achieved by the Knight's romance is as much a function of his various kinds of omissions, the narrative lines he declines or refuses to engage, as of his elaborate descriptions."[37] To devise is to create order, both aesthetic and political, and to create order is to engage in a process of strategic exclusion. The Knight describes, expansively and vividly. But he also abbreviates, and most of those abbreviations come, as Scala points out, at the expense of women. Such a strategy remains consistent with the Knight's self-image as a paternal figure committed to a regime of benign prohibition, a controlled economy of loss and recuperation central, as Aranye Fradenburg has argued, to the production of chivalric culture. "The fantasy of chivalry is a sublime economy that powerfully recuperates the *jouissance* of aggressivity by rewriting it as incalculable, inscrutable love," writes Fradenburg; "it is a structure through which a certain extreme destructivity may be glimpsed and enjoyed, but only to the extent that the gift of death is offered in payment thereof." She continues: "What makes the hypereconomy of sacrifice so effective is that it not only infuses obedience to the command with positivity, it even more radically rationalizes the irrationality of submission and our desire for it through the figure of secrecy: that we cannot know the mysterious reasons of Providence or of the prince is an ideological form of nonknowledge, an *ascesis* of knowledge, a sacrifice of knowledge, that stands in the place of the impossibility of knowing what the law means, and in the place of the *jouissance* signposted by that impossibility."[38] Believing that *jouissance* is in the Other's keeping—believing, in fact, that there exists an Other to keep *jouissance* at all—makes it that much easier for the subject to capitulate to the law not in spite of, but because of, its irrationality. If there is a trade-off for the subject, it is that cultivating the fantasy of the Other as a repository for *jouissance* is in and of itself a form of *jouissance*, one rooted in the choices we make about what will and will not be included in our fictions and fantasies. Scala makes this point when she argues that "the Knight's devising activity transforms 'gyse' (historical difference, epic distance) into romance fabulation, but it does so by making its authority out of these opacities. The Knight does not explain the 'gyse,' the custom of ancient Greece, in his tale. Instead he allows it to stand as a narrative aporia whose very untranslatability marks its significance and superiority."[39] That untranslatability is essential, given that "the enjoyment at stake in how we give credence to the law is . . . supported precisely by that senseless enjoyment that escapes the law."[40] Not only, then, does the Knight use his skill at devising to inoculate his carefully orchestrated version of order against *jouissance*. He also perpetuates the fantasy that *jouissance* is safely prohibited by insisting that it exceeds the symbolic order's ability to name it and thus dissipate it by drawing it into the fabric of the symbolic order itself.

"A structure through which a certain extreme destructivity may be glimpsed and enjoyed," but only at the cost of extreme sacrifice: that would be the same chivalric fantasy-scape cultivated by Troilus, the narrator, and Pandarus, all of whom situate Criseyde so that she shields them from the overproximity of the Thing, thereby allowing them to linger, for a few books at least, in Troy. But unlike the *Knight's Tale*, which is built around a strategically absented narrative, a story the Knight chooses not to translate in the name of order and its attendant *jouissance*, the devise that is *Troilus and Criseyde* spends most of its time trying not to have to translate the one story it must inevitably tell, the narrative of loss that makes the poem itself possible. This too signals a disinclination to engage a particular "narrative line," as Scala calls it, but in this case it is Troilus's story that is being evaded. For as long as he can spend his time devising Criseyde, Troilus (and Pandarus, and the narrator) will not have to confront the fact that it is he who must eventually be absented in the name of order. Troilus's act of devising thus makes it possible for the narrator to put off having to bring his own "devise" to its tragic conclusion. At the same time, it also lays the groundwork for justifying the sacrifices that all of the characters, including the narrator, will be called upon to make in the name of the Other.

The idea I wish to pursue in this section is that the acts of devising performed by Troilus, Pandarus, and the narrator locate Criseyde in the position of the Lady-Object in Lacan's reading of courtly love.[41] Much of what I have to say here will be familiar to anyone who has read the work of Sarah Kay, Fradenburg, Jeffrey Cohen, or Patricia Ingham, all of whom have developed Lacan's idiosyncratic understanding of courtly love for the study of medieval literature and culture.[42] If I have chosen to risk redundancy, it is to bring out the opposition, in *Troilus and Criseyde*, between the real demands of neighbor love and the pleasurable orchestrations of courtly love. This should not be misconstrued as an attempt to revive the Robertsonian opposition between charity and cupidity.[43] On the contrary, one of my arguments in the first chapter of this book was that charity, when reduced to a crude form of altruism, is virtually indistinguishable from courtly love as a means of giving way on the desire of the Other. My aim instead is to show how Criseyde's situation unmasks the poverty of courtly love relative to neighbor love by slowly closing off our access to it as both fantasy and technique—that is, by desublimating courtly love itself.[44]

My thesis is that the singularity imposed on Criseyde by Troilus's initial act of devising moves her into a universal category (the Woman) that only disavows, with destructive consequences for all concerned, the particularity that the imperative to love thy neighbor otherwise enjoins us to embrace.

A sublimated object in the strictest Lacanian sense, the Lady in courtly love is raised "to the dignity of the Thing": located in the "place" where the radically singular, nonsymbolizable, utterly Other Thing "is not."[45] This act of raising the everyday to the singular serves to orchestrate desire by creating a kind of equilibrium. On the one hand, the sublimation of the courtly Lady quickens desire (as happens with Troilus at 1.295–96) by introducing the real, and hence opening up the possibility of *jouissance*, within the symbolic order. Although the Lady-Object is not the Thing itself, which is by its very nature without content, her presence at least makes it seem as though the Thing in whose place she stands, and whose enjoyment she promises, might yet be accessible if only the Lady herself were not off limits. The point, though, is that the ideal Lady must remain inaccessible or, at the very least, only indirectly approachable. This is because the function of the Lady-Object is also to act as a barrier against any direct apprehension of the Thing as traumatically absent, not in the sense of being fully prohibited, but in the much more radical sense of not being in the safekeeping of the Other. As much, then, as the Lady-Object manifests the real Thing, she also advances the comfortingly prohibitory function of symbolic order. And this, as Žižek points out, was always the inherent genius of the Lady as a construct: in her, "*the Object of desire itself coincides with the force that prevents its attainment.*"[46]

The logic of this sublimation begins to play itself out even in Troilus's first encounter with Criseyde, which takes place, as it does in *Il Filostrato*, in a temple: the temple of Pallas Athena, where the Trojans have gathered to "herknen of Palladiones servyce" (1.164). This temple setting might be said to indicate many things: local pagan coloring, a tragic worship of worldly objects, the intertwined fates of Troy and the Palladium. Above all, though, it indicates sublimation in the absence of the Thing. Speaking of the connections between primitive cave painting and the building of temples in the ancient world, Lacan notes that "in the same way that the exercise on the wall [of the cavern] consists in fixing the invisible inhabitant of the cavern, we see the link forged between the temple, as a construction around emptiness that designates the place of the Thing, to the figuration of emptiness on the walls of this emptiness itself."[47] For Lacan, the temple, "as a construction around emptiness that designates the place of the Thing," exemplifies sublimation. That is, the temple, like the cavern, describes a sacred space that allows those entering within it to bear witness to the Thing: to stand within the ambit of the Thing *so as* to acknowledge its radical absence. Shaping emptiness, the temple introduces a space of nothing that, paradoxically, makes present the absence of the Thing. Simply by entering the temple, then, both Troilus and Criseyde have already entered a space defined by the same sublimation that will define them, a space in which the Thing is given shape and, through that shaping, made temporarily approachable.

What truly makes Lacan's discussion of sublimation so applicable to *Troilus and Criseyde* is not, however, the coincidence of temples; it is the fact that his reading of caves and temples as designators of the Thing occurs within a larger analysis of courtly love, one in which he links the radical introduction of sacred space to the equally radical invention, within language, of courtly love practice. Indeed, Lacan's analysis merely serves to remind us, as readers of Chaucer's poem, that something of the same link is implied already in the associations between the temple where Troilus first sees Criseyde, the Palladium on which the safety of Troy depends, and Criseyde herself. Of the Palladium, it might be said that, within the emptiness of the temple, the image of Pallas functions, like "the figuration of emptiness on the walls of . . . emptiness," as an imagistic barrier against any direct encounter with the Thing even in its designated place. Consider as well the strong parallels drawn between the Palladium and Criseyde. Although the Trojans have come to the temple "Palladiones feste for to holde," their attentions are inevitably drawn to Criseyde, whose "goodly lokynge" gladdens the crowd to such an extent that everyone says "[n]as nevere yet seyn thynge to ben preseyd derre"—not even, one assumes, the Palladium itself (1.173–77). Likewise, as Windeatt suggests, "A medieval reader might see the irony that it was to be Diomede who would steal

both Criseyde from Troilus and the Palladium from Troy, so destroying both the hero and the city with which he was identified."[48] Such
a conflation strongly suggests that Criseyde and the Palladium serve
a parallel function: sublime objects—objects raised "to the dignity of
the Thing"—meant to sustain Troy and Troilus alike by preventing an
encounter with the displacement to which each is fated. We saw earlier,
with the brooch, that Troilus must lose Criseyde to fulfill his destiny
and die, as it were, for good this time: both physically and symbolically.
Now we see the obverse: that it is Criseyde who, for most of the poem,
enables Troilus not to have to confront the poignant fact that he is alive
only provisionally—that, from the retroactive vantage point of Chaucer's poem, he has, like Troy itself, already died.[49]

When we first meet her, for example, Criseyde emphasizes her
position as a widow, saying, in response to Pandarus's suggestion that
they "don to May som observaunce,"

> I! God forbede! Be ye mad?
> Is that a widewes lif, so God yow save?
> By God, ye maken me ryght soore adrad!
> Ye ben so wylde, it semeth as ye rave.
> It satte me wel bet ay in a cave
> To bidde and rede on holy seyntes lyves;
> Lat maydens gon to daunce, and yonge wyves.
>   (2.112–19)

Despite the bantering tone here, it is evident that, like Antigone
(Sophocles' Antigone, not Criseyde's niece), Criseyde stands as a figure
of mourning, a figure defined, at least initially, as owing a symbolic
debt to the dead. When Pandarus tries to persuade her, then, over the
course of book 2, that she in fact owes a debt to the living, that only she
can save a living man from death, Criseyde is torn between fulfilling
what her language makes clear, however playfully, is a divine injunction to honor the dead, and a human injunction to take care of the living. Much like Antigone, in fact, Criseyde is under pressure from the
beginning to sacrifice the dead, to give up her commitment to her hus-
band and reenter the symbolic economy of substitution and exchange.

But very much unlike Antigone, Criseyde yields, persuaded, in part, by her dream of substitution: her dream of the eagle who exchanges, violently yet without causing pain or fear, heart for heart (2.925-31). To this extent, Criseyde is enlisted into the service of the Other *as* symbolic order, *as* the impersonal structure of exchange as such. To serve that Other, Criseyde must give up her commitment to the dead. Or at least it seems that way. For of course the point is that, with Troilus, the distinction between living and dead has become suddenly meaningless. Troilus is alive within Chaucer's poem only to the extent that, like the father in a dream analyzed by Freud, the father who "*had really died, only he did not know it,*" he remains pathetically ignorant of the fact that he has already died. Troilus is not simply "alive" as a character for the duration of Chaucer's poem; he is alive *again*, having several times fulfilled his symbolic function of dying before being undead-ened in *Il Filostrato*. No matter how thoroughly we give ourselves over, as readers, to what is happening in *Troilus and Criseyde* at any particular moment, we always know that Troilus *has died* as surely as he *will die*—that the destiny he has to meet he has met already. Troilus, one might say, is less alive than suspended: a pagan character forced to exist beyond his time in the medieval texts that insist on reviving him. One of the complicated ways in which Troilus and the big Other overlap, then, is in their mutual ignorance of their own "death," their own lack of "actual" existence. So long as Troilus remains alive within Chaucer's fictional Troy, there is no having to confront the fact that the Trojan Other does not exist, that it is hastening to meet a doom in fictional time that it has already met in "historical" time. But by the same token, so long as Troilus, the "Little Troy," remains present within the late medieval Other, that Other—the fantasy of a whole, consistent, totalized symbolic order—cannot be said to exist either. And the irony in all of this is that it is Criseyde, a figure whose first allegiance is to the dead, whose very presence points toward death, who should be called upon to save Troilus, to prevent him from confronting directly what he in fact realizes from the first time he sees her: "I mote nedes deye" (1.573).

Although Criseyde's role as the prohibited Lady-Object may not seem immediately apparent, especially given that Pandarus's whole

scheme is directed precisely at *overcoming* her inaccessibility, it nonetheless helps us understand why so much of book 3, the book in which
Criseyde is finally made accessible to Troilus, reads like an act of violation, a treading upon forbidden ground: at once the pinnacle of the
love story and the beginning of its tragic decline. By this I do not mean
merely that book 3 invites us to enter, voyeurlike, into the intimate
space of the bedchamber "as for to looke," alongside Pandarus, "upon
an old romaunce" (3.980). I also have in mind the far more unsettling
feeling we get a little later in the book, when Pandarus "comen was /
Unto his nece" the morning after:

> With that she gan to hire face for to wrye
> With the shete, and wax for shame al reed;
> And Pandarus gan under for to prie,
> And seyde, "Nece, if that I shal be ded,
> Have here a swerd and smyyeth of myn hed!"
> With that his arm al sodeynly he thriste
> Under hire nekke, and at laste hire kyste.
>
> I passe al that which chargeth nought to seye.
> What! God foryaf his deth, and so she al so
> Foryaf, and with her uncle gan to pleye,
> For other cause was ther noon than so.
> But of this thing right to the effect to go:
> Whan tyme was, hom til here hous she wente,
> And Pandarus hath fully his entente.
>
> (3.1569–82)

The question of whether this strange and cryptic passage implies an
act of incest between Pandarus and Criseyde has been a vexed one
among Chaucerians for several years now.[50] But from a psychoanalytic
perspective, what makes this moment so significant is precisely that
it revolves around the *suggestion* of incest rather than its actual *realization*. This is because, in psychoanalytic terms, the incest taboo is
the fundamental (and paradoxical) prohibition of that which is already impossible: the primal, presymbolic *jouissance* associated with

the Thing. More than a means of structuring elementary kinship relations, the incest taboo is put in place to sustain the illusion that primal *jouissance* would be attainable if only it were not prohibited. But of course it is not attainable; on the contrary, as the narrator's passing over "al that which chargeth nought to seye" suggests, there is something at the heart of this scene that remains, not simply unsaid, but unsayable: something that persists in the real. When Pandarus "hath fully his entente," then, it is but a temporary success, though neither he nor Troilus realizes it at the time. For in bringing together Troilus and Criseyde, Pandarus in effect removes Criseyde from the position of the *prohibited* sublime object, thereby exposing the Thing, not as lacking, but as fundamentally impossible: the fragment of the real whose prohibition determines the symbolic order, and whose exposure betokens that order's failure. (Chaucer, as if to drive the point home, attributes the storm that keeps Troilus and Criseyde together to a rare conjunction of Saturn, Jupiter, and the moon [3.624–25]. Saturn, in particular, "is the bringer of disaster," according to John Frankis, "and his involvement indicates that the ensuing events are not intended to have a happy outcome."[51] Meanwhile, Walsingham tells us that just such a conjunction actually took place in 1385 and notes "that it was followed by 'a very great disturbance of kingdoms.'")[52] So yes, Troilus and Criseyde enjoy a temporary bliss. But as the narrator makes clear at the beginning of the next book, "al to litel . . . Lasteth swich joie" (4.1–2): Criseyde's very accessibility marks the beginning of the end, not just for Troilus, but for all of Troy. Pandarus's "hous," his elaborate scheme to unite Troilus and Criseyde, is revealed as having been built, like the temple, around the abyss of the Thing, an abyss into which it will now begin to collapse.

Where Criseyde's status as the Lady-Object becomes most obvious, however, and where the profound trauma of her removal from the empty place of the Thing is felt most deeply, is in Troilus's visit to her empty palace in book 5. The crucial homology here is of course that between *paleys* and *Pallas*—between Criseyde's empty dwelling and Pallas, whose image, if removed from Troy, would signal the city's fall. But the crucial *emphasis* here is on the reality, not simply of a temporary loss, but of utter lack: "O paleys desolat"; "O paleys empty and disconsolat"; "O paleys, whilom day, that now art nyght" (5.540–44). Through the combination of these two elements—the play of homologies (*Troy/Troilus*, *Pallas*/Criseyde's *palace*), and the repeated imagery of emptiness, underscored by the proliferation of *O*'s—we realize that, at this very moment in the text, the Troy matter has been made to confront its own Thing-like quality, configured here as the inherent emptiness at the heart of its own locus. There can be no separation made, in other words, between Troy and Troilus: both share the same desolation, the same constitutive lack at their core.[53]

Strictly speaking, then, the poem has brought us to ground zero in the place between two deaths: the very void of the Thing. For with Criseyde, the Lady-Object, gone, the empty place of the Thing, the void that the Lady-Object had merely covered over, is now exposed. Yet what is "exposed" in this case is not a something, not a place to which, though empty, one could return, but a nothing—a "lanterne of which queynt is the light"—that is itself off limits, sealed up, its every window "shet" and "hire dores spered alle": a no-place at once impossible and prohibited (5.530, 534, 543). We should not be surprised to find, then, that Troilus responds by acknowledging, if only implicitly, the necessity of his own death, saying to Criseyde's empty palace, "Wel oughtestow to falle, and I to dye, / Syn she is went that wont was us to gye!" (5.545–46). Note, however, that Troilus is careful to link his own death to the inevitable fall, along with the rest of Troy, of Criseyde's palace, the "shryne, of which the seynte is oute" (5.553). As with the removal of the Palladium from its temple, Criseyde's absence from her "shryne" signals the end of sublimation, the breakdown of the last barrier between Troy and the Thing at its own heart. What we are given, therefore, as the text draws to a close, is a vivid image fusing Troilus, Troy, and the Thing through a mutual confrontation of the lack to which each is destined. And although it will take the return of the brooch to finally drive Troy-lus to embrace his death, it is at this point that he must confront, through the absence of Criseyde as the sublimated object, the fact that he must die, that there exists no positive support to his being. (Indeed, it is intriguing to note that, after Criseyde has left Troy, Troilus becomes so "feble that he walketh *by potente*"—with a crutch [5.1222, my italics].)

Superficially, perhaps, this reading of Criseyde as Lady-Object may seem willfully out of step with those assessments of her as a woman subject to the exigencies and constraints of Trojan—and therefore, by virtue of association, late medieval—society.[54] It is for this reason, then, that I wish to maintain the crucial distinctions that emerge between Pandarus's "hous," the narrator's often personalized telling of the story, and Chaucer's poem. True, as we have already seen, the narrator is as responsible as either Troilus or Pandarus for "devising" Criseyde as a sublime object. Insofar, then, as the narrator might be understood as Chaucer's at least partial proxy, the latter does seem to acknowledge how thoroughly his text is engaged in maneuvering Criseyde into the position of Lady-Object. Even so, the poem's overall characterization of Criseyde as by turns vulnerable, fearful, reluctant, ambivalent, objectified, confused, tender, regretful, divided, resolute—in every way more complicated and interesting than Troilus—suggests that Chaucer was fully, even painfully, aware of a certain cruelty at the heart of courtly sublimation. Lacan describes this cruelty as follows: "The idealized woman, the Lady, who is in the position of the Other and of the object, finds herself suddenly and brutally positing, in a place knowingly constructed out of the most refined of signifiers, the emptiness of a thing in all its crudity, a thing that reveals itself in its nudity to be the thing, her thing, the one that is to be found at her very heart in its cruel emptiness. That Thing, whose function certain of you perceived in relation to sublimation, is in a way unveiled with a cruel and insistent power."[55]

There are several things to note in this passage. One is that the place of the Thing emerges, not outside of, but *out of,* poetic language, that place having been knowingly "constructed," like the temple, from the material at hand: "the most refined of signifiers." Another is that the artistic practice of courtly love poetry connects "the idealized woman, the Lady," through what might facetiously be called an orifical continuum, to the painted cave and the temple: all three creations, because they posit, in the double sense of fixing and affirming, a "cruel" emptiness, make it possible to experience the *jouissance* associated with the Thing without going so far as to actually disrupt the equilibrium dictated by the pleasure principle. Yet another is that the highly stylized practice of courtly love, precisely because of its reliance on "the most refined of signifiers" as a mediating power, a "go-between," exemplifies the fact that love, in Lacan's view, is what makes up for the lack of any sexual relation. This is why "the Thing . . . is in a way unveiled with a cruel and insistent power" in courtly love. Courtly love, as a radical new way of *not* having a sexual relation, of making up for the traumatic impossibility of the sexual relation, exposes love as a formal means of negotiating sexual difference through the medium of the signifier—of recognizing, in effect, that sexual difference comes down to different ways of relating to the signifier. Above all, though, this passage shows that, like Chaucer, Lacan was fully aware of the potential cost that sublimation, in all its arbitrary suddenness and brutality, might impose upon the subject-made-object. Sublimation may indeed elevate an everyday object to "the *dignity* of the Thing," extracting it from the symbolic circuit of exchange and investing it with the Thing's undiluted singularity. Yet, as the passive language Lacan uses quietly reminds us, no subject ever really asks to find herself "positing . . . the emptiness of a thing in all its crudity." The Lady, if one may put it in these terms, asks to be constructed in the same way that the temple asks to be built, or the cavern sanctified.

Lacan himself tells us as much when he notes that "the poetry of courtly love, in effect, tends to locate in the place of the Thing certain discontents of the culture. And it does so at a time when the historical circumstances bear witness to a disparity between the especially harsh conditions of reality and certain fundamental demands."[56] As the image of cultural discontents being located in the place of the Thing seems to suggest, one might come to embrace one's role as Lady-Object, but only after the fact. The Lady does not locate; she is located. She does not posit the existence of the Thing; she finds herself positing that existence. If this sounds somewhat impersonal and mechanical, it is because the idealized Lady-Object is less an agent than a placeholder serving an exclusively structural function: namely, to manifest the internal failure of structure in a way that allows for the enjoyment of that failure without its being denied or corrected. Note that, for Lacan, courtly culture is defined by a tragic disjunction at its heart. Courtly culture, in his view, produced "certain discontents," in the full Freudian meaning of the term: those who, though they might not have been able to articulate it, were left dissatisfied by the extent of their sacrifice to the interests of symbolic order.[57] Moreover, there is a "disparity," as Lacan puts it, between courtly culture's harsh conditions and the "fundamental demands" of those working to "locate," through the practice of courtly love, some discontented other in the privileged position of the Thing.[58] For Lacan, then, there is a break implied between the theoretical practice of courtly love and the patriarchy, misogyny, exploitation, inequity, and violence that defined the reality of courtly life.[59] What is more, this break replicates the very real disparities between those who, like Criseyde, find themselves located in the place of the Thing, and those who, like Pandarus, the narrator, or Troilus, do the locating. That it should be the discontents of this disjointed culture in particular who occupy the place of the Thing tells us something else, however. Simply put, the Thing, which manifests itself first as that utterly foreign, threatening element in the neighbor with which identification is impossible, is nothing less than the break within courtly culture:[60] the materialization of the lack of relation, the asymmetry between masculine and feminine courtly subjects, that points up the illusory nature of social cohesion. The Lady-Object is deployed to at once acknowledge and screen against the real of social antagonism already signaled by her discontent.

Chaucer, for his part, tries to get at the complexity of this situation by juxtaposing Criseyde's role as Troilus's sublimated Lady-Object with her compromised and vulnerable existence living with Diomede in the Greek camp. Whereas in Troy Criseyde had come to enjoy, however briefly or reluctantly, the dignified place of the Thing in which she had been "devised," among the Greeks she finds herself reduced to her earlier state, before Troilus pursued her, as a "woman in society": as just another object of exchange. In both instances, one might say, Criseyde ultimately finds herself propping up the symbolic order, either as a final barrier against the real or as a mere counter in a power-asymmetrical social structure, to paraphrase Carolyn Dinshaw.[61] Yet even though Criseyde's fortunes seem interchangeable at the most basic structural level, they are clearly not the same; and it is this confusion of Criseyde's role that seems to so trouble the narrator, for it means that, try as he might, he can never fully do her justice. On the one hand, Criseyde's position as the Lady-Object for Troilus, however manufactured it may be, is clearly more dignified than her position as a fish caught unwittingly in Diomede's net (5.775–77). This partly explains why it is so horrible when the operation of the symbolic inevitably asserts itself in book 4 and the Trojans exchange Criseyde for Antenor: We are reminded how contingent the dignity imposed upon Criseyde always was—and how thin the line is between sublimation and degradation (4.211–12). But the irony was always that Criseyde's multifaceted characterization, which includes her eventual willingness to do the pragmatic thing and substitute Diomede for Troilus, makes her the worst possible candidate for the abstracted, ultimately inhuman Lady-Object. If, then, the narrator wishes to tarry awhile in Troy—to ignore, for a few books of his poem, that there is a lack of relation between his own time and place and the pagan past—he must cooperate as Troilus and, especially, Pandarus sublimate Criseyde. But if Chaucer's poem is to complete its principal task of removing Troilus from the space between two deaths, then Criseyde must, like the Palladium, be removed from her singular, privileged position. This, it seems to me, is one important source of the sorrow that permeates much of the final two books of *Troilus and Criseyde*. Chaucer knows from the start that there is no middle ground for Criseyde once Troilus has *devysed* her, any more than there is a middle ground for the Palladium. She is either idealized or ruined, either elevated to the frozen dignity of the Thing or returned to the relative poverty of the symbolic economy. Either way, some aspect of Criseyde is compromised, and the big Other served.

III

As I hope the previous two sections, on the symbolization of Troilus's death and on the devising of Criseyde, have made clear, *Troilus and Criseyde* is a text deeply concerned not only with the costs and demands of maintaining the illusion of the big Other but with the vexed role of poetry—and, in a larger sense, of fiction and artifice—in that maintenance. Although one hesitates to label it a "social" text, considering how aware it is of the breaks and gaps and impossibilities—the eruptions of the real—that preclude the constellation of the social sphere, *Troilus and Criseyde* is at the same time obviously interested in exploring those strategies and pathways whereby the illusion of the Other is perpetuated or, at the very least, negotiated. Of the principal characters in the poem, the two most clearly and self-consciously invested in those strategies are Pandarus and the narrator, both of whom act as makers, as facilitators—even, in the case of the narrator, as a reluctant instrument of destiny. It is for this reason that so much of the narrative is given over to their eventual confrontations with, and reluctant acceptance of, Troilus's symbolic death, since it is that death which, in this case, determines the Other.

Much has been written about the similarities between Pandarus and the narrator, both as "authors" and as the servants of Love's servants. But even in their similarities there remain important differences between the two, and these are worth stressing. To begin with, there is the matter of authorship. Like the narrator, Pandarus relies on written authority both for his knowledge of love and for his construction of the love affair between Troilus and Criseyde. But whereas the poem's central conceit is that the narrator never consciously diverges from his "auctor," Lollius, even when he wants to, Pandarus seems all too willing to take authority into his own hands—to fabricate, to manipulate, to fictionalize—whenever the success of his creation is at stake. Perhaps the most striking example of such improvisation comes in book 3, when Pandarus creates the fiction of Troilus's jealousy to facilitate the latter's access to Criseyde. What truly fascinates about this particular act of manipulation is less its actual invention than how actively Pandarus seeks to disavow it, to hide his role as the author, not merely of the love affair itself, but of Criseyde's seduction in particular. Granted, if one craves a logical explanation for Pandarus's secrecy, one does not have to look very far. As Pandarus himself warns Troilus,

> [W]ere it wist that I, through mine engyn,
> Hadde in my nece yput this fantasie,
> To doon thi lust and holly to ben thyn,

Whi, al the world upon it wolde crie,
And seyn that I the werste trecherie
Dide in this cas, that evere was bigonne,
And she forlost, and thow right nought ywonne.

(3.274–80)

Still, even with this information before us, we are left to wonder, in part because his own motives for helping Troilus remain obscure, why Pandarus is so intent on hiding his participation in the love affair. Why, after all, construct something only to occlude it? Or, to put the matter another way, Why author something only to evade responsibility for its potential consequences?

One possible answer may be found in the sixth stanza of the Prologue to book 3. Praising Love, the narrator observes that

Ye folk a lawe han set in universe,
And this know I by hem that lovers be,
That whoso stryveth with yow hath the werse.
Now lady bryght, for thi benignite,
At reverence of hem that serven the,
Whos clerc I am, so techeth me devyse
Som joye of that is felt in thi servyse.

(3.36–42)

Above all, there is a universal law of love, a law that must be obeyed, even though its workings are obscure. By remaining "on this 'level' of the law . . ." as Fradenburg observes, one might at least experience "the obscene enjoyment at stake in submission to the law": that tiny fragment of *jouissance* derived from obeying the law "not because of its positive qualities, not because it is just, good or beneficial, but because it is the law. True obedience involves obedience to the command as such," writes Fradenburg, "that is, not just whether or not, but insofar as, the command is incomprehensible, traumatic, irrational."[62] The problem for the narrator, however—and it is a problem shared by Pandarus—is that he remains slightly detached from the world of that law, knowing its workings only indirectly, "by hem that lovers be." How, then, is he to experience the obscene enjoyment that comes with submission to the law? The answer hinges on his crucial request to Love, to Venus, to teach him to "dyvyse / Som joye of that is felt" in her service. *Dyvyse*, which I have already noted can mean either "to behold," "to compose or construct," or "to advise," appears repeatedly throughout book 3, much as it did in book 1, when Troilus first saw Criseyde. It is this word *devyse*, then, that enables both the narrator and Pandarus to enjoy, if temporarily, the same position as Troilus: subjects of the law. Troilus "devises"/beholds Criseyde and, in so doing, submits to the inscrutable law of love; Pandarus "devises"/advises Troilus in the seduction of Criseyde, a seduction he of course devises, and, in so doing, enjoys the obscene pleasure of submission to the law; and the narrator, by devising, in verse, "som joye of that is felt" in love's service, also gets to experience the same enjoyment, an enjoyment that would otherwise be unavailable to him, who is only a servant to Love's servants.

And yet, as we have already seen, there is an irony to all of this devising: it cannot be admitted, at least not by Pandarus. For to admit to having devised that which the law itself supposedly mandates is to admit that the symbolic order that hinges on that law is lacking, is not whole—that, indeed, the law itself is not universal.[63] That the law of love is *not* universal has in fact already been intimated in the second stanza of the Prologue to book 3, when the narrator claims that "God loveth, and to love wol nought werne, / And in this world no lyves creature / Withouten love is worth, or may endure" (3.12–14). These are strange lines—strange because they effectively banish both the narrator and Pandarus, each of whom is "withouten love," from the poem's symbolic community, denying them not only worth within its particular economy but also the very possibility of continued existence. Here again, I would argue, we find ourselves between two deaths: between the symbolic death of exclusion from the poem's community of lovers, and physical death, the inability to endure. What is particularly of interest at this point, however, is not that the poem is once again between two deaths—the poem is between two deaths, between Troilus's "historical" death, replayed at the conclusion of *Il Filostrato*, and the medieval symbolization of that death, until its very end—but that the place between two deaths is suddenly occupied, not only by

Troilus, but by Pandarus and the narrator as well. I will discuss what this means in terms of the narrator in a moment. In terms of Pandarus, the realization that he too is between two deaths reminds us, in case we had forgotten, that he too is a Trojan, that he too is a part of the dead matter of Troy. As much as Troilus himself, in other words, Pandarus belongs to Troy-lus, to that little fragment of the pagan at once rejected by medieval European symbolic order and present within it as its cause. Yet unlike the generally passive Troilus, who would just as soon die as pursue Criseyde, Pandarus works very hard to keep Troilus, and thus also himself, as a Trojan, alive between two deaths. Pandarus cannot know this, of course. Like Troilus, he is painfully unaware of his reanimation, of the fact that he exists, as a character in Chaucer's Troy, long after his "historical" time has ended. Pandarus, we might say, is at once the counterpart to the narrator and his greatest rival: a type of artist working to preserve that which the narrator must, in the end, symbolically inter. Pandarus cannot see it at first, but all of his efforts to keep Troilus from dying for love succeed only in covering over the necessity, not merely of Troilus's death, but also of his own, as an inhabitant of Troy.

This explains, perhaps, why there exists an uncanny, if still somewhat muted, affinity between Pandarus and the figure of the courtier in Benjamin's work on the Baroque mourning play. That Pandarus is, in fact, a courtier seems fairly evident. At one point near the beginning of book 5, for example, we are told that "[t]his Pandare . . ."

> Ne myghte han comen Troilus to se,
> Although he on his hed it hadde sworn —
> For with the kyng Priam al day was he
> So that it lay nought in his libertee
> Nowher to gon.
>
> (5.282–86)

This detail serves to remind us that Pandarus, despite having a household of his own, is really an institutional creature, with "access to the prince's cabinet where the projects of high politics are conceived."[64] However much he may run around, hurrying back and forth between palaces, the place to which Pandarus always returns—his natural home, as it were—is the court. Yet it is not just his physical presence at court that makes Pandarus a courtier in the Benjaminian sense. It is the atmosphere of mystery and intrigue that surrounds him, the sense that he knows more, or perhaps fears more, than he lets on. "God and Pandare wist al what this mente," jokes the narrator regarding one of Pandarus's more elaborate schemes (2.1561); but it could just as well be a blanket statement. Almost everything about Pandarus remains a mystery, including his motivations. His last words to Troilus —

> And that thow me bisoughtest don of yore,
> Havyng unto myn honour ne my reste
> Right no reward, I dide al that the leste.

> If I did aught that myghte liken the,
> It is me life; and of this tresoun now,
> God woot that it a sorwe is unto me!
> And dredeles, for hertes ese of yow,
> Right fayn I wolde amende it, wiste I how.
>
> (5.1734–41)

suggest a capacity for self-sacrifice that seems to align him with the type of the faithful servant, "companion in suffering," as Benjamin puts it, "to innocence enthroned."[65] Perhaps, then, Pandarus views his service to Troilus as an extension of his service to the royal family. But might his interest in securing Troilus's "hertes ese" hint at something more than friendly concern—something like a dread of the creaturely suffering, the preoccupation with mortality and corruption, endemic to the princely state? Might the strangeness of Pandarus lie in the fact that he combines both sides of the courtier, the intriguer and the saint? True, he exhibits little of the "power, knowledge, and will intensified to demonic proportions" that Benjamin claims mark the true courtier. But neither does it seem an exaggeration to say that some of his actions— like lying, thrusting Troilus's letter down Criseyde's bosom, feeling around under the covers, and (it seems) watching the consummation moment as if it were an old romance come to life—verge on the sinister.

And what of the role he plays? Pandarus is typically described as a go-between, but the label, which conjures up images of a minor diplomat or bagman, hardly does him justice. Like Benjamin's courtier, he is, quite literally, a plotter: the one who orchestrates the plots and schemes and intrigues that will bring other characters together. It is not only that he is elusive and secretive, reluctant to share his plans even with those he advises. He is also a master of fabrication and manipulation, at times coming close to wresting control of the narrative away from its author, even in spite of its inevitable conclusion. Like an author, in fact, "Pandarus is . . . a master of narratives that are both episodic and highly configured," according to Strohm. Born of long-range planning more than present need, those narratives "possess beginnings, middles, and ends, and feature incidents and observations selected to support predetermined conclusions."[66] As Strohm sees it, Pandarus's reliance on linear narratives—his devotion to *proces*—reflects his "acceptance of time as unavoidable succession." This is undoubtedly true of the first Pandarus we meet, the bustling, garrulous, vaguely overbearing Pandarus of books 1 and 2. By the end of book 3, though, we have encountered another Pandarus, a Pandarus increasingly concerned with the arrangement of space and the staging of scenes, a Pandarus who now channels his creative energies into "making a play for Criseyde."[67] Where Pandarus before had sought to hurry time along, he now seeks to arrest its movement. Indeed, as the culmination of his master plot— book 3's artfully arranged seduction scene—suggests, Pandarus is finally less interested in programming a sequence of temporal events than in choreographing what Benjamin terms a "spatial continuum." Every tale, no matter how embellished, is told "al for som conclusioun," according to Pandarus (2.259); but the conclusion Pandarus has in mind is not the end of a story so much as the continuous realization of his "entente." If he happens to be working toward a particular conclusion, it is only with the aim of deferring, perhaps indefinitely, the end he most fears, which is Troilus's death. The conclusion of his own master plot is arrayed against that of the poem.

Nowhere, in fact, does Pandarus more anticipate the Baroque courtier than when seeking to distract Troilus from his melancholic absorption in suffering and death. This comes through most clearly in Pandarus's preference for *sententia*, for proverbs and maxims. "A proverb . . . ," writes Benjamin, "is a ruin which stands on the site of an old story and in which a moral twines about a happening like ivy around a wall."[68] In contrast to the story, which arises from the craftsman's ability "to fashion the raw material of experience, his own and that of others, in a solid, useful and unique way," the proverb is a mere shard: at best an allegory of its own deracination, at worst the vehicle for a moral having little organic connection to the experiences of either the person rehearsing it or the person hearing it.[69] The story takes the materials of a lived existence and offers them up for contemplation. The proverb, in countering every specific happening with a truism, forecloses contemplation altogether. Pandarus's devotion to proverbs thus says something important about his relation to material history. Pandarus, simply put, is a repository of undead information, information so estranged from the history of its own becoming that it exists only as an "ideogram" of the old story in which it was once embedded. He is a mere preservationist, busily compiling information that is neither timeless nor untimely, but simply out of time: separated from any known source or origin. Ultimately, he can do nothing to help Troilus as a figure bound to history because the knowledge he possesses, his compendium of quotations and citations, is based on forgotten experiences: past happenings about which some morals have since twined themselves, but out of which no useful information can be extracted. The best he has to offer is a collection of ruins. It is all the more ironic, therefore, that Pandarus should compare his work on Troilus's behalf to the building of a house. Viewed from one perspective, the house he envisions is simply the basis for a future ruin. That is what Pandarus is helping to "build," but without knowing it: a story that, over time, will be reduced to a proverb about the treachery of women.

This is why we cannot call Pandarus a storyteller: he lacks the artisan's gift for fashioning the raw materials of experience into something unique and useful. The storyteller, argues Benjamin, "has counsel—not for a few situations, as the proverb does, but for many, like the sage."[70] Pandarus, by contrast, is a courtier; what he deploys are not stories meant to help Troilus make sense of his material existence but proverbs meant to restrain Troilus from thinking about his death. An example of this pattern can be found in book 1, when Pandarus, in the course of trying to rouse Troilus from his lovesick stupor, asks him if he has seen Oenone's letter to Paris (1.652–56). For Pandarus, the contents of the letter are exemplary, almost allegorical. In the same way that Oenone is like Phoebus, so too is Pandarus like Oenone (and, by extension, Phoebus): both are unfortunate in love, despite their talent for advising others on the subject. Pandarus is being doubly proverbial here, offering an instructional story whose implied moral—sometimes the one most disappointed in love makes the best advisor to a would-be lover—not only gives him license to dispense proverbial advice but also confirms the proverbs he has already used (e.g., a whetstone is no carving instrument, but it sharpens carving tools). Yet in his rush to make himself into a proverbial figure—the physician unable to heal himself—Pandarus reveals himself to be a misleading counselor. Or rather, he reveals the aim of the courtier to be, ultimately, that of protecting the status quo from the threatening melancholia of the prince. For in isolating the proverbial aspect of Oenone's story from the narrative that originally contained it, Pandarus not only cuts off the proverb from its source; he also cuts off Troilus, the prince, from the tragic history conveyed by the entire narrative. This is because, as James Simpson puts it, "Pandarus has completely ignored the terrible force of the whole letter in which Oenone attacks Paris for having abandoned her for Helen; predicts the future betrayal of Paris's new lover; and cites Cassandra to prophesy the fall of Troy."[71] The arc of Troilus's sad fate, his abandonment and death, is hinted at in the part of Oenone's letter he never hears about. Not only, then, does Troilus become separated from the past of which the story is itself a part. He becomes separated from the future—his future. One realizes, in fact, how much Troilus could learn from Pandarus's counsel, provided the aim of counsel were to instruct. But in this case, especially, the aim of counsel is to keep the prince from contemplating his doom.

We encounter this pattern again in book 5, when Pandarus convinces Troilus, now given over so completely to melancholia that he has begun to plan his own funeral, to visit their ally Sarpedoun:

> This town is ful of lordes al aboute,
> And trewes lasten al this mene while.

Go we pleye us in som lusty route
To Sarpedoun, nat hennes but a myle;
And thus thow shalt the tyme wel bygile,
And drive it forth unto that blissful morwe
That thow hire se, that cause is of thi sorwe.

(5.400–406)

Pandarus, in the manner of the courtier, hatches a plot to kill time: he and Troilus will pass the ten-day interval of Criseyde's absence delighting in amusements. And Sarpedoun, "as he that honourable / Was evere his lyve, and ful of heigh largesse," doesn't disappoint (5.435–36). There is a great feast, delightful music, and a fair company of ladies to dance with. Everything is superlative. Troilus, however, either cannot or will not be entertained. Instead, he spends his time absorbed in thoughts of Criseyde, even going so far as to imagine that she appears to him as a kind of phantasm. Troilus, in other words, spends his brief sojourn refusing to mourn, eschewing compensation or substitution, turning away from all of the blandishments of the symbolic order. Pandarus, good courtier that he is, had wanted nothing more than to distract Troilus from his melancholic state; but the visit to Sarpedoun's house, because it confronts Troilus with the workings of an order for which he no longer has any use, only seems to intensify it.

Ultimately they cut short their visit, since Troilus, convinced that Criseyde will shortly return to Troy—hoping, in fact, that she will already be there upon his return—is eager to get back home. Pandarus knows better. "Ye, haselwode," he thinks to himself. "God woot, refreynden may this hote fare, / Er Calkas sende Troilus Criseyde!" (5.505–8). Here we catch a glimpse, to cite Benjamin once more, of why "the disillusioned insight of the courtier is just as profound a source of woe to him as it is a potential danger to others, because of the use he can make of it at any time."[72] Pandarus, it turns out, understands perfectly well what Troilus, the prince, has yet to grasp: the latter has already been defeated by the very order of substitution he keeps trying to resist. Ever the courtier, though, Pandarus keeps this knowledge to himself. In fact, he does something that his counterpart in *Il Filostrato* does not: he proceeds to jape and play in his usual manner, trying his best to keep Troilus from realizing that he is, in a manner of speaking, already dead, now that he has been forced aside by the symbolic economy of exchange. In short, Pandarus withholds counsel in order to prevent exactly what ends up happening in the next scene, when Troilus, confronting the emptiness of Criseyde's palace, is forced to confront his own Thingliness.

The aborted visit to Sarpedoun's house and its aftermath thus expose not only a crucial difference between Troilus and Pandarus but also the larger difference, present throughout the poem, between fidelity (in the sense that Badiou has given it) and what Benjamin calls "compromise with the world."[73] Readers often grow impatient with Troilus's melancholic disposition: his passivity, his languishing, his "tendency," as Strohm puts it, "to enter into swoons and trances."[74] But why should we be so quick to dismiss that disposition as mere helplessness, or worse? Why should we not embrace it as Troilus's most admirable, indeed affirmative, quality? Troilus, after all, does something that no other character in the poem can be said to do: he maintains fidelity to the event that has seized and broken him, the event of being in love. Troilus's sudden transformation upon seeing Criseyde in the temple is no mere conventional moment. It is an ethical moment: the moment when Troilus is "induced" as a subject, "convoked," as Badiou might put it, to a truth process.[75] The poem makes it clear, in fact, that Troilus's apparently passive submission is really an affirmative gesture:

> So ferde it by this fierse and proude knyght:
> Though he a worthy kynges sone were,
> And wende nothing hadde had swich myght
> Ayeyns his wille that shuld his herte stere,
> Yet with a look his herte wex a-fere,
> That he that now was moost in pride above,
> Wax sodeynly moost subgit unto love.
>
> (1.225–31)

Before seeing Criseyde, Troilus is little more than "a worthy kynges sone." After he sees her, he becomes part of a love affair that will transform the situation of world (mytho-) history. The event of being in love is Troilus's event, and he knows it. From that point on, he can view his situation—the situation of the Trojan War, of being Priam's son—only from the perspective of the event. This is not to reproach Criseyde, by way of comparison, for doing the pragmatic thing and accepting Diomede. On the contrary, the whole point is that Criseyde does what most of us would do if faced with the same dilemma. Likewise, I am not trying to downplay Troilus's role in Criseyde's sublimation. I simply want to stress that Troilus is the only character who does the truly radical thing and finally rejects the whole economy of exchange, the whole logic of compensatory substitution, that forms the basis of the symbolic order. There is a reason why Criseyde always seems so out of place as the Lady-Object: her sublimation only temporarily masks the fact that it is Troilus, not she, who properly belongs in the place beyond desire, the place of the unchanging Thing. Troilus's melancholia, his final refusal to accept a substitute for Criseyde, is but the outward sign of his ethical subjectivity.

Crucially, though, that melancholic refusal of exchange comes only after Troilus has already capitulated to a monumental act of exchange: the Trojan parliament's exchange of Criseyde for Antenor. The argument could be made, in fact, that Troilus, had he truly maintained fidelity to the event of being in love, would have followed Pandarus's advice and ravished Criseyde—simply taken her out of the economy of exchange altogether. Troilus makes it clear, however, that such a course of action is out of the question: it would upset Criseyde; it would be dishonorable; it would embarrass Priam, who "enseled" her exchange in Parliament; worst of all, it would simply repeat the mistake of "ravysshyng" women "by myght" that first set the Trojans on the path to war (4.547–74). On another level, however, the act is simply unthinkable, not only because Criseyde's exchange for Antenor is a forced choice, but also because that exchange is part of the larger pattern of events that will lead to Troilus's death, the fall of Troy and, in (mytho-historical) time, the founding of England. Strictly speaking, in fact, Troilus's refusal to accept a substitute for Criseyde merely affirms an exchange that, from the retroactive vantage point of Chaucer's poem, has already happened. For if Troilus finally moves to the place of the utterly lacking and impossible Thing, it is only because the advent of a new master signifier, that of the Word itself, has given him that status. This is another way of understanding the poem's preoccupation with destiny: Troilus, the embodiment of Troy and its fate, has already been exchanged *so that* an order of exchange, salvific and translational, might be established. With Criseyde's removal from Troy, the future—the future in which Chaucer will write his poem—comes rushing in just as surely as the Greeks will once the Palladium is removed from its temple.

In the meantime, all of Pandarus's efforts as courtier are meant to forestall exactly that fate, that future. Unlike Troilus, in fact, Pandarus is committed to preserving an economy of substitution and exchange—an economy, in short, of mourning. "But telle me this," he says to Troilus shortly after the Trojan parliament has made its fateful decision to "selle" Criseyde,

> whit how art now so mad
> To sorwen thus? Whi listow in this wise,
> Syn thi desir al holly hastow had,
> So that, by right, it oughte ynough suffise?
> But I, that nevere felte in my servyse
> A friendly cheere or lokyng of an eye,
> Lat me thus wepe and wailen til I deye.
>
> And over al this, as thow wel woost thiselve,
> This town is ful of ladys al aboute;
> And, to my doom, fairer than swiche twelve
> As ever she was, shal I fynde in som route —
> Yee, on or two, withouten any doute.
> Forth be glad, myn owen deere brother!
> If she be lost, we shal recovere an other
>
> (4.393–406)

For Pandarus, exchange is a great salvation precisely because it allows for a future that, grounded in repetition, is really a suspension of temporal movement. Not only has Troilus already fulfilled his desire; he can continue to fulfill it for as long as he wishes. Nothing is ever lost, because an "other" of equal or greater value can always be recovered. Every Trojan woman is fungible—this one "goodly," that one "glad and light" (4.410)—because each one can be made to assume the same role in the spatial continuum wherein Pandarus "hath fully his entente" but desire is never exhausted. This may sound, on the face of it, as though Pandarus is committed to the future, and in a manner of speaking he is. But like his belief in difference (expressed, for example, in his frequent use of oppositional definition), Pandarus's belief in exchange really expresses his profound commitment to an economy of lack. Lack, as we know, institutes desire. Or, to be more rigorous: the fantasy that something lacks, and can be recovered, provides the fundamental support for the symbolic order. But Troilus, by refusing to replace Criseyde—by refusing to sublimate another woman to the place of the Thing, and so maintain the illusion that such a place actually exists to be filled—deprives Pandarus even of the promise associated with lack. This, then, is the radical upshot of Troilus himself moving to the truly "empty" place of the Thing: he goes from being the consummate figure of a desire that supports the symbolic order to a figure of a drive, the death drive, that signals its annihilation. The future for Pandarus—and one wonders to what extent he has known this all along—is no future.

The pathos of Pandarus, then, is the pathos of the courtier, doomed to stand guard against the threatening melancholy of the prince. This makes it all the more ironic that his tragic action should turn out to be precisely that of the melancholic: he transforms Criseyde, a woman who should have remained an object of contemplation, into an object of embrace. In *The Ethics of Psychoanalysis*, Lacan argues that "the function of the beautiful"—and Criseyde, as the narrator tells us both early in the poem (1.99–105) and late (5.806–24), is nothing if not beautiful—"is to reveal to us the site of man's relationship to his own death."[76] For Pandarus, this means that, try as he might to occlude the fact, his own actions spell the end to his continued existence; for by making Criseyde, the sublime Lady-Object, directly available to Troilus, Pandarus also makes undeniable what the poem itself has known from the beginning: Troy-lus is dead. It is something more than mere rhetoric, then, when Pandarus, advocating for Troilus, says to Criseyde such things as

> But if ye late hym deyen, I wol sterve —
> Have here my trouthe, nece, I nyl nat lyen —
> Al sholde I with the knyf my throte kerve.
>
> . . . .
> If that ye don us bothe dyen
> Thus gilteles, than have ye fisshed fayre!
> What mende ye, though that we booth appaire?
>   (2.323–29)

or, a bit later in the same scene,

> But sith I se my lord mot nedes dye,
> And I with hym, here I me shryve and seye
> That wikkedly ye don us bothe dyse.
>
> But sith iy liketh yow that I be ded,
> By Neptunus, that god is of the see,
> Fro this forth shal I nevere eten bred
> Thil I myn owen herte blodd may see;
> For certyn I wol deye as soone as he.
>   (2.439–46)

True, the language here is manipulative, if not outright extortionate. Yet Pandarus speaks a structural truth: his existence is indeed tied to that of Troy-lus, and Troy-lus's continued existence is in turn dependent upon the presence of Criseyde. Thus we should not be surprised, however saddened we may feel, by the most devastating of Pandarus's last lines, delivered just before Troilus leaves to seek his death: "'My brother deer, I may do the namore. / What sholde I seyen? I hate, ywis, Criseyde; / And, God woot, I wol hate hire evermore!'" (5.1731–33). The straightforwardness of these lines is telling. There is no talk here of injustice or betrayal, just a matter-of-fact admission that, with Criseyde gone, there is nothing more that Pandarus can do for Troilus—or himself. He hates Criseyde, in other words, as much for his own sake as for Troilus's, hates her because her absence means that he, no less than his friend, has had an apprehension of his second death. Like the narrator, who in the end answers the call to repudiate the pagan Thing, Pandarus is no longer able to hold out. His words are ironic: he says that he will hate Criseyde "evermore," little realizing that, from the retroactive perspective of Chaucer's poem, his suspension in time is about to end. And after that, he falls deathly silent, as all those connected to Troy-lus must.

The injunction to mourn and the ethical refusal to mourn, the ways of the courtier and the prince: these mark the positions taken up not only by Pandarus and Troilus but also, at different points and under different circumstances, by the narrator. *Troilus and Criseyde*, I have been arguing, is a drama of resistance and submission, which is as much to say that it is, to a large extent, the narrator's drama. Ordinarily, the sheer elusiveness of *Troilus and Criseyde* confounds neat divisions; but it proves surprisingly easy with the narrator. For most of the poem—right up until the end of book 5—the narrator resists submitting to the mandates of the symbolic order, even achieving, at times, a remarkable degree of compassion for, if not identification with, his pagan characters. But then, at the very end of the poem, in a move that early critics such as Curry and Tatlock found dramatically unsatisfying, if not perverse, the narrator suddenly assumes the full weight of his own culture's symbolic mandate, vigorously condemning the same pagan world through which he has led us, his verses weeping as he writes, for nearly five full books. What makes this sudden turnaround so unsettling, however, has nothing to do with either perversity or dramatic disappointment. What makes it so unsettling is that it offers us a vivid representation of the narrator's symbolic castration,[77] his rejection of "feyned loves" in exchange for an identification with the Name-of-the-Father: that fundamental signifier—at once the name affixed to the Other's desire and also the Father's prohibitory "No!"— which grounds the rest of the symbolic order by defining the limit of desire. On the one hand, this representation is surprisingly literal. At almost the very moment he identifies fully with the Name-of-the-Father, the narrator also assumes the voice of a symbolic father figure, appealing to the "yonge, fresshe folkes" of his audience to renounce, in effect, the world of his poem and instead capitulate, as he has done, to the law of their own late fourteenth-century, Christocentric order of meaning: an order structured around "hym the which that right for love / Upon a crois, oure soules for to beye, / First starf, and roos, and sit in hevene above" (5.1842–44). But as striking as this literal identification may be, the true power of the narrator's symbolic castration is ultimately figurative. For in renouncing the poem's pagan world and its inhabitants—in renouncing Troy-lus—the narrator brings to a close his poem's primary subject, refusing once and for all the *jouissance* of the absent Thing as that which is not merely prohibited but fundamentally impossible and replacing it with the only *jouissance* available to the castrated subject: the limited *jouissance* associated with submission to the law.

Central to this endeavor is the narrator's invocation of the crucified Christ. Where the unburied Troilus had been a kind of ghost occupying the place of lack constitutive of the polis, the image of Christ dying and being resurrected—the image, in short, of Christ undergoing the second death—restores lack by decompleting the imaginary fullness of the pagan universe. In the Judeo-Christian fantasy of that universe, where people swear, like Pandarus, "by stokkes and by stones," "the *numen* rises up at every step, at the corner of every road, in grottoes, at crossroads; it weaves human experience together."[78] If "that is something that contrasts greatly with the monotheistic profession of faith," as Lacan puts it, it is because the God that spoke to Moses from out of the burning bush "is a God who introduces himself as an essentially hidden God," one radically absent from the natural world. Before, the gods had been invested in the life of things, their *numena* present at every crossroads. Now God is dead, utterly removed from the cycle of emergence and decay that defines natural history. And it is Christianity that makes that death final. "Only Christianity, through the drama of the passion, gives full content to the naturalness of the truth that we have called the death of God," insists Lacan. "Christianity, in effect, offers a drama that literally incarnates the death of God."[79] That the narrator should want to insist upon the (second) death of God, a death that introduces lack into history, suggests something more, then, than just a simple declaration of faith. Rather, it has to do with the simultaneously cruel and comforting imposition of the law. As Lacan puts it: "So that something like the order of law may be transmitted, it has to pass along the path traced by the primordial drama articulated in *Totem and Taboo*, that is to say the murder of the father and its consequences, the murder at the origin of culture of the figure about whom one can say nothing, a fearful and feared as well as dubious figure, an all-powerful, half-animal creature of the primal horde, who was killed by his sons."[80] Only with his murder, a foundational sacrifice ritually reenacted in the Crucifixion, are the sons of the primal horde finally able to identify with the father, to show him the love they could not show him when he was alive—that is, when they feared and envied him. The act of murder, in other words, allows the sons to assume a particular type of political subjectivity, one organized around an identification with a figure whose symbolic position is now impossible to attain. This is why, for Lacan, "All the mystery is in that act. It is designed to hide something, namely, that not only does the murder of the father not open the path to *jouissance* that the presence of the father was supposed to prohibit, but it, in fact, strengthens the prohibition. The whole problem is there; that's where, in fact as well as in theory, the fault lies. Although the obstacle is removed as a result of the murder, *jouissance* is still prohibited; not only that, but the prohibition is reinforced."[81]

By insisting on the death of God, then, the narrator is able to realize a number of conflicting aims. To begin with, it allows him to affirm the lack, the rupture, that separates the pagan world from the narrator's own. No false universalism here: the narrator, by asserting that God has died out of the natural world, effectively asserts that there is no imaginary correspondence between past and present, that even to fantasize about a return to fullness is already to underscore the gulf that separates the pagan universe from the Christocentric. Second, the narrator's insistence on the death of God reinforces the notion that the law is what keeps the possibility of *jouissance* alive precisely by insisting on its prohibition. Instead of being dispossessed of lack by the suspension of Troilus between two deaths, the narrator now gets the lack he needs and that the polis requires. This is of course to turn away from the affirmation of the Thing as missing from the place of lack, that is, from the idea of a haunted political field. But more than that, it is to accept the excessive nature of the law—the way in which the law does not merely prohibit *jouissance*, holding it in reserve for the mythical figure of the father, but compounds that prohibition through the death of the father. The narrator, unable to handle the *jouissance* evident everywhere in the law, instead insists that *jouissance* is utterly off limits—that lack has somehow ensured the possibility of enjoyment by placing it exclusively in the care of the Other.

Perhaps one should be prepared for this terrible moment from the very beginning of the poem, when the narrator, having invoked Thesiphone to aid him in telling "the double sorwe of Troilus," confesses his "unliklynesse" as "the sorwful instrument, / That helpeth loveres, as [he] kan, to pleyne":

> For I, that God of Loves servantz serve,
> Ne dar to Love, for myn unliklynesse,
> Preyen for speed, al sholde I therfore sterve,
> So fer am I from his help in derknesse.
>
> (1.1–7, 10–11, 15–18)

The *Riverside Chaucer* glosses "unliklynesse" here as "unsuitability"— undoubtedly accurate within the narrowest reading of the context. But the *MED* provides two other meanings for the word, both of which are central to my purposes here. The first of these, "dissimilarity," holds perhaps the farthest-reaching implications, since it means that the narrator effectively denies himself the specular identification with Troilus assumed by the narrator of *Il Filostrato*. What he asserts instead is his dissimilarity, his difference, from the very lovers he serves and about whom he writes. Such a gesture implies a radically different posture, and a more ethical one, than that taken by Boccaccio's narrator. The latter insisted on an equivalency, a mirror likeness, between himself and Troilo that inevitably devolved, as we saw in the previous chapter, into aggression. Chaucer's narrator, by contrast, initially aims not to supplant the pagan other but to serve him, as a servant of Love's servants. Such an attitude implies that what connects the narrator to Troilus—indeed, to all of Love's servants—is not a universalizing equivalency but a mutual estrangement, an acknowledgment of the difference between those able to experience love directly and those who serve them, standing apart from love at one remove. Between these two groups there can never be any real parity; there can only be the recognition of the "unliklynesse" they share between them. And in this respect, the narrator's position also implies a very different principle of neighbor love: one "based," as Kenneth Reinhard puts it, "on structural difference, invoking the recollection of one's own strangeness rather than an imaginary expansion of the category of the self."[82]

As the third definition of *unliklynesse*—"dissatisfaction"—suggests, however, there is something else standing between Chaucer's narrator and Love's servants (who include, one may presume, both Troilo and the narrator of *Il Filostrato*). The essential difference here is that between enjoyment and the sacrifice inherent in service. Simply put, both Troilo and the *Filostrato* narrator can be said to enjoy in ways that the *Troilus* narrator renounces, or at least comes to renounce. Troilo's mode of enjoyment is fairly straightforward: he gains access to Criseida as the privileged Lady-Object. The enjoyment that mainly concerns Chaucer's narrator, by contrast, is the enjoyment gained by his Boccaccian counterpart's exploitation of Troilo. The *Filostrato* narrator, as I tried to show in the previous chapter, transgresses against the traditional order of medieval Trojan historiography by identifying with the pagan Troilo. Seeking to secure his absent Lady's attention, he winds up exploiting Troilo in the most fundamental ways: disinterring him, appropriating his place. Whatever paltry enjoyment the *Filostrato* narrator might be said to achieve as a servant of Love, he achieves it mostly at Troilo's expense. Yet this is the specific form of enjoyment—the form derived not simply from taking advantage of the counterpart but from insisting that the other is an imaginary counterpart in the first place—that the narrator of *Troilus and Criseyde* denies himself. If the *Troilus* narrator acknowledges, then, that he cannot love for his "unliklynesse"—if he cannot align himself, as a counterpart, with either Troilus or the narrator of *Il Filostrato*—he does so partly because he does not have access to the same enjoyment as they. That is, he has already sacrificed the *jouissance*, the painful enjoyment or enjoyed pain, available only to those who serve Love directly. His role, instead, is to serve those who serve—processing their experience, chronicling their pain, cleaning up their mess—and to wait, deferring until some later time the reward he might expect for having acknowledged the impossibility of enjoyment for himself. Proclaiming his "unliklynesse," the narrator assumes his place among the ranks of the big Other's dissatisfied servants, among civilization's discontents.

Another way of putting this is simply to say that the narrator of *Troilus and Criseyde* is like no one so much as Freud in the foundational dream of psychoanalysis, the dream of Irma's injection.[83] In the second part of this dream, after having peered into Irma's mouth only to behold the horrible "white patch" that Lacan will later associate with the real, Freud's "primary desire," according to Joan Copjec, "is a desire *not* to know anything of the real. . . . The abruptness of the transition indicates that Freud *flees* from the real—Irma, her white scabs, the unconscious—into the symbolic community of his fellow doctors."[84] Like Freud, the narrator of *Troilus and Criseyde* flees in horror from the real of Troy, with its "payans corsed olde rites" (5.1849), and turns instead to the multiple symbolic communities either invoked or implied at poem's end: classical writers (5.1789–92); Gower and Strode (5.1856–59); Benoît, Guido, and the other historians of the Trojan War (5.1765–71); even, one might retroactively claim, the imagined community of lovers to whom the poem is initially addressed (1.22). As with Freud, however, the narrator's recoiling from the real has less to do with cowardice than with self-preservation and, beyond that, duty. "Filled with paternal figures," writes Copjec,

> this space [of the second part of Freud's dream] is infused with an air of interdiction, of rules, regulations, and prescriptions, and yet it offers relief from the constricted asphyxiating space that *zusammenchnuren*, that chokes, Freud as well as Irma. In what, then, does this relief consist, and how is it secured? Most simply put, it consists in the setting up of the symbolic as rampart against the real; the symbolic *shields* us from the terrifying real. The climax of the second part [of the dream], the triumphant pronouncement of the word *trimethylamin*, indicates that it is the word itself, or the symbolic itself, that is our salvation.[85]

Again like Freud, the narrator turns to the word—the Word, in fact— for salvation from the Thing, erecting a Christocentric symbolic order against the desire in the Other indexed by the reanimation of Troilus. Indeed, one cannot help but be struck by the uncanny parallel between Freud's longing for the tripartite comfort of *trimethylamin*—which bespeaks, as Lacan puts it, "the intervention of a regulatory third party . . . which would put this distance, the distance of a certain pre-scribed order," between Freud and the real—and the narrator's appeal, not simply to the triumvirate of moral Gower, philosophical Strode, and "that sothfast Crist, that starf on rode," but to the Holy Trinity itself: "Thow oon, and two, and thre, eterne on lyve, / That regnest ay in thre, and two, and oon" (5.1863–64).[86] But what is it, exactly, that the narrator expects in return from his symbolic communities? Speaking of the dream of Irma's injection in his second seminar, Lacan notes that

> the objection which interests Freud is his own guilt, on this occa-sion towards Irma. The object is destroyed, if I can put it like this, and his guilt, which is what is in question, is destroyed with it. As in the story of the kettle with the hole in it, there is no crime here, since *firstly*, the victim was—which the dream says in a thousand different ways—already dead, that is to say was already ill with an organic ailment which is precisely what Freud could not cure, *sec-ondly*, the murderer, Freud, was innocent of any intention to harm, and *thirdly*, the crime in question was curative.[87]

Much the same could be said, I would argue, of the narrator, the vic-tim of whose poem was likewise already dead, whose motives were to "cure" both Troilus and the symbolic, and who appeals to the authority of various symbolic communities, including us readers, not simply to forgive his guilt, but also to share it. After all, has he not taken it upon himself, as a self-proclaimed servant, to pull away from enjoyment and inter Troilus, the "Little Troy"?

Before we begin either to celebrate or to pity the narrator's actions, however, we need to see that his self-proclaimed difference from the servants of Love, because it not coincidentally coincides with Chaucer's rewriting of Boccaccio's poem, also hints at a darker aspect of dissatis-faction. The *Troilus* narrator, after all, is not simply different from the enjoying narrator of *Il Filostrato*; he is actively working to rewrite or overwrite—in essence, undo—the latter's exploitation of Troilo. True enough, he serves the pagan other by providing him with the symbolic interment temporarily denied him. But in performing that particular service, the *Troilus* narrator also takes it upon himself to deny the un-bearable enjoyment in the neighboring text: the enjoyment gained by exploiting Troilo beyond the dictates of historiography. Chaucer's nar-rator, to put the matter another way, is not innocent; he has set out to deny, to overwrite, the neighboring text's enjoyment. One explicit aim of *Troilus and Criseyde*, in other words, is to repudiate an enjoyment of the neighbor that it itself has already repudiated. The *Troilus* narrator, as I suggested earlier, ultimately serves the socio-symbolic big Other by serving the pagan other. Yet that same service also serves his own discontent, his own "unliklynesse," by actively denying enjoyment not only for himself but also for his neighbor.

This troubling fact adds yet another layer of complexity to the idea that the narrator turns, like Freud, to the symbolic order as a defense against the Thing. Recall that, as Copjec puts it, Freud's "triumphant pronouncement of the word *trimethylamin*" at the end of the dream of Irma's injection "indicates that it is the word itself, or the symbolic itself, that is our salvation." But what is it, exactly, that Freud conjures up by pronouncing the word *trimethylamin*? *Trimethylamin*, as it turns out, "plays a role in connection with the decomposition products of sexual substances," according to Lacan. "Indeed . . ." Lacan continues, "trimethylamin is a decomposition product of sperm, and it gives it its ammoniacal smell when it's left to decompose in the air."[88] For Freud, as for the narrator, "there is no other word, no other solution to your problem, than the word."[89] Yet the word that Freud produces as the very essence of the word, the literal solution that is also a metaphor for the solution offered by the word, turns out to be little more than a formula for decay. Could there be a more fitting metaphor for the way in which the death drive is generated by the word itself, a more evoca-tive figure for the way in which the word creates its own opposite: a nongenerative residue that haunts the symbolic order with the specter of its own, self-generated ruin and decay?[90] In short, could there be a more poignant formula for the way in which the foundational word "secretes" the "empty place" of the nonfoundational Thing? "The law is what gives life to desire," Badiou reminds us, apropos of Saint Paul. "But in doing so, it constrains the subject so that he wants to follow only the path of death."[91] By designating the Thing as such, the word creates the possibility of transgression; *jouissance* becomes "the path toward death." That the narrator allows no other solution than the word, which is itself no solution, suggests that there is no protection from the Thing, no escape route from the burden of *jouissance*. There is only an embrace of the unmournable residue—a residue that, never really having been possessed, can never be claimed as lost—manifested in the Thing that haunts the word.

As neatly divisible as the narrator's situation (and its solution) may appear, then, it is profoundly complicated by his ambivalent relationship to the word, an attitude that shapes his equally ambivalent relation to both his "auctor," Lollius, and Criseyde. One reason we cannot call the narrator's repudiation of Troy-lus either unexpected or unconvincing (let alone perverse) is that he has already shown a willingness, if not an actual longing, to obey the law, to submit. One place we see this need to submit is in book 5, when the narrator claims that Criseyde "so sory was for hire untrouthe," he "wolde excuse hire yet for routhe"—would, that is, if his submission to his "auctor" did not demand that he *not* excuse her, or change her fate (5.1098–99). Although we may never know Chaucer's reasons for replacing the name of Boccaccio, his actual source, with that of the fictional "Lollius," Barry Windeatt makes the plausible suggestion that "Chaucer's 'attribution' of his poem to 'Lollius' was always a piece of deliberately transparent artifice . . . designed to foreground the question of sources, and with that the role of interpretation—the relation between this Troilus story and the existing tradition of Troilus narratives."[92] I would like to push this interpretation a bit further by suggesting that *Lollius* serves, in its very lack of authenticity, to articulate three of *Troilus and Criseyde*'s principal concerns. First, as Windeatt suggests, it functions as a sly comment on the imbrication of fantasy and history, underscoring the fact that our relation to the past is always, at some level, fake: as fraudulent as Lollius himself. In the case of *Troilus and Criseyde*, in particular, that fraudulency is redoubled; for here, of course, that relation is to a pagan past from which the narrator and his contemporaries are utterly estranged. Any unmediated connection to the past that they might want to claim is therefore already, and necessarily, bogus. Deliberately transparent artifice though he may be, Lollius is no less authentic than is any other authority on an inherently fabricated past. It is his very lack of authenticity, in fact, that makes Lollius such an accurate representation of a medieval authority on pagan history.

As another name for fantasy, then, Lollius stands for the extent to which authority is called into being by our willful belief in its transparent artifice—that is, by our belief in the consoling fantasy of a masterful Other. As a figure for our investments in the fantasy of the symbolic order, in other words, Lollius stands for the way in which, to paraphrase Žižek, the radically impossible gets changed into the merely prohibited.[93] What, after all, is the status of the name *Lollius?* What structural position does it occupy? One might say that it occupies the place where, instead of encountering the name *Boccaccio,* Chaucer encountered a nameless figure of enjoyment: the narrator of *Il Filostrato.* It is in the place, then, of the Other's unsettling desire, the place where enjoyment "speaks" in the neighboring text, that the *Troilus* narrator imposes authority, imposes prohibition. (Indeed, it is interesting to note that, as Windeatt puts it, "expressions of deference to 'myn auctor' occur when Chaucer is actually writing independently of *Filostrato*"[94]—almost as if Chaucer [or, more properly, the narrator] were simultaneously disavowing his own enjoyment and sanctioning his efforts to overwrite the enjoyment at work in *Il Filostrato.*) *Lollius,* to put the matter slightly differently, stands as a name for the symbolic as such, for the way in which we establish the symbolic order against the traumatic emergence of the real. Here the real emerges in the enjoyment of the *Filostrato* narrator: his transgressions against literary tradition, his simultaneous identification with and exploitation of Troilo. This is an enjoyment that the *Troilus* narrator might also claim—might, that is, if Lollius, the "auctor" whom the narrator has *put* in place, did not prohibit him from doing so. It has sometimes been said that *Troilus and Criseyde,* as a poem ultimately indebted to a Christian notion of salvation, views its pagan characters as necessarily limited and constrained: trapped, so to speak, in an age before grace.[95] But Chaucer's representation of the narrator as beholden to an "auctor" largely invented by himself reminds us that the narrator too, as a subject of the law, is not merely constrained but also deeply implicated: required to maintain the fiction of the Other at the price of his own enjoyment. "Litel myn tragedye," indeed (5.1786).

Here we encounter a paradox, however. For if, on the one hand, *Lollius* is a name for the fantasy of an authoritative Other, he is also a name for exactly what the narrator claims him to be: the true, if unacknowledged, source of his poem, Boccaccio. I have suggested that the name *Lollius* stands in the place of an otherwise nameless enjoyment in the neighboring text, that *Lollius* simply is another name for the symbolic order we exchange for the real, imagining that, by doing so, we will be relieved from the unbearable burden of *jouissance*. Again and again, though, we have seen that such exchanges don't work, that they inevitably produce a residue, an excess of exactly that which the symbolic order is meant to supplant. Like *trimethylamin*, *Lollius* produces a ghost that cannot be mourned because, having never been known, it could never be lost: the name *Boccaccio*. I have described the "book of Troilus" as a tomb. But if it is a tomb, it is one containing a crypt—the secret crypt that conceals the incorporated object. "Incorporation negotiates clandestinely with a prohibition it neither accepts nor transgresses," writes Derrida in his foreword to Abraham and Torok's *The Wolf Man's Magic Word*.

"Secrecy is essential," whence the crypt, a hidden place, a disguise hiding the traces of the act of disguising, a place of silence. Introjection speaks; "denomination" is its "privileged" medium. Incorporation keeps still, speaks only to silence or to ward off intruders from its secret place. What the crypt commemorates, as the incorporated object's "monument" or "tomb," is not the object itself, but its exclusion, the exclusion of a specific desire from the introjection process: A door is silently sealed off like a condemned passageway inside the Self, becoming the outcast safe: "A commemorative monument, the incorporated object marks the place, the date, the circumstances in which such-and-such a desire was barred from introjection: like so many tombs in the life of the Self." The crypt is the vault of a desire.[96]

As opposed to introjection, which names the process by which the ego constructs itself through a progressive series of identifications, incorporation names the process by which the ego refuses to name—that is, encrypts—that part of the other which it takes in without knowing, secreting it away in a no-place at once within and without the ego's cemetery of memory, an "interior . . . partitioned off from the interior."[97] In Chaucer's hands, however, this "cryptic incorporation," as Derrida calls it, marks something more than just an "effect of impossible or refused mourning"; Chaucer's refusal to mourn a name he has never known, to allow it to be exchanged for another, also manifests a profound act of neighbor love. Recall that the neighbor is divided between those aspects with which we can identify, that we can introject, and a Thing with which no identification is possible: a Thing that we incorporate. The crypt is the vault of a desire that is well and truly *extimate*, at once external to the subject, located in the neighbor, and also intimate, a "neighbor" in residence at the heart of the subject. In *Il Filostrato*, that desire is the forward-looking identification with Troilo, manifest in the *Filostrato* narrator's attempt to blast Troilo out of the continuum of history. It was in response to that desire that Chaucer wrote *Troilus and Criseyde*. And yet here Chaucer tacitly, or rather secretly, acknowledges that desire as his own by blasting the name of Boccaccio out of the continuum of history—that is, by allowing his own poem to replicate the very desire from which it recoils. It is a critical commonplace that Chaucer never names Boccaccio, which is of course true. But that is only because he does not mourn Boccaccio by subjecting him to the denominational medium of introjection. Instead, he incorporates Boccaccio, destroying his name, silencing it, only in order to preserve it, to guard it, within a crypt. Transforming the injunction to love the neighbor as himself into a critical paradigm, Chaucer allows his text to be haunted by a name, *Boccaccio*, that he does not know, but that he knows the name of Lollius can never supplant.

It is not only the narrator's qualified submission to his "auctor" that defines the ending of the poem, however. The same ambivalence—the same clandestine negotiation with a prohibition he can neither accept nor transgress, to paraphrase Derrida—is also evident in the narrator's understated devotion to Criseyde. That devotion is expressed in subtle, almost surreptitious ways. It is worth bearing in mind, for example, that before the narrator assumes his own symbolic mandate and repudiates "payens corsed olde rites," Criseyde is told to "lat Troie and Troian from [her] herte pace" by Diomede—arguably the most hard-hearted and unappealing, if prescient, character in the poem (5.1849, 912). The two figures, Criseyde and her narrator, are thus joined through the painful forced choice that each must make: to accept the inevitable loss of Troy in exchange for the promise of "a moore parfit love," be it Christian or Greek (5.919). Still more significant, though, is Troilus's laugh. For if Troilus himself can look down upon his own death and laugh, then how can we continue to hold Criseyde responsible for his supposedly tragic fate? How, in other words, can any poem—or any reader—feel justified in shifting the violence of Troilus's death onto Criseyde when the meaning of that death has been so thoroughly altered, and diminished, by laughter?

Troilus's apotheosis would therefore appear to be staged for Criseyde's benefit as much as for his own. Yet at the same time it can be said to serve the narrator's purpose as well. Throughout this study, I have been concerned to show how Troilus, the "Little Troy," manifests the internal failure—the impossibility—of a late medieval symbolic order. Another way of putting this is simply to state that Troilus, as a figure forever linked to death—his own death in the name of love; the death of the city whose destruction ensured the later advent of another city, London—bodies forth the death drive at work in every symbolic network. By *death drive* here I do not mean simply Troilus's own "living dedication to death," as Spearing calls it: his imagistic and linguistic associations with death, his insistence on dying in battle rather than taking Pandarus's suggestion and seeking a replacement for Criseyde (4.400–406). I also mean that Troilus, as we saw in the previous chapter, manifests the Thing—"the death drive in its 'pure state,'" according to Alenka Zupančič[98]—at the heart of *Il Filostrato* as neighboring text. Troilus, through no fault of his own, becomes associated with that most utterly Other aspect of the other: that foreign Thing in the neighbor with which no identification is possible, which forbids the cohesion of symbolic order—and which, for this reason, intimates the potential annihilation of the symbolic itself. To remove Troilus from the space between two deaths, as Chaucer's narrator does, is thus to serve the big Other by turning away from the traumatic presence of the death drive at its heart.

Yet if Troilus's apotheosis inters the pagan Thing in a symbolically meaningful way, it also complicates matters by leaving behind a surplus in the figure of Criseyde, a Trojan who escapes both the inevitable destruction of Troy and, more important perhaps, the narrator's expressed judgment. The narrator, chafing against the demands of his "auctor," goes out of his way not to condemn Criseyde outright for "betraying" Troilus by falling, out of necessity, back into the symbolic economy of substitution in which she might at least be true to Diomede (5.1071):

> Ne me ne list this sely womman chyde
> Forther than the story wol devyse.
> Hire name, allas, is publysshed so wide
> That for hire gilt it oughte ynough suffise.
> And if I myghte excuse hire any wise,
> For she so sory was for hire untrouthe,
> Iwis, I wolde excuse hire yet for routhe.
>   (5.1093–99)

Criseyde, however, knows all too well of the fate that awaits her, despite the narrator's hesitation. "'Allas,'" she predicts,

>   of me, unto the worldes ende,
> Shal neyther ben ywriten nor ysonge
> No good word, for thise bokes wol me shende.
> O rolled shal I be on many a tonge!
> Thorughout the world my belle shal be ronge!
> And wommen most wol haten me of alle.
> Allas, that swich a cas me sholde falle!
>   (5.1058–64)

In contrast to Troilus, whose "bounded" existence and single-minded devotions—to Criseyde, to death—set him on the path of finitude,

Criseyde's vision of an open-ended future in which she will be repeatedly abused and maligned "unto the worldes ende" suspends her in a kind of undead infinitude. Criseyde's situation is uncertain. On the one hand, she is supposed to be dead to posterity, since the narrator announces at the beginning of book 1 that "she forsook" Troilus "ere she deyde" (1.56). She ought then, from the retroactive perspective of Chaucer's poem, to be always-already dead. On the other hand, Criseyde's own words transport her beyond her physical death into the shadowy space between two deaths: the place of perpetual suffering where the natural cycle of life and death is, if not broken, at least suspended. Lacan, who theorizes the space between two deaths partly through the writings of the Marquis de Sade, notes that, "in the same way . . . the human tradition" has held on to the notion of an afterlife where all our sufferings will end, it has also "never ceased to imagine a second form of suffering, a suffering beyond death that is indefinitely sustained by the impossibility of crossing the limit of the second death. And that is why the tradition of hell in different forms has always remained alive, and it is still present in Sade in the idea he has of making the suffering inflicted on a victim go on indefinitely."[99] In Criseyde, I am suggesting, Chaucer imagines something very close to this Sadeian partner: an indestructible figure who, as Žižek puts it, "can be endlessly tortured and can survive it," who "can endure any torment and still retain her beauty."[100] Granted, Criseyde seems to be worried more about her future reputation than about what might happen to her body—although her use of the word *shende*, which can mean "destroy" or "harm" as well as "disgrace," combined with the highly sensual images of her being rolled on many a tongue and having her "belle" rung throughout the world, suggests that even Criseyde realizes how thoroughly her reputation is tied to her body, and how the treatment of the one "shal be" as sexualized, and as violent, as the other. In a way, however, the question of whether the Sadeian victim is abused in body or in name is a moot one, since the end result of such fantasies is always the same: sublimation. Their purpose, as Žižek goes on to explain, is to insist that, "over and above her natural body (a part of the cycle of generation and corruption)," the victim possesses "a sublime body" that, like the Thing, is composed of an imperishable substance."[101] By refusing to pass final judgment on Criseyde, then, Chaucer's narrator might be said to undo the effect of Criseyde's leaving Troy by allowing Criseyde's own prediction for her future to resublimate her—not as the Lady-Object but as the indestructible body between two deaths.

Yet this gesture is not quite so radical as it sounds, primarily because the Sadeian fantasy scenario is itself not quite so radical as it at first appears. For Lacan, in fact, Sade is a failure, a would-be transgressor who actually ends up revealing the poverty of transgression. It may seem as though the Sadeian fantasy of inflicting perpetual suffering boldly pushes beyond the limits of the law to aim directly at the Thing. But in fact the Sadeian fantasy as such is to make the Other reveal itself—make the big Other appear as whole, an all-encompassing symbolic order—by providing an answer to the enigmatic question of the Other's desire. In the Sadeian fantasy scenario, the Other, embodied in the victim who can never die, is not allowed to desire (and thus to lack) because the void of her desire is "plugged up" by the enjoyment that her torturer claims to provide. The true aim of the Sadeian fantasy is, in the end, rather pedestrian: to fulfill the Other with the gift of *jouissance*, rather than to confront fully the implications of the desire in the Other.

Is it fair to describe the narrator in such terms, as a failed transgressor who unwittingly works on behalf of the Other? At the very least, one can say of the narrator that he remains sincerely, miserably torn. On the one hand, he does not wish to "chyde" Criseyde "forther than the storye wol devyse." That is, he does not wish to enjoy Criseyde, make her suffer, beyond what the symbolic order allows. On the other hand, if he *could* excuse her, and end her suffering, he would. That is, he would forbid the enjoyment of Criseyde altogether, if only the dictates of his story did not demand otherwise. Able neither to add nor to subtract, the narrator simply hands his enjoyment over to the socio-symbolic Other—to the anonymous "men" who say that Criseyde gave Diomede her heart, to "the storye" he feels compelled to follow (5.1050, 1094)—and moves on, leaving Criseyde precisely where her own words have located her: in the space between two deaths.

In other words, the narrator flees at last, like the dutiful political subject he is, from the anxiety-producing burden of his own *jouissance*.

It is that very retreat, however, that lends Criseyde's prophecy its unique power. To be sure, Criseyde's act of self-sublimation, as she herself recognizes only too well, draws her even further into the logic of the symbolic order. Not only has she committed herself to an economy of substitution, exchanging Diomede for Troilus; now she will have to play a particular role in the maintenance of ideology, providing the vehicle by which a succession of male authors might plug up the lack in the Other with the gift of *jouissance*, manifest in the endless suffering of the Sadeian victim: a suffering that never crosses over the limit of the second death. Yet what truly strikes one about Criseyde's prophecy is its utter certainty. In marked contrast to the narrator, who tries repeatedly to avoid confronting Criseyde's fate, Criseyde herself has no doubt about her future. She may regret it, but she makes no effort to deny it. Indeed, one might even go so far as to say that Criseyde embraces her future, and that, in doing so, she affirms the very real that the narrator seeks to evade. It is true, of course, that the future Criseyde envisions for herself is, for Chaucer, a past that has already come to be. Nevertheless, we should not lose sight of the way in which Criseyde's prediction, to the extent that it continues in perpetuity—to the extent that it continues to hold true even in Chaucer's poem—brings out the radical obverse of the Sadeian fantasy scenario. Criseyde, as she herself realizes, stands suspended at the very limit of the second death. She may be prevented from crossing over that limit by the endless suffering inflicted upon her; but that means only that her treatment, by suspending the natural cycles of generation and decay, continues to keep the reader of *Troilus and Criseyde* in contact with the Thing. Criseyde doesn't just have a vision of the future, after all; she has a vision of a future that introduces "the worldes ende," the obliteration of the symbolic universe, into the present. And in that, I would argue, her experience of the present corresponds to Chaucer's own after his encounter with *Il Filostrato*.

In many respects, then, *Troilus and Criseyde* can be read as an inherently anxious text, designed to erect an appropriate barrier between the culture that produced it and a nonhistorical, nonsymbolizable Thing. What saves the poem from a potentially arid and oppressive conservatism, however, is how scrupulously it attends to the complicated position of the subject within the very order it works to maintain. Indeed, what sets the poem apart from, say, Gower's *Vox Clamantis*, with which it might otherwise be broadly compared as a social text, is ultimately the sadness with which it presents the "litel tragedye" of the subject's symbolic castration, the subject's renunciation of *jouissance* and identification with the Name-of-the-Father. One of the things contributing to that sadness is the narrator's seemingly inevitable, if also regrettable, disavowal of Troy, understood as a signifier for the impossibility lurking at the very core of the symbolic order. The narrator could decide not to give way on that impossibility, could choose not to sacrifice *jouissance* to the fantasy of the Other; instead, he opts to evade *jouissance* by retreating into a temporal scheme grounded in the demise of Troy. Confronted by the unbearable impasse generated by the conflicting demands of neighbor love, the narrator simply recoils. But even in this, its most potentially heartbreaking sacrifice, *Troilus and Criseyde* cannot be called overly deterministic. For even as it asks us to submit, to give up the impossible *jouissance* of the Thing in favor of the limited enjoyment of the law, the poem also confronts us with the narrator's ambivalent treatment of Criseyde. And it will be in response to those two ways of bargaining with the real, evasion and ambivalence, that Henryson, at once the most astute and most neighborly of Chaucer's readers, will write his *Testament of Cresseid*.

Epilogue

Once thought to depict an actual occasion when Chaucer read *Troilus and Criseyde* aloud to the Ricardian court, the Frontispiece of Corpus Christi College MS 61 (Fig. 1) is now more commonly read as a sort of vertical diptych, with Richard II and his court listening, in the foreground, as Chaucer at his pulpit "evokes," in the background, the moment in his poem when Criseyde is "swapped" for Antenor and forced to leave Troy.[1] In the view of Elizabeth Salter and Derek Pearsall, who introduced this reading of the Frontispiece, the allusion to Criseyde's departure from Troy is meant to illustrate the Boethian theme of mutability: the vicissitudes of fortune, the inevitable disappointment of worldly love.[2] More recently, James Simpson has suggested that the picture's emphasis on the loss of Criseyde points to the elegiac aspect of Chaucer's poem, its melancholic sense of being "cut off from a remembered but irrecuperable history."[3] I have no wish to dispute either of these readings, which together give us a sense of how profoundly the Frontispiece engages not only with the philosophical and historical dimensions of Chaucer's poem but with its complex portrayal of a narrator torn between admonishment and mourning. I would, however, like to supplement them with two points of my own. The first is that, just because the Frontispiece does not record a historical event doesn't mean it isn't an accurate illustration of history. One of the things that

Figure 1. Chaucer performs before the court. Frontispiece to Corpus Christi College MS 61. Reproduced by permission of the Master and Fellows of Corpus Christi College, Cambridge.

makes the Frontispiece so intriguing, in fact, is that its details manage to reflect, in their very lack of verisimilitude, not only the environment in which Chaucer wrote *Troilus and Criseyde* but the idea of history that structures the poem. More ironically, perhaps, they also look ahead to the way in which Chaucer himself would be treated by the very historical processes he interrogates. The second, closely related, point is that the picture shows that there is no such thing as a history from which we are not cut off—that history names a process not of remembering but of imagining that we remember, or remembering only partially, or misremembering, or strategically forgetting.[4] It is the institution of memory, in other words, that makes all history irrecuperable. In this respect, the exchange of Criseyde for Antenor shown in the top half of the Frontispiece is doubly emblematic, standing in not only for the catastrophic rupture precipitated by that moment of "swapping" but for the fantasy scenarios we swap in exchange for a history too fractured by catastrophic ruptures to be remembered. If the Frontispiece can be described, then, as an astute reading of Chaucer's poem, it is because it too is structured around a series of exchanges— including the exchange of fantasies of imperial continuity for the violent ruptures that both generate and punctuate history.[5]

One notices right away, for example, that the Frontispiece is composed along a vertical axis of visual correspondences and a horizontal axis (albeit one with a curve) of division, with Chaucer situated more or less at the point where the two axes intersect. Since the details of this arrangement matter to an understanding of the whole, it would help to treat each of these axes separately, beginning with the correspondences. We have noted how England, like other medieval European nations, followed the logic of *translatio imperii* in tracing its origins to a legendary Trojan diaspora. We have likewise seen how London, in particular, was fashioned by various parties, including the poet John Gower, the city's sometime mayor, Nicholas Brembre, and even Richard himself, as *Troynovant*, the "New Troy." It is thus significant that the figures in the Trojan background of the Frontispiece are dressed in the same fashions as their counterparts in the Ricardian foreground and that Troy itself looks remarkably like an idealized medieval city. For in such correspondences between foreground and background, between late medieval courtiers and their Trojan counterparts, the Frontispiece registers, in visual terms, precisely the sort of imaginary relation or identification that the English sought in their visions of Troy. In the mirrored scheme of the Frontispiece, Richard and his court truly are the "New Trojans" they proclaimed themselves to be. Indeed, when read literally, the Frontispiece appears to present the Ricardian court as having descended from the Trojans, who are situated above them in the frame.

Superficially, then, the Frontispiece seems to promote a potent ideological fantasy: that of a timeless and coherent big Other, a socio-symbolic order in which the present turns back to find itself reflected, validated, in its own image of the past. As the Frontispiece presents it, Richard and his court are the rightful inheritors of a past that already anticipates them and that seems to flow into their present space. Crucially, though, this fantasy of continuity is shored up by the very moment of exchange depicted in the upper half of the picture, the moment at which Criseyde is exchanged for Antenor. For of course as far as the English were concerned, this was a necessary, even a fortuitous, exchange: the first link in a chain of events that would lead, in time, to the rise of England in Troy's symbolic place. Yet what the moment obscures is the violence implicit in that exchange, the fact that the rise of England could be purchased, so to speak, only at the cost of the intervening destruction of Troy. Lurking behind the Frontispiece is a vision of history as unrelenting catastrophe. But in the sumptuous setting of the Frontispiece itself, one city, one epoch, is exchanged for another without suffering, just as, in book 2 of *Troilus and Criseyde*, Troilus's heart is painlessly swapped for Criseyde's in the latter's dream of the eagle.

This fantasy is quickly undercut, however, by two other of the Frontispiece's prominent features: the inscrutable mass—call it a mountain, a pathway, a ramp[6]—that cuts across the middle of the illustration's visual field, dividing the figures in the foreground, including Chaucer, from the figures positioned in and around the city in the background; and Chaucer's unusual position in the scene: slightly above the assembled courtiers, and standing at his "pulpit" between them and the divisive mass itself.[7] In stark contrast to the Frontispiece's visual correspondences, this second, horizontal axis seems intended to effect a break, a division, between Trojan past and Ricardian present—to insist that the one has been cut off, rather dramatically, from the other. If there is any relation at all between the Ricardian court and their Trojan counterparts, this detail of the Frontispiece reminds us, it is purely imaginary, a fantasy meant to obfuscate the violence inherent in the process of cyclical exchange. Opposing the fantasy of genealogical succession promoted by its own vertical axis, the Frontispiece here presents us with a powerful image of the ceaseless, and ceaselessly violent, cycles of emergence and decay that Benjamin terms "natural history." Like the exchange of Criseyde for Antenor, the barrier hints at a prior moment of "lawmaking" violence, a break that is not so much remembered as detectable, retroactively, in its aftereffects.

Such a moment is not exclusively political or even historical, however. On the contrary, the repeated associations in Chaucer's poem of *Troy* with *joy*, like the associations of *Troy* with lust, aggression, and agitation in the political imaginary of late medieval England, make it difficult not to read the division in the Frontispiece as parabolic in another way, a visual allegory of the renunciation of enjoyment— of *jouissance*—that guarantees the symbolic economy of exchange to which the illustration itself seems so deeply committed.[8] In short, the intrusive, divisive mass depicted in the Frontispiece manifests an image of the structural lack, or rather the *imposition* of such lack, on which the symbolic order is predicated. The split nature of the Frontispiece, to put the matter somewhat differently, calls our attention to the fact that something has already been exchanged—that Troy is encountered, like *jouissance*, only in its lack. Troy, enjoyment: those things can no more be recovered than can Criseyde after she has been traded for Antenor.

The question of exchange becomes yet more complicated with the Frontispiece's depiction of Chaucer. Perhaps responding to the characterization of the *Troilus* narrator in the first four books of the poem, the Frontispiece presents Chaucer as actively cultivating the imaginary correspondence between Troy and London, attributing to him the power to "bring Troy to life," as it were, by conjuring up the scene in the background through the sheer force of his oral delivery (there is no text visible before him on the pulpit). As is typical of late medieval illustrations, however, the Frontispiece incorporates several concurrent narratives; and if Pearsall is right that the Frontispiece draws predominantly on the iconography of preaching and teaching pictures, then it would seem that Chaucer's words to his audience are meant to carry religious as well as didactic overtones.[9] The same is true of Chaucer's unusual position in the scene. Situated so that he stands not only above his listeners, who are gathered like students or congregation about his feet, but in between them and the barrier, Chaucer is here transformed into the very image of a lawgiving father Chaucer: a conflation of Chaucer the poet with the final narratorial voice of book 5, the one that concludes *Troilus and Criseyde* by renouncing Troy, disparaging "swich rascaille" as Jove, Apollo, and Mars, repudiating the "corsed olde rites" of "payans" (5.1853, 1849). What might otherwise be read as frozen gestures (a hand held slightly aloft, a head bent downward and forward, a look of direct appeal) thus come to signify the words of a pointed, if unheard, sermon: though certain imperial ambitions, and certain aspects of aristocratic life, may find validation in English fantasies of Troy, to be interpellated in the Christocentric culture of late medieval Europe is to confront the fact that Troy is prohibited—that the intervening events of dispensation and grace have erected a barrier between the medieval present and the pagan past. It is the divided form of the Frontispiece itself that Chaucer preaches from his pulpit.

Picking up, then, on one dimension of *Troilus and Criseyde*, the Frontispiece busily promotes the idea of Chaucer as a "hero" of lack, in both senses: someone willing to unmask the inherent lack in the Other while at the same time acting as an apologist for the logic of symbolic order by insisting, though his prohibitory gestures, that *jouissance* is securely off limits—that it is even tied, somehow, to its prohibition.[10] This comes through most clearly in the way that the composition of the barrier, which manages to appear both natural seeming, an integral part of the landscape, and also patently artificial, seems to pick up on the role played by courtly love in *Troilus and Criseyde*. Consistent with the sublimating logic of courtly love, the mass appears to screen against a direct apprehension of utter lack, instead cultivating the fundamental illusion of the symbolic order, which is that enjoyment might still be accessible, if not for the external hindrances blocking the way.[11]

Such an arrangement buttresses the logic of the symbolic order in two ways, first by holding out the promise of compensation for what one lacks, second by insisting that it is exchange itself, and the exchange of enjoyment for a place in the symbolic order, in particular, that creates *jouissance*. Like the fantasy of the courtly Lady, the fantasy of father Chaucer—the fantasy, that is, of a figure possessed of the *jouissance* prohibited to the subject—allows his followers to evade the *jouissance* they have but don't want.

Yet if the details of the Frontispiece that commit Chaucer to a "heroism of lack" fail to tell the whole story, it is because they end up drawing our attention to another act of exchange at work in the picture: the exchange of father Chaucer for the confused, ambivalent narrator of *Troilus and Criseyde.* The Frontispiece zeroes in on one ad-monitory moment in the poem, the narrator's hysterical repudiation of the pagan past. Yet by doing so, it ends up transforming Chaucer into an apologist for exchange in a way that subjects him to the very same process of exchange. The Frontispiece, in other words, is not only an interpretation of *Troilus and Criseyde;* it is a misreading of the poem that helps contribute to the politically motivated reinvention of Chaucer as father Chaucer in the years following his death.[12] What gets lost, though, is a Chaucer who resists the logic of exchange, a Chaucer who is reluctant to bury the ghosts produced by natural history. Like the upper half of the Frontispiece, which hints, in its reference to the swapping of Criseyde for Antenor, at two betrayals—Criseyde's be-trayal by the Trojan parliament and Criseyde's betrayal of Troilus— the lower half is also structured around a betrayal: the Frontispiece's betrayal of Chaucer.

Still, as fate would have it, this is not the most powerful thing the *Troilus* Frontispiece ends up having to say about exchange. It also raises the troubling question of whether one can give oneself over to the symbolic economy of exchange—that is, to the merciless logic of natural history—without consequences. At least one detail of the Frontispiece suggests that the answer is no. This is the "detail," surely never intended by the artist(s), in which the Richard figure's face has been rubbed away by a later hand. That act of defacement points, at the very least, to yet another revolution in the cycle of natural history, since it seems likely that whoever carried it out was reacting, albeit some years after the fact, to the imposition of Lancastrian rule in 1399. But what it also makes visible is the stain of aggression, the antagonism, that was already defacing the surface of social relations in England just around the time of the Frontispiece's original composition. Rather than destroying the integrity of the Frontispiece, then, the rubbing away of Richard's face tells us something essential both about the specific historical moment at which the Frontispiece was produced and about the broader workings of history as such. Simply put, the complete picture of late medieval history is realized only once it has been destroyed: once it comes to include an image of its immanent decomposition. As an image of history at once overarching and particular, the Frontispiece is completed only when its future destruction—a destruction already anticipated in the impasse of social antagonism—is included within it.[13]

Yet even this is not the last thing that the defacement of the Richard figure reveals about exchange; it also reminds us that there is no such thing as a complete exchange, an exchange that entirely uproots the order of meaning that precedes it in history. Rather, as we saw in the Introduction, every exchange carried out at the world-historical level, insofar as it perpetuates the violence inherent in the process of natural history, leaves behind "deposits" of suffering, remainders that then serve to "depose" the symbolic order by acting as so many "depositions": testaments that bear witness, by their very muteness or inertness, to an ongoing history of violence.[14] The stain left behind by the defacement of the Richard figure, I am suggesting, is one such deposit—one such holdover from an order that, having been deposed (literally, in Richard's case), returns to depose the order that would supplant it. The fact that it is nothing more than an enigmatic stain, a signifier bereft of any clear signified, only makes its testament that much more compelling.

Like every deposit of suffering thrown up by the cycles of natural history, then, the stain on the Frontispiece persists in a state of what I have called, following Santner (following Benjamin), "petrified unrest": suspended in the continuous expectation of a future that has yet to be.[15] The stain, to put the matter somewhat differently, betrays an inertness, a frozen quality initiated by the traumatic imposition of lawmaking violence; and it is that quality which isolates the stain within the psychoanalytic register of the Thing. References to the Thing in contemporary critical discourse can be traced, as we have seen, to two sources: Lacan, who speaks of it at length in *The Ethics of Psychoanalysis*, referring to it, at various points, as the dumb materiality of the real, the impossible, the lost object, the mother's body after the imposition of the incest taboo, and the Sovereign Good that the subject endeavors to avoid through the intervention of the pleasure principle; and Slavoj Žižek, who describes it as "the materialization of the terrifying, impossible *jouissance*."[16] Strictly speaking, though, the origin of the concept lies, as we have also seen, in Freud's early *Project for a Scientific Psychology*. Recall that, for Freud, self-awareness is gained only through an ethical division of the *Nebenmensch* into "good" elements—"visual perceptions . . . ," as Freud puts it, "[that] coincide in the subject with memories of quite similar visual impressions . . . of his own body"—and "bad" elements: "perceptual complexes" that are, from the subject's point of view, "new and non-comparable." Parsed in this way, says Freud, "the complex of the fellow human-being falls apart into two components, of which one makes an impression by its constant structure and stays together as a *thing*, while the other can be understood by the activity of memory—that is, can be traced back to information from [the subject's] own body." To align the stain with the Thing is thus to recognize, in the first place, that the effacement of Richard marks the eruption of something "new" within the frame of the Frontispiece itself, something that is undeniably in the picture but that comes, as it were, from the future—that registers the point at which the future already impinges upon the imaginary consistency of the present. In this particular case, that future takes the form of Richard's deposition, an event that is already anticipated, as I have suggested, in the antagonistic impasses of Ricardian society. The stain simply materializes a future that is already "in" the picture. The irony of such a future, however, is that it invariably comes from out of the past. What makes the Thing so disturbing, Freud suggests, is not only that it is "new" but also that it is "non-comparable," resistant to the economy of substitutions, exchanges, and comparisons that structures the symbolic order. This is why Lacan refers to the Thing as the *hors-signifié*: it is the "outside-of-the-signifier," "both outside of or beyond signification and the first outside to be signified."[17] The Thing, to put the matter somewhat differently, is created as prehistorical by the order of symbolization that instantiates history. To encounter the utterly alien Thing in the *Nebenmensch* is thus to encounter, in the guise of the future, a return of the past that can only be understood as "new and non-comparable" because it was cast outside of memory at the moment of its creation.

Furthermore, to align the stain with the Thing is to recognize how the Frontispiece, which otherwise depicts a vision of community organized around gestures of sacrifice and affinity, includes within it an element that undermines community as such by precluding identification. It is no coincidence that the Richard figure should be defaced, and so mark the emergence of the Thing, in an illustration concerned with the place of Troy in late medieval fantasies of English nationhood. For *Troy*, as we have seen throughout this study, signified a profound antagonism, a lack of lack, at the heart of fourteenth- and fifteenth-century English civic life, and London civic life in particular. This, too, is a matter foregrounded, and complicated, by the stain. One aspect of the *Nebenmensch* that the subject can identify with, according to Freud, is its scream. The other's pain can serve, in other words, as a basis for our communal bond—provided it happens to correspond to our own memories of suffering or deprivation. If the defacement of the Richard figure elicits any pathos at all, it is because we can identify with the mental and bodily suffering it calls to mind, the knowledge of the natural-historical upheaval that resulted in Richard's deposition and murder. Simply put, we can re-present Richard's pain by making it accord with the memory of our own. As Freud insists, however, there is at the same time an aspect of the *Nebenmensch* with which the subject finds it impossible to identify, a "perceptual complex" that fails to "awaken" even the subject's memory of its own suffering, the sounds of its own screaming. Lacan describes this element "as being by its very nature alien, *Fremde* . . . strange and even hostile on occasion," and he explicitly aligns it, as do his latter-day interpreters, with the death drive.[18] This *thing*-ly aspect of the *Nebenmensch* is also manifest in the defacement of the Richard figure—not in the memories of pain that it awakens in the viewer, but in the inscrutable act of defacement itself. What lies behind that act? Is it fear, anger, disappointment, hostility? Or was the perpetrator just being opportunistic, hoping, perhaps, to replace Richard's face with that of Henry IV? It is because we do not know—because the act defeats memory—that the stain assumes the Thing-like quality that it does. All we know is that, whatever emotion might lurk behind the defacement of the Richard figure, it is one we hasten to attribute to the *Nebenmensch* while simultaneously denying in ourselves.

But why is this? Why is the Thing so "threatening," as Zupančič puts it: "the death drive in its 'pure state'"? It is because, like the drive, the Thing persists as an aftereffect of exchange. The symbolic order, I have argued, is predicated on the subject's willingness to accept the prohibition of *jouissance* instituted by an exchange that has already happened. To detect the Thing in the *Nebenmensch*, by contrast, is to sense that the member of the community most proximate to you refuses to abide by the terms of that exchange—that, in short, the *Nebenmensch* retains a portion of the *jouissance* that you were called upon to sacrifice in the interests of the Other. This is what Lacan seems to be driving at in his characterization of the Thing as not just strange but also hostile: a sense that the *Nebenmensch* derives enjoyment from trying to transgress against exactly those prohibitions erected in the name of community. The stain, I am suggesting, hints at the same refusal to participate in the sacrificial economy of the symbolic order, the same unwillingness to part with *jouissance*. Someone erased the Richard figure's features in a paroxysm of enjoyment; and by doing so he or she gave vent to the very death drive, the very excess of cruelty and suffering, that renders the fantasy of community depicted by the Frontispiece impossible.

Yet it is not the specter of transgression alone that makes the death drive so threatening. On the contrary, if it is true that every attempt at transgression merely ends up strengthening the symbolic order by reinforcing the fantasy that *jouissance* can be experienced only beyond the pleasure principle, then the death drive is in and of itself neither threatening nor radical. What makes the death drive threatening,

rather, is that it points up the poverty of transgression: the realization
that transgression ends, not in the achievement of *jouissance*, but in
the realization that *jouissance* is impossible—that the Thing itself is
utterly lacking. The Thing, recall, was created as such at the moment
of its prohibition. If not for the imposition of the symbolic order, there
would be no Thing—but neither would there be the need for the sus-
taining fantasy that the Thing might still be accessible if only it were
not prohibited. The Thing is that which is lacking in the symbolic
economy of lack. Yet in transgressing against the prohibition of the
Thing—in going beyond the pleasure principle—one merely discovers
that the lacking Thing is itself lacking: missing from the point at which
there ought to be lack. This is why, for Lacan, *jouissance* is ultimately
"the path toward death": because the death drive brings us to the point
of discovering that the very lack that grounds the symbolic order, the
lack that serves as a precondition for desire, is itself lacking.[19] What
we glimpse in the *Nebenmensch*, then, is not only a hostility directed
against us but the possibility of what Žižek calls the "radical effacement" of the symbolic order as a whole.[20]

It is for this reason that I find myself resisting the argument both
that Chaucer was a utopist and, conversely, that he "holds out no hope
for social amelioration."[21] Generally speaking, I agree with Marion
Turner not only that "Chaucer's engagement with the idea of antagonism is more profound than that of his contemporaries" but also that
he appears to have looked with skepticism upon the fantasy of a unified social or corporate body.[22] Part of what I have tried to show here,
in fact, is that the Frontispiece, insofar as it might be considered an interpretation of *Troilus and Criseyde*, is one that emphasizes the poem's
awareness that the consistency of the Other is a fantasy, a trick of our
immersion in the imaginary. At the same time, however, the retroactive exposure of the Thing through the effacement of the Richard
figure ends up revealing something just as important: namely, that
it was Chaucer himself—not the *Troilus* narrator, but Chaucer—who
isolated the alien and hostile Thing, and so exposed the lack of the
Other, through an act of judgment. Note the relationality of Chaucer
to the stain, for example. Now when the Chaucer in the Frontispiece
preaches, he addresses himself directly to the Thing lodged in the place

of the *Nebenmensch*: the place immediately next to him. The retroactive completion of the Frontispiece thus brings into view two Chaucers: the Chaucer that the artist(s) of the Frontispiece wanted us to see, and another Chaucer who holds on to the Thing where it appears, so to speak, on this, the "hither" side of the barrier. The significance of this "holding on" has already been hinted at in the passage from Žižek quoted above: it means that Chaucer affirms the *jouissance* already at work in the symbolic order, that he assumes responsibility for the moment of lawmaking violence recalled in the effacement of Richard. To the extent that he "preaches" the divided form of the Frontispiece, Chaucer thus affirms the reality of lack—the structural fact that an exchange has already happened, that a renunciation is already called for. But to the extent that he also addresses the empty place of the Thing—the place where the Richard figure is neither present nor absent—Chaucer brings the good news of a *jouissance* not based on sacrifice or transgression, an enjoyment that derives from something other than the violation of prohibitions, that isn't safely beyond the pleasure principle.

This act of addressing the Thing matters for two reasons. In the first place, it speaks directly to the question of critical practice. The isolation of the Thing in the Frontispiece, a retroactive gesture that in turn reveals Chaucer's own affirmation of the Thing, transforms the Frontispiece from a simple interpretation to a work of genuine critique: a work that brings out the truth of another work, and so helps it achieve a kind of "self-recognition," only through an act of destruction.[23] Coming to include the future element that decompletes its image of the present, revealing it already to be looking ahead to its own ruination, the Frontispiece ends up capturing an aspect of Chaucer overlooked by its original artist(s): his openness to the possibility of a community organized not around fantasies of specularity or the call to sacrifice but around a recognition of the Thing that makes community impossible. Second, the Frontispiece Chaucer's affirmation of the Thing assumes an aesthetic dimension, insofar as it allows us to reopen the question of what it means to call *Troilus and Criseyde* a tragedy. For the tragedy here, as we learn through the experience of the narrator, is that the political subject is invariably called upon to betray the Thing that haunts him. The price of remembrance, as Chaucer's poem makes only too clear, is always betrayal.

But as the Frontispiece's critique of *Troilus and Criseyde* also makes clear, there is always an alternative to such betrayal; for it is the Frontispiece that materializes, in its own decompleted composition, how the conjoined acts of reading and criticism might be understood as acts of neighbor love. Earlier, I tried to spell out my resistance both to the argument that "Chaucer . . . holds out no hope for social amelioration" and to the utopist claim that the "lies" promoted by Chaucer's *Troilus* "are wishful as well as willful, based on a hope for an impossible future" by suggesting that Chaucer in fact perceived something beyond the economy of lack, the economy of the "not now" and the "not yet," that antagonism and utopianism both perpetuate.[24] Another way of putting this would be to say that, with *Troilus and Criseyde*, Chaucer figured out a particular way of loving the neighbor as himself. This is a form of neighbor love, as the visual context of the Frontispiece seems to suggest, that comes down to holding on to the Thing, refusing either to give it up or to give up on it. This is a gesture, in the first place, of recognition—specifically, the recognition that the "fundamental evil/ suffering which dwells within [the] neighbor . . . also dwells within me."[25] The neighbor's drive to transgress against us, the strange desire of which he himself seems unaware, the *jouissance* he refuses to sacrifice: those things belong to us as much as to our neighbor. Indeed, our impulse to "cognize," as Freud puts it, is already an expression of the very death drive that we impute to the neighbor. This is no less true of our encounters with the neighboring text, the *jouissance* of which is reflected in our own impulse, as readers and critics, to subject that text to acts of destruction: to dissect it, to mortify it, to take it apart. For those, too, are acts of neighbor love: at once an acknowledgment and an enactment of the Thing one shares with the neighbor, the Thing that is one's neighbor.

NOTES

Introduction

1. Line 545. All references to Chaucer's work are to *The Riverside Chaucer*, gen. ed. Larry D. Benson (Boston: Houghton Mifflin, 1987).

2. W. H. Clemen writes of the dreamer's interactions with the eagle: "Nowhere in the works of Chaucer's early period do we ever again have so varied and amusing an instance of the poet's self-depreciation." *Chaucer's Early Poetry*, trans. C. A. M. Sym (London: Methuen, 1968), 90. On the possibility that *The House of Fame* offers us a privileged glimpse of Chaucer's working life as controller of customs, see Derek Pearsall, *The Life of Geoffrey Chaucer: A Critical Biography* (Oxford: Blackwell, 1992), 98–99.

3. Keith Wrightson, "The 'Decline of Neighbourliness' Revisited," in *Local Identities in Late Medieval and Early Modern England*, ed. Norman L. Jones and Daniel Woolf (New York: Palgrave, 2007), 27. I should note that Wrightson's focus is on the continuation of "medieval" forms of neighborliness into the early modern period and what that continuation might tell us about "the process of social change in the local communities of [that] period" (21). I should also stress that, in Wrightson's words, "the more abundant documentary evidence available from the sixteenth century offers us our first real opportunity to explore many types of social relationship that can only be conjectured from earlier centuries" (21).

4. Ibid., 23–26. As Wrightson puts it: "The neighbours alluded to in such sources as petitions, court depositions, diaries or letters are usually near-dwellers, fellow parishioners, tenants of the same manor, inhabitants of the same street and so on. Such neighbourhoods might or might not have clearly defined geographical parameters. They might be more, or less, institutionally structured. They were certainly not rigidly bounded, or autonomous: their members moved

for a variety of purposes in larger worlds and they were subject to external authorities. Yet, clearly, the common use of the term was indicative of a peculiarly significant kind of local social space, be it a nucleated village, the scattering of farmsteads in an upland valley, or one of the 'mosaic of neighborhoods' that constituted the city of London. To be accounted, a neighbour seems to have implied a specific sense of belonging; it conferred an identity through membership of a localized grouping" (23).

5. The only example I know of is Kenneth Reinhard, "Kant with Sade, Lacan with Levinas," *Modern Language Notes* 110, no. 4 (1995): 785–808. Individual citations alone cannot convey my indebtedness to Reinhard's groundbreaking essay.

6. I am thinking, in particular, of Patricia Clare Ingham, *Sovereign Fantasies: Arthurian Romance and the Making of Britain* (Philadelphia: University of Pennsylvania Press, 2001); Michelle Warren, *History on the Edge: Excalibur and the Borders of Britain, 1100–1300* (Minneapolis: University of Minnesota Press, 2000); Kathleen Biddick, *The Shock of Medievalism* (Durham: Duke University Press, 1998); and Kathleen Davis, *Periodization and Sovereignty: How Ideas of Feudalism and Secularization Govern the Politics of Time* (Philadelphia: University of Pennsylvania Press, 2008). And of course this is to say nothing of those works of feminist medievalism, such as Carolyn Dinshaw's *Chaucer's Sexual Poetics* (Madison: University of Wisconsin Press, 1989), Gayle Margherita's *The Romance of Origins: Language and Sexual Difference in Middle English Literature* (Philadelphia: University of Pennsylvania Press, 1994), and Jennifer Summit's *Lost Property: The Woman Writer and English Literary History, 1380–1589* (Chicago: University of Chicago Press, 2000), that have done so much to challenge masculinist paradigms of literary history.

7. Ethan Knapp, *The Bureaucratic Muse: Thomas Hoccleve and the Literature of Late Medieval England* (University Park: Pennsylvania State University Press, 2001), 107. "Despite recent debate over the content and function of literary canons, and despite theoretical critiques of organic, continuous historical models, the implicit frame within which we read and teach is still grounded, in the last resort, on notions of sources and influence thoroughly genealogical at their core," contends Knapp. "It is, indeed, hard to imagine a form of literary history that would not be genealogical." To his credit, though, Knapp himself does indeed try to imagine just such a nongenealogical form: a kind of "poetic usurpation" by which a belated writer like Hoccleve might "lay claim to an inherited poetic authority and also interrogate the notions of origins and authority that underwrite the idea of generational succession" (109).

8. As far as medieval commentators were concerned, "Any text which has anything to do with human behavior 'subponitur ethice' [is classified as ethics]," according to Judson Boyce Allen. By this reckoning, "Narrative poetry,

obviously, one must take as ethics; I have found in commentary on the *Thebaid* of Statius no exception to this rule. Ovid's *Heroides* are ethics; so is the *Facta et dicta* of Valerius Maximus, so is Boethius' *Consolation of Philosophy*, so, by clear implication, are at least some of the various genres of Languedoc lyric, so, by virtue of Dante's own accessus, is the *Divina commedia*, so, to descend into medieval trivia, are the pseudo-Virgilian *Copa* and John Garland's *Cornutus.*" Judson Boyce Allen, *The Ethical Poetic of the Later Middle Ages: A Decorum of Convenient Distinction* (Toronto: University of Toronto Press, 1982), 6, 10.

9. Jessica Rosenfeld, "Narcissus after Aristotle: Love and Ethics in *Le Roman de la Rose*," *New Medieval Literatures* 9 (2007): 2–3. "In a sense," argues Rosenfeld, "scholastic philosophy followed the lead of poetry, which had addressed issues of love, pleasure, and despair from the beginning of its entrée into romantic love. The ethical stakes of vernacular love poetry had always far exceeded the dutiful *ethica supponitur* with which medieval commentators tagged classical poetry, from Virgil to Ovid to Boethius. . . . By the time enjoyment became a main topic in philosophy, its terms and questions had been contemplated in poetry for quite some time."

10. See the introduction to Mark Miller, *Philosophical Chaucer: Love, Sex, and Agency in the "Canterbury Tales"* (Cambridge: Cambridge University Press, 2004), especially 14–19.

11. J. Allan Mitchell, *Ethics and Eventfulness in Medieval English Literature* (New York: Palgrave, 2009). I derive my definition of the event from Alain Badiou, *Ethics: An Essay on the Understanding of Evil*, trans. Peter Hallward (London: Verso, 2001): "Events are irreducible singularities, the 'beyond-the-law' of situations. Each faithful truth-process is an entirely invented immanent break within the situation" (44). But Mitchell's definition, borrowed from François Dastur, is also helpful: "The event in the strong sense of the word is . . . always a surprise, something which takes possession of us in an unforeseen manner, without warning, and which brings us toward an unanticipated future." François Dastur, "Phenomenology of the Event: Waiting and Surprise," *Hypatia* 15, no. 4 (2000): 182, quoted in Mitchell, *Ethics and Eventfulness*, 2. Mitchell's book came out just as I was finishing my own, and I regret that I was not able to engage with it more fully.

12. Although its focus is not on miscellaneity per se, the introduction to Elizabeth Scala's *Absent Narratives, Manuscript Textuality, and Literary Structure in Late Medieval England* (New York: Palgrave, 2002) articulates an understanding of manuscript culture that has been particularly influential on the one found here. As Scala writes, "The multiplicity of medieval texts appears not only in its various witnesses, but the medieval text is also 'multiple' in each of its singular manifestations. . . . The multiplicity and variation of texts in individually copied manuscripts also contribute to our overall picture of this culture,

offering here a snapshot of textual dissemination, something that takes its effect at the level of reception. . . . The issue, for us, is not—or not simply—the
difference between the literature of print culture and manuscript culture but
the differences within the texts of manuscript culture itself" (7–8).

13. On "the structure of the lineage family" as a "perceptual 'grid' . . . in
medieval historiography," see Gabrielle M. Spiegel, *The Past as Text: The Theory
and Practice of Medieval Historiography* (Baltimore: Johns Hopkins University
Press, 1997), 103. "While typology is possibly the most common organizing
'grid' in medieval historiography," writes Spiegel, "it is by no means the only
one, nor do they all originate in previously existing forms of thought. Another
perceptual 'grid,' more social than intellectual in origin, yet important for the
shape of vernacular history in thirteenth-century France, is the structure of the
lineage family, which expressed its existence in written form as genealogy. . . .

"Genealogy intrudes into historical narrative at precisely the time when
noble families in France where beginning to organize themselves into vertical
structures based on agnatic consanguinity, to take the form, in other words, of
lignages. . . . Written above all to exalt a line and legitimize its power, a medieval genealogy displays a family's intention to affirm and extend its place in
political life. . . . Whether aristocratic or royal, genealogies were expressions of
social memory and, as such, could be expected to have a particular affinity with
historical thought and, at least to a certain extent, to impose their consciousness
of social reality upon those whose task it was to preserve for future generations
images of society in the record of history" (103–4).

14. Wrightson, "'Decline of Neighbourliness' Revisited," 22.

15. Ibid., 20.

16. Ibid.

17. L. O. Aranye Fradenburg, *Sacrifice Your Love: Psychoanalysis, Historicism, Chaucer* (Minneapolis: University of Minnesota Press, 2002), 84.

18. Psychoanalysis has been "*in* medieval studies . . . in a variety of acknowledged and unacknowledged ways" for so long now as to allow for a verita-
ble Homeric catalog of medievalists whose work is informed by psychoanalytic
principles. Louise O. Fradenburg, "We Are Not Alone: Psychoanalytic Medievalism," *New Medieval Literatures* 2 (1998): 250. A partial list would include
the following: Fradenburg, *Sacrifice Your Love*; Paul Strohm, *England's Empty
Throne: Usurpation and the Language of Legitimation, 1399–1422* (New Haven:
Yale University Press, 1998) and *Theory and the Premodern Text* (Minneapolis:
University of Minnesota Press, 2000), esp. ch. 11, "What Can We Know about
Chaucer That He Didn't Know about Himself?"; Jeffrey Jerome Cohen, *Of
Giants: Sex, Monsters, and the Middle Ages* (Minneapolis: University of Min-
nesota Press, 1999) and *Medieval Identity Machines* (Minneapolis: University
of Minnesota Press, 2003), esp. ch. 3, "Masoch/Lancelotism," and ch. 6, "On

Saracen Enjoyment"; Patricia Clare Ingham, *Sovereign Fantasies* and "Amorous Dispossessions: Knowledge, Desire, and the Poet's Dead Body," in *The Post-historical Middle Ages*, ed. Elizabeth Scala and Sylvia Federico (New York: Palgrave, 2009), 13–35; Scala, *Absent Narratives*, as well as Scala's indispensable "Historicists and Their Discontents: Reading Psychoanalytically in Medieval Studies," *Texas Studies in Literature and Language* 44, no. 1 (2002): 108–31; Sylvia Federico, *New Troy: Fantasies of Empire in the Late Middle Ages* (Minneapolis: University of Minnesota Press, 2003); Sarah Kay, *Courtly Contradictions: The Emergence of the Literary Object in the Twelfth Century* (Stanford: Stanford University Press, 2001); Miller, *Philosophical Chaucer*; Erin Felicia Labbie, *Lacan's Medievalism* (Minneapolis: University of Minnesota Press, 2006); Britton J. Harwood, "Psychoanalytic Politics: Chaucer and Two Peasants," *ELH* 68, no. 1 (2001): 1–27; and Peter W. Travis, "White," *Studies in the Age of Chaucer* 22 (2000): 1–66.

19. Fradenburg, in particular, has several important things to say about the status of the neighbor in psychoanalysis, in medieval studies, and in the Chaucerian text, most of which inform the argument I am trying to develop here. See especially, in *Sacrifice Your Love*, ch. 5, "Loving Thy Neighbor: *The Legend of Good Women*," 176–98 and 37–39, as well as, to a lesser degree, ch. 3, "The Ninety-six Tears of Chaucer's Monk." There is an obvious overlap between the figure that I call "the neighbor" and the "intimate stranger" of Cohen's pioneering *Of Giants*. If I have opted to use the former term and not the latter, it is largely because the neighbor is a figure developed by both Freud and Lacan. In my view, this lends the concept a stronger theoretical foundation while at the same time more firmly connecting psychoanalysis to the Western religious and philosophical traditions. The neighbor, moreover, embodies a paradox that the stranger does not. Where any encounter with the stranger is, by definition, out of the ordinary, even marvelous, our encounters with the neighbor are fundamentally quotidian—and thus all the more unsettling for their uncanniness. The stranger is strange. The neighbor is both strange and familiar. It is therefore all the more disturbing when the neighbor appears to be not only a stranger to himself but the site of our own self-estrangement. See Cohen, *Of Giants*, esp. the introduction, "The Intimate Stranger," xi–xx.

20. What makes Jesus's parable so radical, according to Reinhard, is that it treats the lawyer's "typically Talmudic" question ("And who is my neighbor?") "as an ontological question: what *is* a neighbor, that is, who merits inclusion into the category of the Neighbor, now, moreover, meaning the subject as much as the object of 'compassion' (Luke 10:33). Jesus transforms the Levitical scenario of *having* a neighbor to whom you owe love . . . into the metaphysical imperative to *become* a neighbor." Kenneth Reinhard, "Freud, My Neighbor," *American Imago* 54, no. 2 (1997): 169–70.

21. Sigmund Freud, *Project for a Scientific Psychology,* in *The Complete Standard Edition of the Psychological Works of Sigmund Freud,* ed. and trans. James Strachey (London: Hogarth Press, 1966), 1:331.

22. Jacques Lacan, *The Ethics of Psychoanalysis, 1959–60,* trans. Dennis Porter, Seminar 7 (New York: Norton, 1997), 52.

23. Kenneth Reinhard, "Toward a Political Theology of the Neighbor," in Slavoj Žižek, Eric L. Santner, and Kenneth Reinhard, *The Neighbor: Three Inquiries in Political Theology* (Chicago: University of Chicago Press, 2005), 32.

24. Sigmund Freud, "The Uncanny," in *Complete Standard Edition,* 17:222–23.

25. Ibid., 225–26.

26. Sigmund Freud, *Beyond the Pleasure Principle,* in *Complete Standard Edition,* 18:17.

27. I mean for *imaginary* and *real* in this case to carry their full Lacanian weight, with the former designating the order of spatial and visual relations and involving the subject in fantasies of wholeness, cohesion, totality, and closure, and the latter designating the realm of materiality—of all that is fixed, stubborn, absolutely resistant to symbolization. If the imaginary provides us with the illusory comforts of the ego, the real confronts us with the horror of being flesh.

28. Augustine, *On Christian Doctrine,* trans. D. W. Robertson Jr. (Upper Saddle River, NJ: Prentice-Hall, 1958), 2:40.

29. Paul Zumthor, *Speaking of the Middle Ages,* trans. Sarah White (Lincoln: University of Nebraska Press, 1986), 28–29.

30. Kenneth Reinhard, "Kant with Sade," 785.

31. Freud, *Beyond the Pleasure Principle,* 18:14–17.

32. Ingham, *Sovereign Fantasies,* 8.

33. Ibid., 9.

34. See Andrew Taylor, *Textual Situations: Three Medieval Manuscripts and Their Readers* (Philadelphia: University of Pennsylvania Press, 2002). "The field of manuscript studies has often been seen as an intensely conservative one, not least by its practitioners, who are much given to presenting it as a bastion of certainty against the rages of modernity and the over-ingenuity of literary critics," writes Taylor, who continues: "But this is not how I would choose to justify my interest. The three manuscripts I examine offer not some absolute origin but rather a testimony to the complexity of textual production and a measure of the difference between our cultural categories and those of earlier times" (9). Taylor is even more pointed a few pages later: "By stabilizing the textual tradition and isolating 'literary' texts from the diversity of their earlier circulation, traditional textual editing has produced an origin for vernacular literature. It has excerpted texts from their codices in accordance with generic categories that are central to

Romantic philology, concentrating on those vernacular texts that most readily conform to the category of 'literature,' secular poetry expressing the genius of a people and the creative imagination of the artist" (13).

35. Warren, *History on the Edge,* 2 and passim.

36. This would be a highly reductive distillation of Žižek's argument in *The Sublime Object of Ideology* (London: Verso, 1989). See esp. 30–33 and 118–28.

37. "If intensified (almost) to the point of unpleasure, pleasure, now in the form of *jouissance,* shares pain's ability to focus subjectivity on the fact of its sentience and therefore on its embodiment," explains Fradenburg. *"Jouissance* is the point at which pleasure and pain crisscross, when there are no more objects, and the only thing left for desire to desire is the unknowable beyond of insentience. With the loss of its objects, the *I* also loses its self-presence—or, at least, the vulnerability of its self-presence becomes felt experience. Pleasure protects us from *jouissance* by delivering as much *jouissance* as the *I* can bear and still be there to bear it." *Sacrifice Your Love,* 18.

38. Lacan, *Ethics of Psychoanalysis,* 150.

39. Žižek, *Sublime Object of Ideology,* 118.

40. Fradenburg has been stressing this point for some time now, and nowhere more urgently than in *Sacrifice Your Love.* The core argument of that book, as I understand it, is that medieval studies intersects with chivalric techniques of living at the point where both disciplines teach—or perhaps simply allow—their subjects to turn sacrifice into its own, highly attenuated, not to mention aestheticized, form of *jouissance.* Reading Fradenburg's visionary work, it is not always clear (at least not to me) whether she allows for any line of flight away from this dynamic, other than yet another act of sacrifice, this time of the sacrifice (of *jouissance*) itself. What I am proposing is that the imperative to neighbor love provided medieval subjects with just such a line of flight, and one that did not involve still more sacrifice. This held true, moreover, regardless of whether that imperative was (mis)interpreted as a version of the Golden Rule or a call to altruism, precisely because the real remains embedded in the literal wording of the imperative itself. There was always, at the core of medieval life, an immanent alternative to the enjoyment of sacrifice, always an alternative to the dialectic of prohibition and transgression. Now whether this represents a departure from Fradenburg's argument or an extension of it, I cannot quite say. Perhaps it is neither one nor the other, or a bit of both. At any rate, I would resist reducing, as Fradenburg tends to do, the neighbor relation to yet another form of group identity (as on p. 32, for example).

41. Ingham, *Sovereign Fantasies,* 2.

42. Žižek, *Sublime Object of Ideology,* 47.

43. Sigmund Freud, *Civilization and Its Discontents,* in *Complete Standard Edition,* 21:109.

44. Ibid.

45. Ibid., 21:110.

46. Ibid., 21:112, 125–26.

47. Lacan, *Ethics of Psychoanalysis*, 186.

48. M. S. Kempshall, *The Common Good in Late Medieval Political Thought* (Oxford: Clarendon Press, 1999), 105.

49. *Speculum Christiani*, ed. Gustaf Holmstedt, EETS, o.s., 182 (London: H. Milford, 1933), 1.

50. Ibid., 38.

51. Eric L. Santner, *On the Psychotheology of Everyday Life* (Chicago: University of Chicago Press, 2001), 36.

52. Eric L. Santner, *On Creaturely Life: Rilke, Benjamin, Sebald* (Chicago: University of Chicago Press, 2006), 33.

53. Reinhard, "Toward a Political Theology," 31.

54. For the concept of "petrified unrest," see Santner, *On Creaturely Life*, 81.

55. Reinhard, "Freud, My Neighbor," 183. As Lacan puts it, "My neighbor possesses all the evil Freud speaks about, but it is no different from the evil I retreat from in myself. To love him, to love him as myself, is necessarily to move toward some cruelty. His or mine?, you will object. But haven't I just explained to you that nothing indicates they are distinct?" Lacan, *Ethics of Psychoanalysis*, 198.

56. Alenka Zupančič, *Ethics of the Real: Kant, Lacan* (London: Verso, 2000), 225.

57. As Freud famously says of the Rat Man: "At all the more important moments while he was telling his story his face took on a very strange, composite expression. I could only interpret it as one of *horror at pleasure of his own of which he himself was unaware.*" Sigmund Freud, "Notes on a Case of Obsessional Neurosis," in *Complete Standard Edition*, 10:166.

58. On this point, see Slavoj Žižek, *The Fragile Absolute—Or, Why Is the Christian Legacy Worth Fighting For?* (London: Verso, 2000), 107–13.

59. As Lacan puts it, "The resistance to the commandment 'Thou shalt love thy neighbor as thyself' and the resistance that is exercised to prevent [the subject's] access to *jouissance* are one and the same thing." *Ethics of Psychoanalysis*, 194. I have found Paul Moyaert's commentary on Lacan's understanding of neighbor love very helpful: "Responding to my neighbor according to the extreme description offered by Freud brings me into contact with that in the other which the light of the good and grace cannot penetrate. In a certain respect, it therefore concerns not *his*, but *my Hilflosigkeit* [helplessness]. For, indeed, what would it mean to seek the good for someone to whom it is inaccessible? And the problem with this is not so much that I must let go of my own subjective representations of the good and so far as possible accede to his obscure desires.

It is not a question here of whether or not I am prepared to set aside or shift my subjective limits of the good. I come up against the limits of the good as such, against that for which I cannot open myself. In the love of the neighbor, it is not a question of whether I can accept *what* the other desires and whether I can agree with it. I must instead relate to what it is impossible for me to admit and accept—and not because it is irreconcilable with my representations but instead because it simply is unacceptable and objectionable. In order to clarify this, Lacan appeals to the example of radical evil and speaks of '*la jouissance nocive*.' In other words, in love of the neighbor, I must relate myself to something unbearable and unforgivable, to '*le hors-signifié*,' to what can only awaken in me reactions of aggression, offence, hate, and aversion whenever it comes close to me. At the limit of the unbearable, there arises love of the neighbor." Paul Moyaert, "Lacan on Neighborly Love: The Relation to the Thing in the Other Who Is My Neighbor," *Epoché* 1 (1996): 25.

60. On this point, see Reinhard: "The 'hearing' of the commandments, in Lacan's expression, should not be understood only as the reception and transmission of their message, but implies as well an incomprehensible speech that takes place in the present, not as the mediation of a past event but as an ever-renewed revelation that, Lacan writes, we 'cannot help hearing.' In such a structure, the fore-runner becomes a neighbor, not father-to-son but shoulder-to-shoulder, no longer the source of a distant memory but the fellow participant in a traumatic experience of singularity. . . .

"Freud's horror at the commandment [to love thy neighbor as thyself] not only colors his rejection of an injunction that asks something unreasonable and even irresponsible, but is also symptomatic of the presence of the neighbor in and as the commandment itself. In *The Ethics of Psychoanalysis*, Lacan encounters the commandment as itself Freud's neighbor, not merely latent in Freud's thinking as its repressed ground in a genealogy of morals, but 'in Freud more than Freud,' a piece of Scriptural discourse that enters Freud's writing as neither cancelled nor acknowledged, but as the unassimilated remnant of the historical processes of annulment and recognition." "Freud, My Neighbor," 189–90.

61. Lacan, *Ethics of Psychoanalysis*, 188.

62. Here again I am drawing on Reinhard: "To have a neighbor means to put myself in the neighbor's place, to substitute myself for him or her—not to imagine myself as like my neighbor, to constitute myself as his or her mirror or antithesis, but to serve my neighbor's *jouissance*, no matter how strange or traumatic or not to my 'taste' it may be." "Kant with Sade," 801.

63. "Can we imagine a practice of reading," asks Reinhard, "not instead of, but preliminary to, comparison, a mode of interpretation that would begin by asking what the responsibility of one text to another is, and, in turn, of a reader to a text? If the relationships produced by critical juxtaposition first imply and

conceal the traumatic fact of proximity without resemblance, hence both a singularity of encounter and an infinity of responsibility for that encounter, would this nearness take priority to and restrict the self-sameness of each text, the fixity of its place in literary genealogy, the autonomy of its reader, and the rationality of possible intertextual or comparative relationships?" Ibid., 796.

64. One of those directions is suggested by Nicholas Perkins's essay "Haunted Hoccleve? *The Regiment of Princes*, the Troilean Intertext, and Conversations with Dead," *Chaucer Review* 43, no. 2 (2008): "For Hoccleve . . . Chaucer's sometimes painful absence, sometimes reverent presence, work at these multiple levels, as a contributor to anxiety or lack, but also as an impetus to the development of Hoccleve's own poetic identity. . . . If Hoccleve is haunted, then the ghost of father Chaucer is 'gentle' as well as forbidding, and that wider textual hauntology proposed in Derrida's reading of Marx can also provide a model for the shady intertextual relations between the *Regiment* and *Troilus and Criseyde* as they inhabit overlapping spaces, each changed by the other's presence, and each spending time with the dying author, divided self, and therapeutic dialogue of *De consolatione Philosophiae*; in these texts, the spectral author certainly '(re)pays us a visit'" (120–21).

65. Federico, *New Troy*, 2, 3.

66. David Wallace, *Chaucerian Polity: Absolutist Lineages and Associational Forms in England and Italy* (Stanford: Stanford University Press, 1997), 179.

67. Sheila Lindenbaum, "The Smithfield Tournament of 1390," *Journal of Medieval and Renaissance Studies* 20, no. 1 (1990): 10.

68. Regarding the location of Smithfield "outside the city to the north," see Caroline M. Barron, *London in the Later Middle Ages* (Oxford: Oxford University Press, 2004), 52.

69. Federico, *New Troy*, 19–28.

70. Richard Maidstone, *Concordia (The Reconciliation of Richard II with London)*, ed. David R. Carlson, trans. A. G. Rigg (Kalamazoo, MI: Medieval Institute Publications, 2003), 39.

71. Pamela Nightingale, "Capitalists, Crafts and Constitutional Change in Late Fourteenth-Century London," *Past and Present* 124 (1989): 34, quoted in Carlson, introduction to Maidstone, *Concordia*, 2.

72. Marion Turner, *Chaucerian Conflict: Languages of Antagonism in Late Fourteenth-Century London* (Oxford: Clarendon Press, 2007), 60.

73. "Ethnic and racial violence, Žižek argues, is an attempt to snatch or destroy ('strike a blow against') what might be called the 'unbearable surplus-enjoyment' of the other," writes Cohen. "Powerful fantasies structure the relationship between subjects and their own 'lost' enjoyment, which (against all evidence to the contrary) they see as being possessed by this other. . . .

"Enjoyment in the Other saturates *The Sultan of Babylon*, a text that invokes almost every medieval fantasy about the exorbitance of Islam. The Sultan

Laban hoards a wealth beyond measure, and a key scene involves his daughter commanding that the royal treasury be hurled over the city walls to confound her own father's army. Saracen maidens willingly offer their bodies to Christian men. Abundant food, drink, sex, and magic characterize Sultan culture." Cohen, *Medieval Identity Machines*, 213–14.

74. Slavoj Žižek, *The Indivisible Remainder: An Essay on Schelling and Related Matters* (London: Verso, 1996), 93.

75. Lee Patterson, *Chaucer and the Subject of History* (Madison: University of Wisconsin Press, 1991), 200.

76. On this point, see Santner, *On Creaturely Life*, 17.

77. Reinhard, "Toward a Political Theology," 20.

78. Walter Benjamin, "Theologico-Political Fragment," quoted in Reinhard, "Toward a Political Theology," 20.

79. Carla Freccero, *Queer/Early/Modern* (Durham: Duke University Press, 2006), 70.

80. Michel de Certeau, *The Writing of History*, trans. Tom Conley (New York: Columbia University Press, 1988), 2. Under such a necrological regime, Freccero argues, "the others, ghosts of historiography, do indeed haunt the present, but the response to that haunting is a kind of anxious appeasement." Against this model of necrological historiography, Freccero proposes a counter-model based on the Derridean categories of spectrality and hauntology. "Spectrality is, in part, a mode of historicity," she argues: "it describes the way in which the time is out of joint; that is, the way the past or the future presses upon us with a kind of insistence or demand, a demand to which we must somehow respond. 'Hauntology' as the practice of attending to the spectral, is then a way of thinking and responding ethically within history, as it is a way of thinking ethics in relation to the project of historiography by acknowledging the force of haunting." *Queer/Early/Modern*, 70–71.

81. Freccero, *Queer/Early/Modern*, 71.

82. I borrow the phrase "deposits of suffering" from Eric Santner. Every act of succession carried out at the world-historical level, insofar as it perpetuates the violence inherent in the process of a Benjaminian "natural history," leaves behind "deposits" of suffering, remainders that then serve to "depose" the symbolic order by acting as so many "depositions": testaments that bear witness, by their very muteness or inertness, to an ongoing history of violence. See Santner, *On Creaturely Life*, 95, but also see 114–15.

83. Lacan, *Ethics of Psychoanalysis*, 114.

84. Walter Benjamin, "Theses on the Philosophy of History," in *Illuminations: Essays and Reflections*, trans. Harry Zohn (New York: Schocken Books, 1968), 262.

85. Lacan, *Ethics of Psychoanalysis*, 71, 139. The concept of *extimacy* has a widespread currency in medieval studies. See, for example, Cohen, *Of Giants*

("The monster exposes the *extimité*, the 'extimacy' or 'intimate alterity,' of identity: its inescapable self-estrangement, the restless presence at its center of everything it abjects in order to materialize and maintain its borders. To be fully human is to disavow the strange space that the inhuman, the monstrous, occupies within every speaking subject" [4]), and Gila Aloni, "Extimacy in the *Miller's Tale*," *Chaucer Review* 41, no. 2 (2006): 163–84.

86. Žižek, for example, describes symbolic death variously as "the 'settling of accounts'" and "the accomplishment of symbolic destiny." See *Sublime Object of Ideology*, 135.

87. On the matter of Cligès between two deaths, see Kay, *Courtly Contradictions*, 216–58. For Lancelot, Tristan, and Cligès (again), see Simon Gaunt, *Love and Death in Medieval French and Occitan Courtly Literature* (Oxford: Oxford University Press, 2006), 104–37. On Richard II, see Strohm, *England's Empty Throne*, 101–27. On Antigone and the ghost of Hamlet's father, see Žižek, *Sublime Object of Ideology*, 135.

88. Strohm, *England's Empty Throne*, 101, 103.

89. Lee Patterson, review of *England's Empty Throne*, by Paul Strohm, *Studies in the Age of Chaucer* 22 (2000): 542.

90. Lacan, *Ethics of Psychoanalysis*, 248.

91. Žižek, *Sublime Object of Ideology*, 135.

92. Ibid., 135.

93. Lacan, *Ethics of Psychoanalysis*, 295.

94. Ibid., 248.

95. See Robert Henryson, the *Testament of Cresseid*, lines 8 and 28. All references to Henryson's works are to the edition by Denton Fox, *The Poems of Robert Henryson* (Oxford: Clarendon Press, 1981).

96. See Giovanni Boccaccio, *Il Filostrato*, Proem, p. 7. All references to *Il Filostrato* are to the dual-language edition by Robert P. apRoberts and Anna Bruni Seldis (New York: Garland, 1986).

97. As Laplanche and Pontalis explain, "It is not lived experience in general that undergoes a deferred revision but, specifically, whatever it has been impossible in the first instance to incorporate fully into a meaningful context. The traumatic event is the epitome of such unassimilated experience." J. Laplanche and J.-B. Pontalis, *The Language of Psychoanalysis*, trans. Donald Nicholson-Smith (New York: Norton, 1973), 112.

CHAPTER 1.   Henryson's Doubt

1. Such descriptions of the *Testament* are commonplace. Representative examples might include the following: Douglas Gray, *Robert Henryson* (Leiden:

Brill, 1979), 170 ("continuation" and "companion"); Derek Pearsall, *Old and Middle English Poetry* (London: Routledge, 1977), 276 ("sequel"); Barry Windeatt, *Troilus and Criseyde*, Oxford Guides to Chaucer (Oxford: Clarendon Press, 1992), 369 ("sequel" and "pendant"); Gregory Kratzmann, *Anglo-Scottish Literary Relations, 1430–1550* (Cambridge: Cambridge University Press, 1980), 63 ("dependent"); Melvin Storm, "The Intertextual Cresseida: Chaucer's Henryson or Henryson's Chaucer?" *Studies in Scottish Literature* 28 (1993): 119 ("sequel"); C. David Benson, "Critic and Poet: What Lydgate and Henryson Did to Chaucer's *Troilus and Criseyde*," in *Writing after Chaucer: Essential Readings in Chaucer and the Fifteenth Century*, ed. Daniel J. Pinti (New York: Garland, 1998), 235 ("Rather than retell the love story so that it becomes more conventional, Henryson produces a new narrative that is fully worthy of its source"); and Nicholas Watson, "Outdoing Chaucer: Lydgate's *Troy Book* and Henryson's *Testament of Cresseid* as Competitive Imitations of *Troilus and Criseyde*," in *Shifts and Transpositions in Medieval Narrative: A Festschrift for Elspeth Kennedy*, ed. Karen Pratt, Penny Eley, and Elspeth Kennedy (Cambridge: D. S. Brewer, 1994), 91 ("The process of supplanting England's nearest thing to a classical epic was—for these writers and their contemporaries—a kind of *translatio auctoritatis*: a necessary displacement of a literary father in the very texts that defined him as such for centuries"). Opposed to this is an important countertradition, in which the *Testament* is read as a "critical" or "dialectical" rewriting of the *Troilus*. See, for example, A. C. Spearing, *Medieval to Renaissance in English Poetry* (Cambridge: Cambridge University Press, 1985), 167–68; Florence H. Ridley, "A Plea for the Middle Scots," in *The Learned and the Lewed: Studies in Chaucer and Medieval Literature*, ed. Larry D. Benson (Cambridge, MA: Harvard University Press, 1974), 175–81, 196; and R. James Goldstein, "Writing in Scotland, 1058–1560," in *The Cambridge History of Medieval British Literature*, ed. David Wallace (Cambridge: Cambridge University Press, 1999), 240–41.

2. Gayle Margherita, "Criseyde's Remains: Romance and the Question of Justice," *Exemplaria* 12 (2000): 274. Margherita asserts, as a way of buttressing her own argument, that "several readers have noted . . . a filial relationship between Henryson's work and Chaucer's."

3. Reinhard, "Toward a Political Theology," 20.

4. Katherine H. Terrell, "Subversive Histories: Strategies of Identity in Scottish Historiography," in *Cultural Diversity in the British Middle Ages: Archipelago, Island, England*, ed. Jeffrey Jerome Cohen (New York: Palgrave, 2008), 153–72.

5. Robert Henryson, *Testament of Cresseid*, 61–63. All references to Henryson's works are to the edition by Denton Fox, *The Poems of Robert Henryson* (Oxford: Clarendon Press, 1981).

6. See, for example, the excerpts from these writers in *Chaucer: The Critical Heritage*, vol. 1, *1385–1837*, ed. Derek Brewer (London: Routledge and Kegan Paul, 1978).

7. Nicholas Watson makes a similar point when he writes that, "in spite of a challenge to the older writer, 'Chauceir' and 'sum poeit' indeed emerge from this stanza [lines 64–70] as colleagues, not as senior and junior ('poeit' is a term of dignity)." Watson, "Outdoing Chaucer," 104.

8. Seth Lerer, *Chaucer and His Readers: Imagining the Author in Late-Medieval England* (Princeton: Princeton University Press, 1993), 3, but see also 14–16.

9. For a concise account of Thynne's edition and its influence, see Windeatt, *Troilus and Criseyde*, 369.

10. Louise O. Fradenburg, "The Scottish Chaucer," in Pinti, *Writing after Chaucer*, 168.

11. Emmanuel Levinas, *Otherwise Than Being, or Beyond Essence*, trans. Alphonso Lingis (Pittsburgh: Duquesne University Press, 1998), 86–89, 99–102, and passim.

12. Fradenburg, "Scottish Chaucer," 175.

13. Walter Scheps, "A Climatological Reading of Henryson's *Testament of Cresseid*," *Studies in Scottish Literature* 15 (1980): 81.

14. Spearing, *Medieval to Renaissance*, 166.

15. Scheps, "Climatological Reading," 81.

16. Ibid., 82.

17. Ibid.

18. Walter Bower, *Scotichronicon*, gen. ed. D. E. R. Watt (Aberdeen: Aberdeen University Press, 1996), 7.13.25, pp. 19–51.

19. Sigmund Freud, *Civilization and Its Discontents*, in *Complete Standard Edition*, 21:110.

20. Along these same lines, Scheps notes that "the Scottish attitude is perhaps best summarized by James III, who, in noting the reluctance of his magnates to support the truce with England, concluded that the Scots were 'so made they could not agree with the English.'" Scheps, "Climatological Reading," 80.

21. Beryl Smalley, *English Friars and Antiquity in the Early Fourteenth Century* (New York: Barnes and Noble, 1960), 13–14.

22. Ibid., 13. In Gray's own words: "Si deueint corious et penßiue, com geris nauoit en le hour autre chos afair, a treter et a tranßlater en plus court sentence lez cronicles del Graunt Bretaigne, et lez geßtez dez Engleßßez." Sir Thomas Gray, *Scalacronica: A Chronicle of England and Scotland*, ed. J. Stevenson (Edinburgh, 1836), 2.

23. Smalley, *English Friars and Antiquity*, 13.

24. Žižek, *Sublime Object of Ideology*, 126.

25. See John H. Fisher, "A Language Policy for Lancastrian England," *PMLA* 107, no. 5 (1992): 1173–74, 1176–77, 1178. It is perhaps worth noting that Lydgate's *Troy Book*, which Fisher cites, was one of the more enthusiastic vehicles of that promotion.

26. Freud, *Civilization and Its Discontents*, in *Complete Standard Edition*, 21:110.

27. On this point, see Terrell, "Subversive Histories," 160–63 and passim.

28. Jacques Lacan, *The Four Fundamental Concepts of Psychoanalysis*, trans. Alan Sheridan, Seminar 11 (New York: Norton, 1981), 35.

29. Joan Copjec, *Read My Desire: Lacan against the Historicists* (Cambridge, MA: MIT Press, 1994), 121.

30. Ibid., 122.

31. Ibid., 121.

32. For the complete transcript of the dream of Irma's injection (parts of which I have quoted here) and, more important, for Freud's analysis of it, see *The Interpretation of Dreams*, in *Complete Standard Edition*, 4:106–21.

33. Copjec, *Read My Desire*, 123.

34. Ibid., 122–23.

35. "Shall I say that Freud makes one more step . . . when he invites us to integrate in the text of the dream what I shall call the *colophon of doubt*—the colophon, in an old text, is that small pointing hand that used to be printed, back in the days when we still had a typography, in the margin" (Lacan, *Four Fundamental Concepts*, 44). Lacan, speaking off the cuff, is confusing his terms. He says *colophon*, but what he describes is a manicule. I am grateful to Liz Scala for calling this to my attention.

36. Margherita, "Criseyde's Remains," 257.

37. See Boccaccio, *Il Filostrato*, 8.29-30.

38. See Geoffrey Chaucer, *Troilus and Criseyde*, 5.1807–27.

39. Suggesting that Lydgate and Henryson were each "attempting to rectify a different absence in *Troilus*," C. David Benson writes that the "Chaucerian absence that Henryson wants to fill is the narrator's admission that he does not know what Criseyde felt in her heart toward Diomede and the refusal of *Troilus* to tell the end of her story" ("Critic and Poet," 228).

40. Julia Kristeva, *Powers of Horror: An Essay on Abjection*, trans. Leon S. Roudiez (New York: Columbia University Press, 1982), 16, quoted in Felicity Riddy, "'Abject Odious': Feminine and Masculine in Henryson's *Testament of Cresseid*," in *The Long Fifteenth Century: Essays for Douglas Gray*, ed. Helen Cooper and Sally Mapstone (Oxford: Clarendon Press, 1997), 246 n. 41. It may seem, given this essay's obvious debt to Riddy's, like an exercise in theoretical hairsplitting to quibble with the latter's characterization of Cresseid as abject, in the Kristevan sense of the term: excluded matter that stands "for the danger to identity that

comes from without: the ego threatened by the non-ego, society threatened by its outside; life by death" (Kristeva, quoted in Riddy, "Abject Odious," 234 n. 10). As I see it, however, the fact that Cresseid's abject status has been conflated with the neighboring text's unsettling desire emphasizes that the problem for the *Testament* is not a simple one of inside versus outside. The problem, rather, is that the outside, the object as rejected matter, is never truly that: outside. As the category of the neighbor suggests, we seek to impute to the outside, to the other, what we in fact recognize to be the most intimate, horrible truth about our own being. Negation, rejection, is forever linked with affirmation, inclusion.

41. On this point, see Jana Mathews, "Land, Lepers, and the Law in *The Testament of Cresseid*," in *The Letter of the Law: Legal Practice and Literary Production in Medieval England*, ed. Emily Steiner and Candace Barrington (Ithaca: Cornell University Press, 2002), 49–51.

42. Much of Cresseid's actual testament, we should recall, is given over to the most mundane of legal procedures: distributing property.

43. Copjec, *Read My Desire*, 121.

44. Another way of addressing Cresseid's status is to consider where she goes, the spaces she occupies, over the course of the poem. The court, the oratory, the hospital, and, finally, the tomb all serve as metaphors for Cresseid's awkward position: marginal, abject and alone, yet always fully inside, incorporated into some structure. Far from being excluded, Cresseid can't seem to escape, either from judgment or from enclosed spaces implying judgment.

45. Copjec, *Read My Desire*, 121.

46. Saul Brody, *The Disease of the Soul: Leprosy in Medieval Literature* (Ithaca: Cornell University Press, 1974), 176–77.

47. For a provocative reading of these lines, see James Simpson, *The Oxford English Literary History*, vol. 2, *1350–1547: Reform and Cultural Revolution* (Oxford: Oxford University Press, 2002), 189.

48. Spearing, *Medieval to Renaissance*, 178. For a more detailed description of the laws governing lepers in the late Middle Ages, see Mathews, "Land, Lepers," 57–58.

49. I take the term *bare life* or *mere life* from Giorgio Agamben's analysis and elaboration of Walter Benjamin's "Critique of Violence," in *Homo Sacer: Sovereign Power and Bare Life* (Stanford: Stanford University Press, 1998). Benjamin's "analysis of this figure [i.e., the figure of bare life]," writes Agamben, "establishes a link between bare life and judicial violence. Not only does the rule of law over the living exist and cease to exist alongside bare life"; bare life also hastens "the dissolution of juridical violence," insofar as the punishment "purifies," according to Benjamin, "the guilty, not of guilt, however, but of law," thereby calling the justice and efficacy, even the legality, of the law into question. Agamben, *Homo Sacer*, 65. "With mere life," writes Benjamin, "the rule of

law over the living ceases," meaning not that they somehow elude the law but that their reduction to mere life reveals the extralegal violence embodied in the law itself. Bare life means that one is subject not to the law but to the extralegal sovereign suspension of the law. See Walter Benjamin, "Critique of Violence," in *Reflections: Essays, Aphorisms, Autobiographical Writings*, ed. Peter Demetz, trans. Edmund Jephcott (New York: Schocken Books, 1986), 297. I also have in mind Paul Strohm's interpretation of "bare life" as "life stripped down and prepared for the imposition of symbolic meaning"—an accurate enough description of Cresseid's state at this point in the *Testament*. Paul Strohm, *Politique: Language of Statecraft between Chaucer and Shakespeare* (Notre Dame: University of Notre Dame Press, 2005), 209.

50. See Spearing, *Medieval to Renaissance*, 173; and Margherita, "Criseyde's Remains," 279.

51. Riddy, "Abject Odious," 243.

52. "In the exercise of violence over life and death . . . ," writes Benjamin, "law reaffirms itself. But in this very violence something rotten in law is revealed." Benjamin, "Critique of Violence," 286. Can one not associate Cresseid's leprous flesh with that "something rotten"?

53. Reinhard, "Freud, My Neighbor," 177.

54. Several readers have found Cresseid's punishment to be cruel, excessive, or unjust. See, for example, A. C. Spearing, *Criticism and Medieval Poetry*, 2nd ed. (New York: Barnes and Noble, 1972), 189; Lee Patterson, "Christian and Pagan in *The Testament of Cresseid*," *Philological Quarterly* 52 (1973): 700–703; Simpson, *Reform and Cultural Revolution*, 189; and Mathews, "Land, Lepers," 54–57.

55. Introduction to Henryson, *Testament of Cresseid*, ed. Denton Fox (London: Thomas Nelson and Sons, 1968), 30–31.

56. Lacan, *Ethics of Psychoanalysis*, 178.

57. Reinhard, "Freud, My Neighbor," 187–88.

58. Fox, *Poems of Robert Henryson*, 342 n. 34.

59. On Henryson's use of *doolie*, see Fox, *Poems of Robert Henryson*, 38 n. 1.

60. Although I am not the first to note them: Gregory Kratzmann has written that "the figure who is prevented by the cold (both external and internal) from praying to Venus is clearly associated with the character whose story he is about to tell." Kratzmann likewise points out that "the link between heroine and narrator is underlined by the metaphors of flowering and fading which are applied to both, in the 'doolie season' in which the narrative is set." Kratzmann, *Anglo-Scottish Literary Relations*, 76.

61. This is a paraphrase of Lacan, *Ethics of Psychoanalysis*, 186.

62. Spearing, *Medieval to Renaissance*, 179.

63. For a powerful critique of "the getting-of-wisdom reading" of the *Testament*, see Riddy, "Abject Odious," 237–39.

64. Riddy defines those subject positions as "the 'I' of the moralizing mirror, as it occurs in *The Three Dead Kings* or *The Buke of the Howlat*; the *ubi sunt* 'I' from the Body and Soul tradition; the testamentary 'I' of contemporary wills; the 'I' of the forsaken woman, as in Chaucer's *Anelida and Arcite*; the 'I' of the outcast." Ibid., 244.

65. Regarding Cresseid's epitaph, see Spearing, *Medieval to Renaissance*, 171.

66. Riddy, "Abject Odious," 248.

67. Much of my thinking in this section has been inspired by Jeffrey Cohen's meditations on megaliths and giants' teeth in "Time Out of Memory," in *The Post-historical Middle Ages*, ed. Elizabeth Scala and Sylvia Federico (New York: Palgrave, 2009), 37–57.

68. Lacan, *Ethics of Psychoanalysis*, 188.

69. On Benjamin's concept of redemption, see Reinhard, "Toward a Political Theology," 20.

70. Derek Pearsall, "'Quha wait gif all that Chauceir wrait was trew?': Henryson's *Testament of Cresseid*," in *New Perspectives on Middle English Texts: A Festschrift for R. A. Waldron*, ed. Susan Powell and Jeremy J. Smith (Cambridge: D. S. Brewer, 2000), 177.

71. Lacan, *Ethics of Psychoanalysis*, 186.

72. R. James Goldstein, *The Matter of Scotland: Historical Narrative in Medieval Scotland* (Lincoln: University of Nebraska Press, 1993). See especially chs. 2 and 3, 57–103.

73. Ibid., 58, 63–64.

74. Ibid., 66–73.

75. *Anglo-Scottish Relations, 1174–1328, Some Selected Documents*, ed. and trans. E. L. G. Stones (Oxford: Clarendon Press, 1965), 225–27. Commenting on the Scots' legal strategy, Goldstein notes that "the appeal to a specifically Scottish legend enables the Scots to derive their origins from a parent race as old as the Trojan remnant. The parallel even extends to the historical role fulfilled by each parent race: both "losers" in their narrative settings, the Egyptians and the Trojans yet achieved their destiny in the West by founding a daughter race of conquerors." Goldstein, *Matter of Scotland*, 74.

76. Margherita, "Criseyde's Remains," 273.

77. Fradenburg, *Sacrifice Your Love*, 38.

CHAPTER 2.   *Fremde* and Neighbor

1. *Chaucer Life-Records*, ed. Martin M. Crow and Clair C. Olson (Oxford: Clarendon Press, 1966). Those records relevant to Chaucer's two known journeys to Italy are on 32–40 and 53–61. I rely heavily, both for its narrativization of

these events and for its learned speculations about their significance, on Pears-all's *Life of Geoffrey Chaucer*, 102–9.

2. C. S. Lewis, "What Chaucer Really Did to *Il Filostrato*," in *Chaucer's "Troilus": Essays in Criticism*, ed. Stephen A. Barney (Hamden, CT: Archon Books, 1980), 39.

3. Wallace, *Chaucerian Polity*, 395 n. 2. A variation on the theme is offered by Derek Brewer: "Chaucer responded both consciously and unconsciously to the stimulus of Italy. It was exactly what he needed to reinforce his own characteristic attitudes and interests. . . . Italy has always had a vividness and splendour for certain types of Englishmen. The milder air and bluer sky warm and loosen their responses and clarify their minds. The splendour of Italian cities and art, the liveliness of ordinary life, vivify more northern temperaments." Continuing this "awakening of the Englishman" motif, Brewer goes on to list the many ways that Italy, which "led European cultural life" in the fourteenth century, would likely have impressed Chaucer. Derek Brewer, *Chaucer and His World* (New York: Dodd, Mead, 1978), 124–25.

4. Wallace, *Chaucerian Polity*, 13.

5. Taken together, the detailed studies by David Wallace and Barry Windeatt amply demonstrate that, as Wallace puts it, "Chaucer—unlike many of his modern critics—was a serious student of the Italian language, not just a cheerful dilettante." "Comparative study of the *Filostrato* and *Troilus and Criseyde* suggests that Chaucer's understanding of Italian was extraordinarily acute . . . ," argues Wallace. "It appears that Chaucer, in reading the *Filostrato*, was concerned not simply to catch the drift of a given stanza, but to analyze and worm his way into the language from which the stanza is fashioned. Before transforming the *Filostrato*, Chaucer understood what the *Filostrato* meant." David Wallace, *Chaucer and the Early Writings of Boccaccio* (Woodbridge: D. S. Brewer, 1985), 107. Likewise, Windeatt contends that, "when they are compared, it soon becomes clear that for long stretches *Troilus* follows *Filostrato* so closely that Chaucer must have worked with a copy of the Italian in front of him as he created the draft of his poem: so much of the outline of *Troilus* is in fact the outline of *Filostrato*. The distribution of narrative and dialog into stanzas is identical in the two poems for substantial stretches: over and over again, the first line of Chaucer's stanzas is very closely rendered from the parallel Italian line, stanza by stanza. . . . There is much syntactical closeness in such passages, and also a very real and sustained lexical influence from Italian." Barry Windeatt, "Chaucer and the *Filostrato*," in *Chaucer and the Italian Trecento*, ed. Piero Boitani (Cambridge: Cambridge University Press, 1983), 164.

6. Freud, "Constructions in Analysis," in *Complete Standard Edition*, 23:258–59.

7. Reinhard, "Kant with Sade," 804. By "originary non-relation," Reinhard means not that there exists a stable point of origin but that there is "no original common ground" shared by texts prior to "the act of comparison that symbolizes their relations" within a family of texts. Extrapolating somewhat, I am suggesting that an originary nonrelation also obtains between readers and the neighboring text: that they share no common ground prior to the moment of ethical encounter. What we get instead is a chain of originary moments—ruptures and discontinuities—grounded, like subjectivity itself, in the reader's traumatic encounter with the Thing in the *Nebenmensch*.

8. For this conception of the neighbor, and of the neighboring text derived from it, see the Introduction. On the related matter of *Il Filostrato*'s isolation from the traditions familiar to Chaucer at the time, I refer to Maria Gozzi, who observes that "in design, in tone and even in size the *Filostrato* is a work that is very different from medieval narratives ('storie') of Troy." Maria Gozzi, "Sulle fonti del *Filostrato:* Le narrazioni di argomento troiano," *Studi sul Boccaccio* 5 (1968): 126, quoted in Wallace, *Chaucer and the Early Writings*, 74.

9. Reinhard, "Toward a Political Theology," 31.

10. John Gower, *Mirour de l'Omme (The Mirror of Mankind)*, trans. William Burton Wilson (East Lansing, MI: Colleagues Press, 1992), lines 25, 429–25, 452.

11. Lacan, *Ethics of Psychoanalysis*, 198.

12. Lewis, "What Chaucer Really Did," 37.

13. My thinking here is indebted to Paul Strohm's meditations on the multiple temporalities of *Troilus and Criseyde*. See the chapter "Chaucer's *Troilus* as Temporal Archive," in his *Theory and the Premodern Text*, 80–96.

14. Gregory B. Stone, *The Death of the Troubadour: The Late Medieval Resistance to the Renaissance* (Philadelphia: University of Pennsylvania Press, 1994), 3.

15. On the privileging of particular situations over general categories, and on the definition of fidelity as the decision to think the situation according to the event, see Badiou, *Ethics*, 41 and passim.

16. Ibid., 52, but see also 47.

17. Freud, *The Ego and the Id*, in *Complete Standard Edition*, 19:29–30. For an influential elaboration of the (latent) political implications of Freud's theory, see Judith Butler, *The Psychic Life of Power: Theories in Subjection* (Stanford: Stanford University Press, 1997), 190–91.

18. Santner, *On Creaturely Life*, 24. "The meaning of *excitare*," Santner reminds us, is "to call or summon out."

19. Ibid., 15.

20. On the relationship between *Il Filostrato* and the *cantari*, see Wallace, *Chaucer and the Early Writings*, 76–93.

21. Wallace, *Chaucerian Polity*, 52.

22. Here is the original Italian:

da piú utile consiglio mosso, mutai proposto e pensai di volere con alcuno onesto ramarichio dare luogo a quella e uscita del tristo petto, acciocché io vivessi e vi potessi ancora vedere e piú lungamente vostro dimorassi vivendo. Né prima tal pensiero nella mente mi venne, che il modo subitamente con esso m'occorse; del quale avvenimento, quasi da nascosa divinitá spirato, certissimo augurio presi di futura salute. E il modo fu questo: di dovere in persona d'alcuno passionato si come io era e sono, cantando narrare li miei martiri.

Mecco adunque con sollicita cura cominciai a rivolgere l'antiche storie per trovare cui io potessi fare scudo verisimilmente del mio segreto e amoroso dolore. Né altro piú atto nella mente mi venne a tale bisogno, che il valoroso giovane Troiolo, figliuolo di Priamo nobilissimo re di Troia, alla cui vita, in quanto per amore e per lontananza della sus donna fu dolorosa, se fede alcuna alle antiche lettere si puó dare, poi che Criseida da lui sommamente amata fu al suo padre Calcas renduta, é stata la mia similissima dopo la vostra partita. Per che della persona di lui e de' suoi accidenti ottimamente presi forma alla mia intenzione, e susseguentement in leggier rima e nel mio fiorentino idioma, con stilo assai pietoso, li suoi e li miei dolori parimente compuosi; li quali e una e altra volta cantando, assai gli ho utili trovati secondo che fu nel principio l'avviso.

23. Donald R. Howard, *Chaucer: His Life, His Works, His World* (New York: Fawcett Columbine, 1987), 198. Giulia Natali also makes a case for the innovativeness of *Il Filostrato*. See "A Lyrical Version: Boccaccio's *Filostrato*," in *The European Tragedy of Troilus*, ed. Piero Boitani (Oxford: Clarendon Press, 1989), 50–51.

24. For what has become the definitive account of the relationship between identification and ideology, see Žižek, *Sublime Object of Ideology*, 100–110. One important aspect of identification that must be stressed at the outset is the primacy of symbolic identification over imaginary identification. This is a situation nicely summarized by Phillippe Julien, as follows:

Even before birth, the child is inscribed in a symbolic universe that determines its place. Indeed, the symbolic order subordinates the imaginary, and the speech that names the subject in the Other (locus of signifiers) eventually coincides with the vision of the other. The imaginary alienation, in which the subject *sees* his or her desire in the image of the other, is coupled with symbolic alienation, in which the subject's desire is *recognized* as desire of the Other's desire. The subject sees the ego in the ideal ego, but without recognizing it there. However, on the return trip the subject can, by means of the *speech* that answers the subject's demand for love, come to recognize himself or herself in what he or she sees. Thus the third, symbolic element situates the subject at a point where his or her own image is "fixed."

To the symbolic introjection of the ego-ideal into the ego, there comes to correspond an imaginary projection of the ego into the ideal ego. Such is the incessant movement of *going and coming* that marks the history of the subject.

Phillippe Julien, *Jacques Lacan's Return to Freud*, trans. Devra Beck Simiu (New York: New York University Press, 1994), 50. I emphasize this primacy of symbolic identification only to suggest how a radical act of imaginary identification, an identification not sanctioned by the symbolic, can imply, paradoxically, a lack of symbolic domination.

25. As Reinhard puts it: "It is not that aggressivity is a primal force overcome by the civilizing motives of society, but rather, aggressivity is simultaneously repudiated and produced as murderous enjoyment by the identifications that create the common-places of a community." Reinhard, "Freud, My Neighbor," 178.

26. In the original:

Icist Daires dont ci oëz
Fu de Troie norriz e nez;
Dedenz esteit, onc n'en eissi
Desci que l'oz s'en departi;
Mainte proëce i fist de sei
E a asaut e a tornei.
En lui aveit clerc merveillos
E des set arz esciëntos:
Por ço qu'il vit si grant l'afaire
Que ainz ne puis ne fu nus maire,
Si voust les faiz metre en memoire:
En grezeis en escrist l'estoire.
Chascun jor ensi l'escriveit
Come il o ses ieuz le veeit.
Tot escriveit la nuit apres
Icist que je vos di Dares:
Onc por amor ne s'en voust taire
De la verté dire e retraire.
Por ço, s'il ert des Troïens,
Ne s'en pendié plus vers les suens,
Ne mais que vers les Grezeis fist:
De l'estoire le veir escrist.

Lonc tens fu sis livres perduz,
Qu'il ne fu trovez ne veüz;
Mais a Athenes le trova
Cornelius, quil translata:
De greu le torna en latin
Par som sen e par son engin.
Mount en devons mieuz celui creire
E plus tenir s'estoire a veire
Que celui qui puis ne fu nez
De cent anz o de plus assez,
Qui rien n'en sot, iço savon,
Se par oïr le dire non.

(Pr. 93–128)

All references to Benoît de Sainte-Maure's *Roman de Troie* are to the edition by Léopold Constans, 6 vols. (Paris: Firmin-Didot, 1904–12). The translation is taken from the abridged version by R. K. Gordon, in *The Story of Troilus* (Toronto: University of Toronto Press, 1978), 3–22.

27. A. J. Minnis, *Chaucer and Pagan Antiquity* (Woodbridge: D. S. Brewer, 1982), 22.

28. "What is my desire?" asks Lacan. "What is my position in the imaginary structuration? This position is only conceivable in so far as one finds a guide beyond the imaginary, on the level of the symbolic plane, of the legal exchange which can only be embodied in the verbal exchange between human beings. This guide governing the subject is the ego-ideal." Jacques Lacan, *Freud's Papers on Techniques, 1953–1954*, trans. John Forrester, Seminar 1 (New York: Norton, 1991), 141.

29. Žižek, *Sublime Object of Ideology*, 109.

30. On Chaucer approaching *Il Filostrato* as a "historical poet," see Lewis, "What Chaucer Really Did," 40.

31. Wallace, *Chaucer and the Early Writings*, 74.

32. Benjamin, "Theses on the Philosophy of History," in *Illuminations*, 262.

33. Ibid., 263–65.

34. Slavoj Žižek, *For They Know Not What They Do: Enjoyment as a Political Factor* (London: Verso, 1991), 266–67.

35. "From the very beginning," notes Boitani, "Troilus is an epic figure who lives in an exclusively tragic dimension. It is his death, and his death alone, that interests classical art and that part of the medieval tradition which is directly or indirectly influenced by it. From the epic cycles collected in the *Kypria* to Homer . . . and on to Joseph of Exeter in the twelfth [century] and Albert von Stade in the thirteenth, to the *Ovid Moralisé* and the erudite Boccaccio of the

Amorosa Visione, the *De Casibus,* the *Genealogie,* and the *Esposizioni* on the *Divine Comedy,* the constant feature of Troilus' figure is his death at the hands of Achilles." Troilus, Boitani argues, "is not primarily a character but a 'function.' He is his death and the fall of Troy in that war which, being the first and most famous of all, constitutes the archetypal World War." Piero Boitani, "Antiquity and Beyond: The Death of Troilus," in Boitani, *European Tragedy of Troilus,* 2–3, 5.

36. Santner, *On Creaturely Life,* 18.

37. Walter Benjamin, *The Origin of German Tragic Drama,* trans. John Osborne (London: Verso, 1977), 233.

38. Santner, in his excavations of what he calls the "creaturely" dimension of human life, argues that the notion of a messianic "awakening" found in Benjamin's work "should be understood not as a resurrection, an animation of the dead, but . . . as *a deanimation of the undead,* an interruption of the 'ban,' the captivation at work in the spectral fixations—the petrified unrest—that cringes/curves the psychic space of human subjects." *On Creaturely Life,* 88.

39. Troilo, to put the matter somewhat differently, is transformed, through the narrator's creative act of identification, into *homo sacer:* the figure that can be killed (repeatedly, in this case) but not sacrificed, the figure toward whom every man can act as sovereign. Identifying with the other but not substituting himself for the other, assuming the place of the one made prostrate for love, but only up to a point, the narrator ironically, inadvertently, transforms himself not into the *homo sacer* with whom he identifies but into its obverse: the sovereign.

40. Of interest is this description of Troilus's funeral from *The Laud Troy Book,* a paraphrase of Guido dating from about 1400, the year of Chaucer's death:

> The Troyens haue at Gregays ben,
> And trew is taken hem be-twen.
> And precious tombe for Troyle was wrought,
> And his body ther-In was broght;
> And leyde him ther-In bischopis thre
> With wonder gret solempnite:
> Ther was for him a riche offerynges
> Off Erles, Dukes, and of kynges.
> . . . .
> And whan that seruice was al y-done
> To her mete thei wente sone,
> Thei dight hem to her mete.

The Laud Troy Book, ed. J. Ernst Wülfing, EETS, o.s., 121–22 (London: Kegan Paul, 1902), 15, 245–15, 259. This is, admittedly, a more detailed "account" of

Troilus's burial than Guido provides (the mourners are even served dinner). Yet therein lies its value, since the elaboration here gives us a stronger sense of what Chaucer's immediate contemporaries would have expected by way of "proper" symbolic internment, complete with "bischopris thre," "riche offerynges," and "gret solempnite."

41. In the Italian:

O giovinetti, ne' quai con l'etate
surgendo vien l'amoroso disio
per Dio vi priego che voi raffreniate
i pronti passi all'appetito rio,
e nell'amor di Troiol vi specchiate,
il qual dimostra suso il verso mio;
per che, se ben col cuor gli leggerete,
non di leggieri a tutte crederete.

42. See, for example, Barbara Nolan's chapter "From History into Fiction: Boccaccio's *Il Filostrato* and the Question of Foolish Love," in her *Chaucer and the Tradition of the "Roman Antique"* (Cambridge: Cambridge University Press, 1992), 119–54; and Natali, "Lyrical Version," 49–73.

43. Natali, "Lyrical Version," 73.

44. Ibid., 60.

45. Giorgio Agamben, *Stanzas: Word and Phantasm in Western Culture*, trans. Ronald L. Martinez (Minneapolis: University of Minnesota Press, 1993), 20.

46. Lacan, *Ethics of Psychoanalysis*, 320.

47. Žižek, *Sublime Object of Ideology*, 135.

48. Lacan, *Ethics of Psychoanalysis*, 257–83.

49. Žižek, *Sublime Object of Ideology*, 132.

50. "And it is because we know better than those who went before how to recognize the nature of desire . . . ," says Lacan, "that a reconsideration of ethics is possible, that a form of ethical judgment is possible, of a kind that gives this question the force of a Last Judgment: Have you acted in conformity with the desire that is in you?" Lacan, *Ethics of Psychoanalysis*, 314.

51. Freud, *Interpretation of Dreams*, in *Complete Standard Edition*, 5:430–31.

52. Zupančič, *Ethics of the Real*, 172–73.

53. On the significance of Troilus's name, Boitani (*European Tragedy of Troilus*, 5) is worth quoting at some length:

"Troilus" is the hypocoristic, i.e. the pet-name of "Tros," Troy's eponymous hero, the mythological figure who gave his name to the city. Troilus—for some the son not of Priam but of Apollo himself—represents the very origin of his town and bears her name. . . . If we were medieval etymologists we could try to play with Troilus' name in two different ways. One could see it, on the one hand, as the sum and conflation of "Tros" and "Ilos," Troy's founders. One could also, on the other, speculate on a more fanciful association of "Troiï," the city of Troy, and the verb *lyÿ*, which means "to destroy," "to annihilate." These are of course mere games. But there is no doubt that the ancients were aware of the connection between "Troilus" and Troy's fate. There are, says Chrysalus in Plautus's *Bacchides*, "three fateful events which will prove Troy's downfall": the disappearance of the Palladium from the citadel, the tearing away of the upper lintel of the Phrygian gate, and "Troili mors"—the death of Troilus.

Elsewhere, Boitani notes that "a prophecy reported by the First Vatican Mythographer states that if Troilus reached the age of twenty Troy could not be destroyed. This is of course partly tied to his name, but in a peculiar fashion. Troilus, who bears his city's name, cannot achieve an age that would allow him to perpetuate the species by begetting children. 'Troy' must die with him." Boitani, "Antiquity and Beyond," 4–5.

54. Federico, *New Troy*, xii.

55. Ibid., xii.

56. Sylvia Federico, "Old Stories and New Trojans: The Gendered Construction of English Historical Identity" (PhD diss., Indiana University, 1997), 1. John Gower was one of those contemporaries; so were the Carmelite Richard Maidstone, author of the *Concordia facta inter regem Riccardum II et civitatem Londonie*, Nicholas Brembre, the sometime mayor of London, and Richard II. See Federico, *New Troy*, 3–6.

57. Lacan, *Four Fundamental Concepts*, 22.

58. Patterson, *Chaucer and the Subject*, 123.

59. I have in mind here those lines from book 5 of *Troilus and Criseyde*:

And for ther is so gret diversite
In Englissh and in writyng of oure tonge,
So prey I God that non myswrite the,
Ne the mysmetre for defaute of tonge;
And red wherso thow be, or elles songe,
That thow be understonde, God I biseche!
(5.1793–99)

60. Žižek, *Sublime Object of Ideology*, 133, 135.

61. Zupančič, *Ethics of the Real*, 144.

62. Copjec, *Read My Desire*, 118.

63. Zupančič, *Ethics of the Real*, 145.

64. Monica E. McAlpine, *The Genre of "Troilus and Criseyde"* (Ithaca: Cornell University Press, 1978), 116.

65. Henry Ansgar Kelly, *Chaucerian Tragedy* (Cambridge: D. S. Brewer, 1997), 40.

66. Benjamin, *Origin of German Tragic Drama*, 107. On the "germ of authentic tragedy" in *Troilus and Criseyde*, see McAlpine, *Genre*, 117.

67. This point is made, in virtuoso fashion, by D. Vance Smith in "Crypt and Decryption: *Erkenwald* Terminable and Interminable," *New Medieval Literatures* 5 (2002): 59–85. The custodians of Chaucer's "tomb" in Poets' Corner have likewise long understood the importance of a foundational tomb. See Thomas A. Prendergast, *Chaucer's Dead Body: From Corpse to Corpus* (New York: Routledge, 2004), and the chapter "At Chaucer's Tomb: Laureation and Paternity in Caxton's Criticism," in Lerer, *Chaucer and His Readers*.

68. See Paul Strohm, review of *Chaucerian Tragedy*, by Henry Ansgar Kelly, *Journal of English and Germanic Philology*, 98, no. 2 (1999): 259.

69. Julia Reinhard Lupton, "Tragedy and Psychoanalysis: Freud and Lacan," in *A Companion to Tragedy*, ed. Rebecca Bushnell (Malden, MA: Blackwell, 2005), 96–97.

70. Lewis, "What Chaucer Really Did," 38–39.

71. See, for example, Bruce Holsinger, *The Premodern Condition: Medievalism and the Making of Theory* (Chicago: University of Chicago Press, 2005), 79–82.

72. Lacan, *Ethics of Psychoanalysis*, 136.

73. Kay, *Courtly Contradictions*, 270.

74. Jacques Lacan, *On Feminine Sexuality, the Limits of Love and Knowledge, 1972–1973*, trans. Bruce Fink, Seminar 20 (New York: Norton, 1998), 69.

75. Reinhard, "Toward a Political Theology," 51.

76. Bruce Fink, *The Lacanian Subject: Between Language and Jouissance* (Princeton: Princeton University Press, 1995), 111.

77. Reinhard, "Toward a Political Theology," 58–59.

78. Santner, *On Creaturely Life*, 31.

79. Lacan, *Ethics of Psychoanalysis*, 150.

80. Mladen Dolar, "At First Sight," in *Gaze and Voice as Love Objects*, ed. Renta Salecl and Slavoj Žižek (Durham: Duke University Press, 1996), 132–33, 134.

81. James Simpson, "Chaucer as a European Writer," in *The Yale Companion to Chaucer*, ed. Seth Lerer (New Haven: Yale University Press, 2006), 75.

82. Karl Marx, *Capital*, vol. 1, trans. Eden Paul and Cedar Paul (London: Everyman's Library, 1957), 371–72.

83. To paraphrase Badiou's definition of the event. See his *Ethics*, 42–43.

84. See E. Talbot Donaldson, "The Ending of *Troilus*," in his *Speaking of Chaucer* (New York: Norton, 1970), esp. 99–100.

85. Reinhard, "Freud, My Neighbor," 172.

86. Lacan, *Ethics of Psychoanalysis*, 152.

87. Fradenburg offers a typically luminous meditation on this aspect of courtly love in *Sacrifice Your Love*, 40–41.

88. Lacan, *On Feminine Sexuality*, 83. For a concise account of the Other *jouissance* and its role in courtly love, see Bruce Fink, *Lacan to the Letter: Reading "Écrits" Closely* (Minneapolis: University of Minnesota Press, 2004), 162.

89. On the deficiencies of phallic *jouissance*, and the related matter of the imaginary compensations of the Other *jouissance*, see Fink, *Lacan to the Letter*, 155–158.

90. Spearing, *Medieval to Renaissance*, 12.

91. See, for example, the seminal essays by Morton W. Bloomfield, "Distance and Predestination in *Troilus and Criseyde*" and "Chaucer's Sense of History," in his *Essays and Explorations: Studies in Ideas, Language, and Literature* (Cambridge, MA: Harvard University Press, 1970), 200–216 and 12–26 respectively; John P. McCall, "The Trojan Scene in Chaucer's *Troilus*," in *Critical Essays on Chaucer's "Troilus and Criseyde" and His Major Early Poems*, ed. C. David Benson (Toronto: University of Toronto Press, 1991), 57–67; Patterson, *Chaucer and the Subject*, esp. ch. 2; Federico, "Old Stories," esp. ch. 1.

92. My frame of reference here is that of Emmanuel Levinas in *Time and the Other:* "The future is what is in no way grasped. The exteriority of the future is totally different from spatial exteriority precisely through the fact that the future is absolutely surprising. Anticipation of the future and projection of the future, sanctioned as essential to time by all theorists from Bergson to Sartre, are but the present of the future and not the authentic future; the future is what is not grasped, what befalls us and lays hold of us. The other is the future. The very relationship with the other is the relationship with the future." Emmanuel Levinas, *Time and the Other*, trans. Richard A. Cohen (Pittsburgh: Duquesne University Press, 1987), 76–77.

93. A. J. Gurevich, *Categories of Medieval Culture*, trans. G. L. Campbell (London: Routledge and Kegan Paul, 1985), 125.

94. I take the phrase "impossible present" from Paul Strohm. See "Chaucer's *Troilus* as Temporal Archive," in *Theory and the Premodern Text*, 81.

95. Simpson, *Reform and Cultural Revolution*, 1.

96. My use of the term *gaze* may require some clarification. I do not mean the all-encompassing, panoptic gaze typically associated, in Anglo-American critical discourse, with early film theory. I mean the gaze that Lacan, in *Four Fundamental Concepts*, situates in the place of the Other's inscrutable desire. As Joan Copjec has put it:

Lacan does not ask you to think of the gaze as belonging to an Other who cares about what or where you are, who pries, keeps tabs on your whereabouts, and takes note of all your steps and missteps, as the panoptic gaze is said to do. When you encounter the gaze of the Other, you meet not a seeing eye but a blind one. The gaze is not clear or penetrating, not filled with knowledge or recognition; it is clouded over and turned back on itself, absorbed in its own enjoyment. The horrible truth, revealed to Lacan by Petit-Jean, is that *the gaze does not see you*. So, if you are looking for confirmation of the truth of your being or the clarity of your vision, you are on your own; the gaze of the Other in not confirming; it will not validate you.

Copjec, *Read My Desire*, 36. Lacan himself has this to say in *Four Fundamental Concepts*: "From the outset, we see, in the dialectic of the eye and the gaze, that there is no coincidence, but, on the contrary, a lure. When, in love, I solicit a look, what is profoundly unsatisfying and always missing is that—*you never look at me from the place from which I see you*" (102–3).

97. All references to *Il Teseida* are to the translation by N. R. Havely in *Chaucer's Boccaccio: Sources of "Troilus" and the Knight's and Franklin's Tales* (Woodbridge: D. S. Brewer, 1980).

98. Lacan, *Four Fundamental Concepts*, 95.

99. M. Bloomfield, "Distance and Predestination," 207.

100. On the matter of a work's outward "material contents" as containing its "truth content," see Walter Benjamin's early essay "Goethe's Elective Affinities," in Walter Benjamin, *Selected Writings*, vol. 1, *1913–1926*, ed. Marcus Bullock and Michael W. Jennings (Cambridge, MA: Belknap Press, 1996), 298.

101. See the chapter "The *Knight's Tale* and the Crisis of Chivalric Identity," in Patterson, *Chaucer and the Subject*, 165–230.

102. Jennifer Summit comes to a similar conclusion, but from a materialist perspective: "If Chaucer is the first poet to dare to place English writing alongside the classical canon, this placement also reveals their incommensurability. Not only the changeable nature of a living language but also the contingency of manuscript culture make the English text an eminently unstable entity" (*Lost Property*, 49).

CHAPTER 3. Troilus and Criseyde between Two Deaths

1. Patrick J. Geary, *Living with the Dead in the Middle Ages* (Ithaca: Cornell University Press, 1994), 1; Bruce Gordon and Peter Marshall, eds., *The Place of the Dead: Death and Remembrance in Late Medieval and Early Modern Europe* (Cambridge: Cambridge University Press, 2000), 6.

2. B. Gordon and Marshall, *Place of the Dead*, 4–5.

242 Notes to Pages 136–138

3. Ibid., 8. B. Gordon and Marshall cite the examples of C. Platt, *King Death: The Black Death and Its Aftermath in Late-Medieval England* (London: UCL Press, 1996), 105–7, and R. N. Swanson, *Religion and Devotion in Europe, c. 1215–c. 1515* (Cambridge: Cambridge University Press, 1995), 233–34.

4. Jean-Claude Schmitt, *Ghosts in the Middle Ages: The Living and the Dead in Medieval Society*, trans. Teresa Lavender Fagan (Chicago: University of Chicago Press, 1998), 5.

5. Quoted in B. Gordon and Marshall, *Place of the Dead*, 3.

6. See the Introduction.

7. Schmitt, *Ghosts in the Middle Ages*, 186.

8. "The Fifth Commandment ['Honor thy father and thy mother'] both introduces human dealings and contrasts the exclusive familial scene that unfolds over time with the incessantly contemporary, necessarily accidental, and singularly interchangeable experience of the neighbor." Reinhard, "Freud, My Neighbor," 188.

9. John M. Bowers, *The Politics of "Pearl": Court Poetry in the Age of Richard II* (Cambridge: D. S. Brewer, 2001). See especially chs. 6 and 8.

10. Ibid., 125.

11. Ibid., 126.

12. Ibid., 162, 156.

13. That Chaucer's poetry is fundamentally commemorative—and thus also, at some level, forgetful—was noted by L. O. Aranye Fradenburg as far back as 1990. See her "'Voice Memorial': Loss and Reparation in Chaucer's Poetry," *Exemplaria* 2, no. 1 (1990): 171 and passim.

14. Whatever his amount of direct knowledge of the classical tradition, or even of classical notions of tragedy, Chaucer clearly grasped that there was something terrible about a body left suspended between two deaths. Kathy Lavezzo, for example, argues that the *Clerk's Tale* subverts the medieval rhetoric of death as leveler through its potentially radical concern with "everyday death," including the vulnerability of unburied peasant bodies. "Chaucer and Everyday Death: The *Clerk's Tale*, Burial, and the Subject of Poverty," *Studies in the Age of Chaucer* 23 (2001): 255–87. More immediately, Catherine Sanok has shown just how significant it is that Criseyde and her female companions should be reading from Statius's *Thebaid* when Pandarus comes to inform Criseyde of Troilus's love in book 2. "Statius' epic seems at first an extraordinary text to give to female characters," notes Sanok. "But the *Thebaid* departs from traditional epic in addressing a specifically female perspective, both in Hypsipyle's long narrative of the anger of the Lemnian women at being abandoned by their warring husbands . . . and in the final book of the poem, *which recounts the grief of the Argive women who have been prevented from burying their dead by the tyrant Creon*." Catherine Sanok, "Criseyde, Cassandre, and the *Thebaid*: Women and

the Theban Subtext of Chaucer's *Troilus and Criseyde*," *Studies in the Age of Chaucer* 20 (1998): 42–43, my italics.

15. Steve Ellis, "The Death of the *Book of the Duchess*," *Chaucer Review*, 29, no. 3 (1995): 253, 256.

16. Schmitt, *Ghosts in the Middle Ages*, 173.

17. Ibid., 194.

18. For a wonderfully sly and subtle treatment of the "Is he or isn't he?" question of Troilus's status as a virtuous pagan, see Frank Grady, *Representing Righteous Heathens in Late Medieval England* (New York: Palgrave, 2005), 103–9.

19. As Fradenburg puts it: "Troy's desire *wants* to let the 'traitor' out of its sight and thus let the death drive run loose in the world." *Sacrifice Your Love*, 229. Josephine Bloomfield makes a similar point when she observes that "the deepest irony is that when Troilus is able to carry on his affair [with Criseyde], the effects on him appear to be extremely advantageous for the polity: he is more noble, more courageous, a better leader, a better friend, in every way a better member of the polis. His fighting ability, inspired by his love, would probably be of much more value to Troy than Antenor's (if indeed Antenor were loyal rather than a traitor). . . . Again, Chaucer seems to be suggesting that polities at times blindly advance the wrong set of values, demanding sacrifices in areas where such sacrifice actually hinders rather than furthers their goals." Josephine Bloomfield, "Chaucer and the Polis: Piety and Desire in the *Troilus and Criseyde*," *Modern Philology* 94, no. 3 (1997): 296.

20. Windeatt, *Troilus and Criseyde*, 235. See also his essay "Chaucer and the *Filostrato*," 172.

21. The classic statement of this position is that of Mary F. Wack: "Love figured as an illness is of course a commonplace of medieval literature." "Lovesickness in *Troilus*," *Pacific Coast Philology* 19 (1984): 55. For a comprehensive treatment of the subject, see her *Lovesickness in the Middle Ages: The "Viaticum" and Its Commentaries* (Philadelphia: University of Pennsylvania Press, 1990).

22. Windeatt speaks of "the added reference to death" in *Troilus and Criseyde*, noting that "Chaucer floods his translating with an alertness to death: death that the lovers feel; death until which and beyond they will endure." "Chaucer and the *Filostrato*," 172. A. C. Spearing, meanwhile, notes that "Troilus's life has been a mere rehearsal for death, so that death, when it comes, even so senselessly, is felt as a fulfilment . . . a logical culmination of his living dedication to death." A. C. Spearing, *Chaucer: "Troilus and Criseyde"* (London: Edward Arnold, 1976), 31. Stephen A. Barney likewise refers to "Troilus' death wish." Stephen A. Barney, "Troilus Bound," in *Chaucer's "Troilus and Criseyde": "Subgit to alle Poesye*," ed. R. A. Shoaf (Binghamton, NY: Medieval and Renaissance Texts and Studies, 1992), 11 n. 30, but see also 11–12.

23. Boitani, "Antiquity and Beyond," 5.

24. Žižek, *Sublime Object of Ideology*, 135.

25. Lacan, *Ethics of Psychoanalysis*, 83.

26. Patterson, *Chaucer and the Subject*, 86.

27. Indeed, I agree with Patterson that Chaucer's poem goes "far beyond the *Filostrato* in exploring the idea of antiquity—not in its own right precisely (whatever that might mean) but rather for what it could tell him about his own place in historical time." *Chaucer and the Subject*, 84.

28. C. David Benson, *The History of Troy in Middle English Literature* (Woodbridge: D. S. Brewer, 1980), 134.

29. "Once human life has sunk into the merely creaturely," notes Benjamin, "even the life of apparently dead objects secures power over it." And a bit later: "The passionate stirrings of creaturely life in man—in a word, passion itself—bring the fatal property into the action." Benjamin, *Origin of German Tragic Drama*, 132.

30. Sigmund Freud, "A Disturbance of Memory on the Acropolis," in *Complete Standard Edition*, 22:239–48.

31. Strohm, *England's Empty Throne*, 103.

32. Julia Reinhard Lupton, *Afterlives of the Saints* (Stanford: Stanford University Press, 1996), 60–61.

33. On this point, see Kay, *Courtly Contradictions*, 219–31.

34. C. David Benson, *Chaucer's "Troilus and Criseyde"* (London: Unwin Hyman, 1990), 68.

35. Matthew Giancarlo, *Parliament and Literature in Late Medieval England* (Cambridge: Cambridge University Press, 2007), 85.

36. Schmitt, *Ghosts in the Middle Ages*, 5.

37. Scala, *Absent Narratives*, 103.

38. Fradenburg, *Sacrifice Your Love*, 163.

39. Scala, *Absent Narratives*, 123.

40. Fradenburg, *Sacrifice Your Love*, 163.

41. It should be noted that Lacan himself nowhere uses the term *Lady-Object*. I take the term from Žižek, who coins it to describe how the courtly Lady is made to function as the *objet a*, the object-cause of desire. See his chapter "Courtly Love, or, Woman as Thing," in *The Metastases of Enjoyment: Six Essays on Woman and Causality* (London: Verso, 1994), 89–112.

42. Ingham's essay "Amorous Dispossessions" has been especially helpful to me here. "Taken together, Finucci and Duff mark the double relevance of ['Petrarch's'] grave to the desiring structure of courtly love," observes Ingham: "not only does courtly love figure the poet's relation to Laura, it figures, as the problem of the poet's dead body makes clear, the relation of devoted admirers to the poets they love. The yearning for possession that is always deferred,

the dispossession of the beloved that structures the state of amorousness itself, the desire that is impossible of satisfaction—this is the amorous dispossession to which we, like Petrarch, are consigned" (14). Ingham's observation clarified for me that the fundamental ethical misstep of courtly love is that it revolves around the Kierkegaardian fantasy of the *dead* neighbor criticized by Žižek: "The dead neighbor means the neighbor deprived of the annoying excess of *jouissance* that makes him or her unbearable. So it is clear where Kierkegaard cheats: in trying to sell us, as the authentic difficult act of love, what is in fact an escape from the effort of authentic love. Love for the dead neighbor is an easy feast: it basks in its own perfection, indifferent to its object." Slavoj Žižek, *Revolution at the Gates: Žižek on Lenin* (New York: Verso, 2002), 214, quoted in Reinhard, "Toward a Political Theology," 23.

43. I refer to D. W. Robertson's controversial encapsulation of a medieval exegesis derived from Augustine's *On Christian Doctrine*: "Those passages which promote charity or condemn cupidity are to be left with their literal significance; but all figurative interpretations must promote the love of God and of one's neighbor. If they do not, the interpreter is either deceived or deceiving, and the interpretations are false." D. W. Robertson Jr., *A Preface to Chaucer: Studies in Medieval Perspectives* (Princeton: Princeton University Press, 1962), 295.

44. "Courtly love designs the future of amorous European subjectivity by subliming sublimation," contends Fradenburg. "The technique of raising the object to the dignity of the Thing is itself exalted, as a consequence of which its object—the Lady—is doubly fascinating, as not only 'she,' but the artifice that makes her, now points us toward our *jouissance*. What, then, could be more courtly than European historiography's fascination with courtly love—with the topics of desire, spectacular language, and their interdependence in the history of styles of European feeling?" *Sacrifice Your Love*, 19.

45. "The most general formula that I can give you of sublimation is the following," says Lacan: "it raises an object . . . to the dignity of the Thing." *Ethics of Psychoanalysis*, 112. Žižek's concise gloss on this formula is helpful: "What Lacan means by sublimation . . . is shifting the libido from the void of the 'unserviceable' Thing to some concrete, material object of need that assumes a sublime quality the moment it occupies the place of the Thing." *Metastases of Enjoyment*, 96.

46. Žižek, *Metastases of Enjoyment*, 96.

47. Lacan, *Ethics of Psychoanalysis*, 140.

48. Windeatt, *Troilus and Criseyde*, 174.

49. As Federico puts it, "Criseyde is the one ultimately responsible for the death of Troilus and, by extension, for the death of the city as well. Serving as a marker for this connection between the woman and the fate of the city, 'joie' is what Troy and Troilus have when Criseyde is present, and it is what they lose

when she leaves." Sylvia Federico, "Chaucer's Utopian Troy Book: Alternatives to Historiography in *Troilus and Criseyde*," *Exemplaria* 11, no. 1 (1999): 88.

50. For a helpful overview of the criticism on this scene, as well as for an important reading in its own right, see Richard W. Fehrenbacher, "'Al that which chargeth nought to seye': The Theme of Incest in *Troilus and Criseyde*," *Exemplaria* 9, no. 2 (1997): 341–69.

51. John Frankis, "Paganism and Pagan Love in *Troilus and Criseyde*," in *Essays on "Troilus and Criseyde,"* ed. Mary Salu (Cambridge: D. S. Brewer, 1979), 60.

52. See the notes for 3.624–26 in *Riverside Chaucer*, 1039–40.

53. As John P. McCall has put it, "In Book Five Chaucer not only continues to paint the declining picture of Troy with an eye on his failing hero, but he effectively identifies the two. . . . By this point, it would appear that Diomede, Criseyde, and the narrator are all explicitly aware that Troy and Troilus are one." John P. McCall, *Chaucer among the Gods: The Poetics of Classical Myth* (University Park: Pennsylvania State University Press, 1979), 100–101.

54. See, for example, David Aers's chapter on "Chaucer's Criseyde: Woman in Society, Woman in Love," in his *Chaucer, Langland, and the Creative Imagination* (London: Routledge and Kegan Paul, 1980), 117–42; Arlyn Diamond, "*Troilus and Criseyde:* The Politics of Love," in *Chaucer in the Eighties*, ed. Julian N. Wasserman and Robert J. Blanch (Syracuse: Syracuse University Press, 1986), 93–103; McAlpine, *Genre*, esp. ch. 6; Dinshaw, *Chaucer's Sexual Poetics*, esp. ch. 1; and, to a lesser degree, Elizabeth Salter, "*Troilus and Criseyde:* A Reconsideration," in *Critical Essays on Chaucer's "Troilus and Criseyde" and His Major Early Poems*, ed. C. David Benson (Toronto: University of Toronto Press, 1991), 92–109.

55. Lacan, *Ethics of Psychoanalysis*, 163.

56. Ibid., 150.

57. For Freud, the tragic irony of civilization is that the more we, as subjects, sacrifice our libido and aggressivity in the interests of communal harmony, the more discontented we, as subjects, become. To be civilized is thus, in Freud's view, automatically to become one of civilization's discontents.

58. In the same chapter of Seminar 7, "Courtly Love as Anamorphosis," Lacan suggests the following: "What man demands, what he cannot help but demand, is to be deprived of something real." I take this to mean that those defined by masculine structure demand to have something real, that is, the Thing, *jouissance*, located just out of reach. The Lady-Object serves to meet this demand. *Ethics of Psychoanalysis*, 150.

59. Lacan is hardly alone in thinking this, of course. David Aers, for example, suggests that "one of the central problems" explored by Chaucer in *Troilus and Criseyde* is precisely "the contradictions between aristocratic love conventions, in which woman was an exalted and powerful figure, and the

reality in which she was a subordinate being to be manipulated and made serviceable to men." Aers, "Chaucer's Criseyde," 123.

60. See Lacan, *Ethics of Psychoanalysis*, 152.

61. Dinshaw, *Chaucer's Sexual Poetics*, 30.

62. Fradenburg, *Sacrifice Your Love*, 162.

63. Of Pandarus's secretive machinations, Dinshaw says that "his perfect willingness to engage in this activity *and* his reluctance to have it known suggest both that he views women as things to be traded and that this is an operant truth Trojans (especially those ostensible courtly lovers) would perhaps rather not acknowledge." Dinshaw, *Chaucer's Sexual Poetics*, 58. I would add to this that such trafficking in women, such circulation and exchange, is among the most rudimentary ways of screening against lack by constantly transferring enjoyment to the Other. Women, and the right to traffic in them, are what masculine subjects get in exchange for sacrificing their enjoyment to the big Other. (In this respect, "the traffic in women" is but the most elemental metaphor for the trade-off made by all subjects, male and female.) There is a direct correspondence, then, between Pandarus's active participation in the exchange economy that underlies the Other and in his keeping Troilus from his death. Both activities serve the same end.

64. Benjamin, *Origin of German Tragic Drama*, 97.

65. Ibid., 98.

66. Paul Strohm, *Social Chaucer* (Cambridge, MA: Harvard University Press, 1989), 121.

67. In Saul Brody's felicitous phrase. See his "Making a Play for Criseyde: The Staging of Pandarus's House in Chaucer's *Troilus and Criseyde*," *Speculum* 73, no. 1 (1998): 115–40.

68. Walter Benjamin, "The Storyteller," in *Illuminations*, 108.

69. Ibid.

70. Ibid.

71. Simpson, *Reform and Cultural Revolution*, 139.

72. Benjamin, *Origin of German Tragic Drama*, 97.

73. Ibid., 98.

74. Strohm, *Social Chaucer*, 119.

75. See Badiou, *Ethics*, 51.

76. Lacan, *Ethics of Psychoanalysis*, 295.

77. The Lacanian concept of symbolic castration, as Bruce Fink explains, "clearly has nothing to do with biological organs or threats thereto." Rather, it "has to do with the fact that, at a certain point, we are required to give up some *jouissance*." Fink, *Lacanian Subject*, 73, 99. Or, as Lacan himself puts it, "Castration means that *jouissance* has to be refused in order to be attained on the inverse scale of the Law of desire." Jacques Lacan, *Écrits*, trans. Bruce Fink (New York: Norton, 2006), 700.

78. Lacan, *Ethics of Psychoanalysis*, 172.

79. Ibid., 193.

80. Ibid., 176.

81. Ibid.

82. Reinhard, "Freud, My Neighbor," 172.

83. On this dream, see chapter 1 of this book, note 32.

84. Copjec, *Read My Desire*, 120.

85 Ibid., 120–21.

86. Jacques Lacan, *The Ego in Freud's Theory and in the Technique of Psychoanalysis, 1954–55*, trans. Sylvia Tomaselli, Seminar 2 (New York: Norton, 1991), 169.

87. Ibid., 168.

88. Ibid., 158.

89. Ibid.

90. I am indebted to my colleague Klaus Mladek for bringing this to my attention.

91. Alain Badiou, *Saint Paul: The Foundation of Universalism* (Stanford: Stanford University, 2003), 79.

92. Windeatt, *Troilus and Criseyde*, 39.

93. Žižek, *Metastases of Enjoyment*, 95.

94. Windeatt, *Troilus and Criseyde*, 41.

95. The classic statement of this position is that of Robertson, *Preface to Chaucer*, 472–503.

96. Jacques Derrida, "Foreword: *Fors*: The Anglish Words of Nicholas Abraham and Maria Torok," trans. Barbara Johnson, in Nicholas Abraham and Maria Torok, *The Wolf Man's Magic Word: A Cryptonymy*, trans. Nicholas Rand (Minneapolis: University of Minnesota Press, 1986), xvii.

97. Ibid., xix.

98. Zupančič, *Ethics of the Real*, 155.

99. Lacan, *Ethics of Psychoanalysis*, 295.

100. Žižek, *Sublime Object of Ideology*, 134. Fradenburg comes to a similar conclusion regarding Arcite's body in Chaucer's *Knight's Tale*. See *Sacrifice Your Love*, 167–69.

101. Žižek, *Sublime Object of Ideology*, 134.

Epilogue

1. Elizabeth Salter and Derek Pearsall, "Pictorial Illustration of Late Medieval Poetic Texts: The Role of the Frontispiece or Prefatory Picture," in *Medieval Iconography and Narrative: A Symposium*, ed. Flemming G. Andersen et al. (Odense: Odense University Press, 1980), 100–123, but see esp. 123.

Strictly speaking, this essay derives from Pearsall's version of a talk that Professor Salter was unable to deliver because of illness. The essay appears in print under joint authorship, "as the two scholars had worked closely together on the subject for some years." Marianne Powell, introduction to *Medieval Iconography and Narrative*, 9.

2. Ibid., 123.

3. Simpson, *Reform and Cultural Revolution*, 148.

4. My perspective here, extrapolated from the individual to the collective, is that of Freud in his essay "Screen Memories": "It may indeed be questioned whether we have any memories at all *from* our childhood: memories *relating to* our childhood may be all that we possess. Our childhood memories show us our earliest years not as they were but as they appeared at the later periods when the memories were aroused. In these periods of arousal, the childhood memories did not, as people are accustomed to say, *emerge*; they were *formed* at that time. And a number of motives, with no concern for historical accuracy, had a part in forming them, as well as in the selection of the memories themselves." See *Complete Standard Edition*, 3:322.

5. Molly Murray, "The Value of 'Eschaunge': Ransom and Substitution in *Troilus and Criseyde*," *ELH* 69, no. 2 (2002): 335–58, discusses "the poem's preoccupation with double sense, surrogacy, and substitution" in light of "the medieval chivalric practice of ransom" (335). "In its depiction of character, in its narrative structure, and even in its insistently metaphoric language," writes Murray, "the poem makes use of the resonances of ransom to suggest that value and meaning are not threatened, but rather generated by separation and exchange" (335–36).

6. Elizabeth Salter describes the mass as "a diagonal line of soft-modeled rock." See "The *Troilus* Frontispiece," in *Troilus and Criseyde: A Facsimile of Corpus Christi College Cambridge MS 61* (Cambridge: D. S. Brewer, 1978), 19. Laura Kendrick, more elaborately, argues that the illuminator of the Frontispiece "uses the steep diagonal ramp of a mountain in the upper register . . . to represent by means of a concrete mountain or *puy*—with courtly figures climbing it, and others coming down to give them a loving welcome—the abstract notion of the *puy* as literary society involving friendship, striving, and aspiration." Laura Kendrick, "The *Troilus* Frontispiece and the Dramatization of Chaucer's *Troilus*," *Chaucer Review* 22 (1987): 87–88. Interestingly, Kendrick claims to "have found no very convincing iconographical precedents for the diagonal ramp of the frontispiece" (88), which to my mind suggests not only a degree of inventiveness on the artist's part but an attempt to translate into visual terms the singular and original emphasis on division in *Troilus and Criseyde*.

7. Kendrick notes that Chaucer's position would have signaled a "radical reversal of the usual deferential dedicatory image of the kneeling poet presenting his work to his patron" and contends that "such a reversal of positions of

authority would be extremely daring . . . even though 'corrected' to some extent by an image of the prince on the ramp of the mountains above the poet's head." Kendrick, "*Troilus* Frontispiece," 81.

8. On the concatenation of *Troy* and *joy*, see Mark Lambert, "*Troilus*, Books I–III: A Criseydan Reading," in *Critical Essays on Chaucer's "Troilus and Criseyde" and His Major Early Poems*, ed. C. David Benson (Toronto: University of Toronto Press, 1991), 110–27.

9. Derek Pearsall, "The *Troilus* Frontispiece and Chaucer's Audience," *Yearbook of English Studies* 7 (1977): 68–74.

10. On the concept of a "heroism" of lack, see Zupančič, *Ethics of the Real*, 240.

11. This is a point repeatedly stressed by Žižek. See, for example, his *For They Know Not*, 266–67.

12. On the often politically motivated "construction" of father Chaucer by "his later fifteenth-century scribes, readers and poetic imitators," see Lerer, *Chaucer and His Readers*, 3, 14–16.

13. This idea of a past that returns from the future—that is, from a past that "was already in itself pregnant with the open dimension of the future," that already contains a dormant future that, once reanimated, will destroy the present—is heavily indebted to Žižek's explication of Walter Benjamin's "Theses on the Philosophy of History." See *Sublime Object of Ideology*, 136–42.

14. Santner, *On Creaturely Life*, 95, also 114–15.

15. Ibid., 81.

16. See, for example, Lacan, *Ethics of Psychoanalysis*, 55, 159, 52, 67, 70–73, and passim; Žižek, *Sublime Object of Ideology*, 71.

17. Julia Reinhard Lupton and Kenneth Reinhard, *After Oedipus: Shakespeare in Psychoanalysis* (Ithaca: Cornell University Press, 1993), 165; Lacan, *Ethics of Psychoanalysis*, 65, 83.

18. Lacan, *Ethics of Psychoanalysis*, 52.

19. Jacques Lacan, *The Other Side of Psychoanalysis, 1969–70*, trans. Russell Grigg, Seminar 17 (New York: Norton, 2007), 18.

20. Žižek, *Sublime Object of Ideology*, 132.

21. Turner, *Chaucerian Conflict*, 5.

22. Ibid., 5.

23. My point of reference here is Benjamin's early essay "The Concept of Criticism in German Romanticism," filtered through Lacan's *Ethics of Psychoanalysis*. "Experiment consists in the evocation of self-consciousness and self-knowledge in the things observed," writes Benjamin, "experiment" being the critical process by which the concealed "truth content" of a work of art is brought to light through painstaking analysis. "To observe a thing means only to arouse it to self-recognition. Whether an experiment succeeds depends on the extent

to which the experimenter is capable, through the heightening of his own consciousness, through magical observation, as one might say, of getting nearer to the object and of finally drawing it into himself. . . . Observation fixes in its view only the self-knowledge nascent in the object; or rather it, the observation, *is* the nascent consciousness of the object itself. . . . Simultaneous with any cognition of an object is the actual coming-to-be of this object itself." As Benjamin would have it, the critical practice described here is one not of judgment but of observation. Invariably, though, to bring an object (and Benjamin is quick to assert that "all the laws that hold generally for the knowledge of objects in the medium of reflection also hold for the criticism of art") to self-knowledge involves bringing it to a knowledge about itself that it didn't know it possessed. For Benjamin, the unity of the work of art, by which he means the link between its material content and its truth content, must be "dissolved" for it to realize its own "self-judgment," the genuine insight that its material contents otherwise obscure and that the critic must work to disclose. Framed in Lacanian terms, the act of criticism means isolating the Thing from which the object in question is self-estranged—an act that necessarily involves the ethical judgment by which the observer distinguishes the "good" (those parts of the work that reflect the myths of its time, the common stories that people told themselves about themselves, and that are therefore familiar enough to lend themselves to commentary) from the "bad" (that part of the work, its self-judgment, that is a mystery even to itself but that nonetheless constitutes its repressed truth). To return, for a moment, to the point elaborated in note 13, above: the work of art already preserves within itself, buried among its other representations, the trace of its future dissolution, later to be revealed through an observation that sunders material content from truth content, the elements that, according with memory, lend themselves to commentary, from the new and noncomparable Thing that can be disclosed only through patient critique. Particularly telling, however, is the fact that Benjamin should describe the culminating moment of observation as one in which the experimenter gets so near to the object that he finally draws it into himself, worrying it, dissolving it, setting it up within himself: a process that sounds uncannily like the psychoanalytic concept of incorporation. The same process of criticism that dissolves the unity of the object also dissolves that of the observer. See "The Concept of Criticism in German Romanticism," in Benjamin, *Selected Writings*, vol. 1, *1913–1926*, 148, 151, 182, and passim.

24. Federico, *New Troy*, 73.

25. Lacan, *Ethics of Psychoanalysis*, 186. As the translator's note on 179 points out, "'Le mal' in French [which Lacan uses in the passage cited here] includes the ideas both of 'evil' and of 'suffering.'"

BIBLIOGRAPHY

Aers, David. *Chaucer, Langland, and the Creative Imagination*. London: Routledge and Kegan Paul, 1980.

———. *Community, Gender, and Individual Identity: English Writing, 1360–1430*. London: Routledge, 1988.

Aers, David, and Lynn Staley. *The Powers of the Holy: Religion, Politics, and Gender in Late Medieval English Culture*. University Park: Pennsylvania State University Press, 1997.

Agamben, Giorgio. *Homo Sacer: Sovereign Power and Bare Life*. Stanford: Stanford University Press, 1998.

———. *Stanzas: Word and Phantasm in Western Culture*. Translated by Ronald L. Martinez. Minneapolis: University of Minnesota Press, 1993.

Allen, Judson Boyce. *The Ethical Poetic of the Later Middle Ages: A Decorum of Convenient Distinction*. Toronto: University of Toronto Press, 1982.

Aloni, Gila. "Extimacy in the *Miller's Tale*." *Chaucer Review* 41, no. 2 (2006): 163–84.

Augustine. *On Christian Doctrine*. Translated by D. W. Robertson Jr. Upper Saddle River, NJ: Prentice-Hall, 1958.

Badiou, Alain. *Ethics: An Essay on the Understanding of Evil*. Translated by Peter Hallward. London: Verso, 2001.

———. *Saint Paul: The Foundation of Universalism*. Stanford: Stanford University Press, 2003.

Barney, Stephen A. "Troilus Bound." In *Chaucer's "Troilus and Criseyde": "Subgit to alle Poesye,"* edited by R. A. Shoaf, 1–16. Binghamton, NY: Medieval and Renaissance Texts and Studies, 1992. Previously published in *Speculum* 47 (1972): 445–58.

Barrell, A. D. M. *Medieval Scotland*. Cambridge: Cambridge University Press, 2000.

Barron, Caroline M. *London in the Later Middle Ages*. Oxford: Oxford University Press, 2004.

Barrow, G. W. S. *Scotland and Its Neighbors in the Middle Ages*. London: Hambledon Press, 1992.

Bellamy, Elizabeth J. *Translations of Power: Narcissism and the Unconscious in Epic History*. Ithaca: Cornell University Press, 1992.

Benjamin, Walter. *Illuminations: Essays and Reflections*. Translated by Harry Zohn. New York: Schocken Books, 1968.

———. *The Origin of German Tragic Drama*. Translated by John Osborne. London: Verso, 1977.

———. *Reflections: Essays, Aphorisms, Autobiographical Writings*. Edited by Peter Demetz. Translated by Edmund Jephcott. New York: Schocken Books, 1986.

———. *Selected Writings*. Vol. 1. *1913–1926*. Edited by Marcus Bullock and Michael W. Jennings. Cambridge, MA: Belknap Press, 1996.

Benoît de Sainte-Maure. *Le Roman de Troie par Benoît de Sainte-Maure*. 6 vols. Edited by Léopold Constans. Paris: Firmin-Didot, 1904–12.

Benson, C. David. *Chaucer's "Troilus and Criseyde."* London: Unwin Hyman, 1990.

———, ed. *Critical Essays on Chaucer's "Troilus and Criseyde" and His Major Early Poems*. Toronto: University of Toronto Press, 1991.

———. "Critic and Poet: What Lydgate and Henryson Did to Chaucer's *Troilus and Criseyde*." In *Writing after Chaucer: Essential Readings in Chaucer and the Fifteenth Century*, edited by Daniel J. Pinti, 227–41. New York: Garland, 1998. Previously published in *Modern Language Quarterly* 53 (1992): 23–40.

———. *The History of Troy in Middle English Literature*. Woodbridge: D. S. Brewer, 1980.

———. "Troilus and Criseyde in Henryson's *Testament*." *Chaucer Review* 13 (1979): 263–71.

Biddick, Kathleen. *The Shock of Medievalism*. Durham: Duke University Press, 1998.

Binski, Paul. *Medieval Death: Ritual and Representation*. London: British Museum Press, 1996.

Birns, Nicholas. "The Trojan Myth: Postmodern Reverberations." *Exemplaria* 5, no. 1 (1993): 45–78.

Bloch, R. Howard. *Etymologies and Genealogies: A Literary Anthropology of the French Middle Ages*. Chicago: University of Chicago Press, 1983.

Bloom, Harold. *The Anxiety of Influence: A Theory of Poetry*. Oxford: Oxford University Press, 1973.

Bloomfield, Josephine. "Chaucer and the Polis: Piety and Desire in the *Troilus and Criseyde*." *Modern Philology* 94, no. 3 (1997): 291–304.

Bloomfield, Morton W. "Chaucer's Sense of History." In *Essays and Explorations: Studies in Ideas, Language, and Literature,* 12–26. Cambridge, MA: Harvard University Press, 1970. Previously published in *JEGP* 51 (1952): 301–13.

———. "Distance and Predestination in *Troilus and Criseyde.*" In *Essays and Explorations: Studies in Ideas, Language, and Literature,* 201–16. Cambridge, MA: Harvard University Press, 1970. Previously published in *PMLA* 72 (1957): 14–26.

Boase, T. S. R. *Death in the Middle Ages: Mortality, Judgment and Remembrance.* London: Thames and Hudson, 1972.

Boccaccio, Giovanni. *Il Filostrato.* Edited by Vincenzo Pernicone. Translated with an introduction by Robert P. apRoberts and Anna Bruni Seldis. New York: Garland, 1986.

Boitani, Piero. "Antiquity and Beyond: The Death of Troilus." In *The European Tragedy of Troilus,* edited by Piero Boitani, 1–20. Oxford: Clarendon Press, 1989.

Bower, Walter. *Scotichronicon.* Vol. 7. Edited by D. E. R. Watt. Aberdeen: Aberdeen University Press, 1996.

Bowers, John M. *The Politics of "Pearl": Court Poetry in the Age of Richard II.* Cambridge: D. S. Brewer, 2001.

Brewer, Derek. *Chaucer and His World.* New York: Dodd, Mead, 1978.

———, ed. *Chaucer: The Critical Heritage.* Vol. 1. *1385–1837.* London: Routledge and Kegan Paul, 1978.

Brody, Saul. *The Disease of the Soul: Leprosy in Medieval Literature.* Ithaca: Cornell University Press, 1974.

———. "Making a Play for Criseyde: The Staging of Pandarus's House in Chaucer's *Troilus and Criseyde.*" *Speculum* 73, no. 1 (1998): 115–40.

Brown, Jennifer M., ed. *Scottish Society in the Fifteenth Century.* New York: St. Martin's Press, 1977.

Butler, Judith. *The Psychic Life of Power: Theories in Subjection.* Stanford: Stanford University Press, 1997.

Canning, Raymond, O.S.A. "The Distinction between Love for God and Love for Neighbor in St. Augustine." In *Christian Life: Ethics, Morality, and Discipline in the Early Church,* edited by Everett Ferguson, 103–39. New York: Garland, 1993.

Certeau, Michel de. *The Writing of History.* Translated by Tom Conley. New York: Columbia University Press, 1988.

Chaucer, Geoffrey. *The Riverside Chaucer.* Gen. ed. Larry D. Benson. Boston: Houghton Mifflin, 1987.

———. *Troilus and Criseyde: A New Edition of "The Book of Troilus."* Edited with an introduction by Barry Windeatt. London: Longman, 1984.

Clemen, W. H. *Chaucer's Early Poetry.* Translated by C. A. M. Sym. London: Methuen, 1968.

Cohen, Jeffrey Jerome. *Medieval Identity Machines.* Minneapolis: University of Minnesota Press, 2003.

———. *Of Giants: Sex, Monsters, and the Middle Ages.* Minneapolis: University of Minnesota Press, 1999.

———. "Time Out of Memory." In *The Post-historical Middle Ages,* edited by Elizabeth Scala and Sylvia Federico, 37–57. New York: Palgrave, 2009.

Coleman, Janet. "English Culture in the Fourteenth Century." In *Chaucer and the Italian Trecento,* edited by Piero Boitani, 33–63. Cambridge: Cambridge University Press, 1983.

Colonne, Guido delle. *Historia destructionis Troiae.* Translated by Mary Elizabeth Meek. Bloomington: University of Indiana Press, 1974.

Copjec, Joan. *Read My Desire: Lacan against the Historicists.* Cambridge, MA: MIT Press, 1994.

Crow, Martin M., and Clair C. Olson, eds. *Chaucer Life-Records.* Oxford: Clarendon Press, 1966.

Cullen, Mairi Ann. "Cresseid Excused: A Re-reading of Henryson's *Testament of Cresseid.*" *Studies in Scottish Literature* 20 (1985): 137–59.

Daniel, Christopher. *Death and Burial in Medieval England, 1066–1550.* London: Routledge, 1997.

Davis, Kathleen. *Periodization and Sovereignty: How Ideas of Feudalism and Secularization Govern the Politics of Time.* Philadelphia: University of Pennsylvania Press, 2008.

Derrida, Jacques. "Foreword: *Fors*: The Anglish Words of Nicholas Abraham and Maria Torok." Translated by Barbara Johnson. In Nicholas Abraham and Maria Torok, *The Wolf Man's Magic Word: A Cryptonymy,* translated by Nicholas Rand, xi–xlviii. Minneapolis: University of Minnesota Press, 1986.

———. *The Gift of Death.* Translated by David Wills. Chicago: University of Chicago Press, 1995.

Diamond, Arlyn. "*Troilus and Criseyde*: The Politics of Love." In *Chaucer in the Eighties,* edited by Julian N. Wasserman and Robert J. Blanch, 93–103. Syracuse: Syracuse University Press, 1986.

Dinshaw, Carolyn. *Chaucer's Sexual Poetics.* Madison: University of Wisconsin Press, 1989.

Dolar, Mladen. "At First Sight." In *Gaze and Voice as Love Objects,* edited by Renta Salecl and Slavoj Žižek, 129–53. Durham: Duke University Press, 1996.

Donaldson, E. Talbot. *Speaking of Chaucer.* New York: Norton, 1970.

Duncan, Douglas. "Henryson's *Testament of Cresseid.*" *Essays in Criticism* 11 (1961): 128–35.

Edwards, Robert R. "Pandarus,' 'Unthrift' and the Problem of Desire in *Troilus and Criseyde.*" In *Chaucer's "Troilus and Criseyde": "Subgit to alle Poesye,"* edited by R. A. Shoaf, 74–87. Binghamton, NY: Medieval and Renaissance Texts and Studies, 1992.

Ellis, Steve. "The Death of the *Book of the Duchess.*" *Chaucer Review*, 29, no. 3 (1995): 249–58.

Evans, Murray J. "'Making Strange': The Narrator (?), the Ending (?), and Chaucer's *Troilus.*" In *Critical Essays on Chaucer's "Troilus and Criseyde" and His Major Early Poems,* edited by C. David Benson, 164–75. Toronto: University of Toronto Press, 1991. Previously published in *Neuphilologische Mitteilungen* 87 (1986): 218–28.

Federico, Sylvia. "Chaucer's Utopian Troy Book: Alternatives to Historiography in *Troilus and Criseyde.*" *Exemplaria* 11, no. 1 (1999): 79–106.

———. "A Fourteenth-Century Erotics of Politics: London as a Feminine New Troy." *Studies in the Age of Chaucer* 19 (1997): 121–55.

———. *New Troy: Fantasies of Empire in the Late Middle Ages.* Minneapolis: University of Minnesota Press, 2003.

———. "Old Stories and New Trojans: The Gendered Construction of English Historical Identity." PhD diss., Indiana University, 1997.

Fehrenbacher, Richard W. "'Al that which chargeth nought to seye': The Theme of Incest in *Troilus and Criseyde.*" *Exemplaria* 9, no. 2 (1997): 341–69.

Fink, Bruce. *Lacan to the Letter: Reading "Écrits" Closely.* Minneapolis: University of Minnesota Press, 2004.

———. *The Lacanian Subject: Between Language and Jouissance.* Princeton: Princeton University Press, 1995.

Fisher, John H. "A Language Policy for Lancastrian England." *PMLA* 107, no. 5 (1992): 1168–80.

Foucault, Michel. "Nietzsche, Genealogy, History." In *Aesthetics, Method, and Epistemology,* edited by James D. Faubion, translated by Robert Hurley et al., 369–91. New York: New Press, 1998.

Fox, Denton, ed. *The Poems of Robert Henryson.* Oxford: Clarendon Press, 1981.

Fradenburg, L. O. Aranye. "'Be not far from me': Psychoanalysis, Medieval Studies, and the Subject of Religion." *Exemplaria* 7, no. 1 (1995): 41–54.

———. "Narrative and Capital in Late Medieval Scotland." In *Literary Practice and Social Change in Britain, 1380–1530,* edited by Lee Patterson, 285–333. Berkeley: University of California Press, 1990.

———. *Sacrifice Your Love: Psychoanalysis, Historicism, Chaucer.* Minneapolis: University of Minnesota Press, 2002.

———. "The Scottish Chaucer." In *Writing After Chaucer: Essential Readings in Chaucer and the Fifteenth Century,* edited by Daniel J. Pinti, 167–76. New York: Garland, 1998. Previously published in *Proceedings of the Third*

International Conference on Scottish Language and Literature, 177–90. Stirling: William Culcross, 1981.

———. "'Voice Memorial': Loss and Reparation in Chaucer's Poetry." *Exemplaria* 2, no. 1 (1990): 169–202.

———. "We Are Not Alone: Psychoanalytic Medievalism." *New Medieval Literatures* 2 (1998): 249–76.

Frankis, John. "Paganism and Pagan Love in *Troilus and Criseyde.*" In *Essays on "Troilus and Criseyde,"* edited by Mary Salu, 57–72. Cambridge: D. S. Brewer, 1979.

Frantzen, Allen J. *"Troilus and Criseyde": The Poem and the Frame.* New York: Twayne, 1993.

Frazer, R. M., trans. *The Trojan War: The Chronicles of Dictys of Crete and Dares the Phrygian.* Bloomington: Indiana University Press, 1966.

Freccero, Carla. *Queer/Early/Modern.* Durham: Duke University Press, 2006.

Freud, Sigmund. *The Complete Standard Edition of the Psychological Works of Sigmund Freud.* Edited and translated by James Strachey. London: Hogarth Press, 1966.

Gaunt, Simon. *Love and Death in Medieval French and Occitan Courtly Literature.* Oxford: Oxford University Press, 2006.

Geary, Patrick J. *Living with the Dead in the Middle Ages.* Ithaca: Cornell University Press, 1994.

Geoffrey of Monmouth. *The History of the Kings of Britain.* Translated by Lewis Thorpe. Harmondsworth: Penguin Books, 1966.

Giancarlo, Matthew. *Parliament and Literature in Late Medieval England.* Cambridge: Cambridge University Press, 2007.

Goldstein, R. James. *The Matter of Scotland: Historical Narrative in Medieval Scotland.* Lincoln: University of Nebraska Press, 1993.

———. "Writing in Scotland, 1058–1560." In *The Cambridge History of Medieval British Literature,* edited by David Wallace, 229–54. Cambridge: Cambridge University Press, 1999.

Goodman, Anthony. "The Anglo-Scottish Marches in the Fifteenth Century: A Frontier Society?" In *Scotland and England, 1286–1815,* edited by Robert A. Mason. Edinburgh: John Donald, 1987.

Gordon, Bruce, and Peter Marshall, eds. *The Place of the Dead: Death and Remembrance in Late Medieval and Early Modern Europe.* Cambridge: Cambridge University Press, 2000.

Gordon, Ida L. *The Double Sorrow of Troilus: A Study of Ambiguities in "Troilus and Criseyde."* Oxford: Clarendon Press, 1970.

Gordon, R. K. *The Story of Troilus.* Toronto: University of Toronto Press, 1978.

Gower, John. *Mirour de l'Omme (The Mirror of Mankind).* Translated by William Burton Wilson. East Lansing, MI: Colleagues Press, 1992.

Grady, Frank. *Representing Righteous Heathens in Late Medieval England*. New York: Palgrave, 2005.

Gray, Douglas. *Robert Henryson*. Leiden: Brill, 1979.

Gray, Sir Thomas. *Scalacronica: A Chronicle of England and Scotland*. Edited by J. Stevenson. Edinburgh, 1836.

Gurevich, A.J. *Categories of Medieval Culture*. Translated by G.L. Campbell. London: Routledge and Kegan Paul, 1985.

Hanning, Robert W. "Come in Out of the Code: Interpreting the Discourse of Desire in Boccaccio's *Filostrato* and Chaucer's *Troilus and Criseyde*." In *Chaucer's "Troilus and Criseyde": "Subgit to alle Poesye*," edited by R.A. Shoaf, 120–37. Binghamton, NY: Medieval and Renaissance Texts and Studies, 1992.

Harwood, Britton J. "Psychoanalytic Politics: Chaucer and Two Peasants." *ELH* 68, no. 1 (2001): 1–27.

Havely, N.R., ed. and trans. *Chaucer's Boccaccio: Sources of "Troilus" and the Knight's and Franklin's Tales*. Woodbridge: D.S. Brewer, 1980.

Henryson, Robert. *The Poems of Robert Henryson*. Edited by Denton Fox. Oxford: Clarendon Press, 1981.

———. *Testament of Cresseid*. Edited by Denton Fox. London: Thomas Nelson and Sons, 1968.

Holmstedt, Gustaf, ed. *Speculum Christiani*. EETS, o.s., 182. Oxford: Oxford University Press, 1933.

Holsinger, Bruce. *The Premodern Condition: Medievalism and the Making of Theory*. Chicago: University of Chicago Press, 2005.

Howard, Donald R. *Chaucer: His Life, His Works, His World*. New York: Fawcett Columbine, 1987.

Ingham, Patricia Clare. "Amorous Dispossessions: Knowledge, Desire, and the Poet's Dead Body." In *The Post-historical Middle Ages*, edited by Elizabeth Scala and Sylvia Federico, 13–35. New York: Palgrave, 2009.

———. *Sovereign Fantasies: Arthurian Romance and the Making of Britain*. Philadelphia: University of Pennsylvania Press, 2001.

Ingledew, Francis. "The Book of Troy and the Genealogical Construction of History: The Case of Geoffrey of Monmouth's *Historia regum Britanniae*." *Speculum* 69 (1994): 665–704.

Julien, Phillippe. *Jacques Lacan's Return to Freud*. Translated by Devra Beck Simiu. New York: New York University Press, 1994.

Kay, Sarah. *Courtly Contradictions: The Emergence of the Literary Object in the Twelfth Century*. Stanford: Stanford University Press, 2001.

Kelly, Henry Ansgar. *Chaucerian Tragedy*. Cambridge: D.S. Brewer, 1997.

Kempshall, M.S. *The Common Good in Late Medieval Political Thought*. Oxford: Clarendon Press, 1999.

Kendrick, Laura. "The *Troilus* Frontispiece and the Dramatization of Chaucer's *Troilus.*" *Chaucer Review* 22 (1987): 81–93.

Knapp, Ethan. *The Bureaucratic Muse: Thomas Hoccleve and the Literature of Late Medieval England.* University Park: Pennsylvania State University Press, 2001.

Kratzmann, Gregory. *Anglo-Scottish Literary Relations, 1430–1550.* Cambridge: Cambridge University Press, 1980.

Labbie, Erin Felicia. *Lacan's Medievalism.* Minneapolis: University of Minnesota Press, 2006.

Lacan, Jacques. *Écrits.* Translated by Bruce Fink. New York: Norton, 2006.

———. *The Ego in Freud's Theory and in the Technique of Psychoanalysis, 1954–55.* Translated by Sylvia Tomaselli. Seminar 2. New York: Norton, 1991.

———. *The Ethics of Psychoanalysis, 1959–60.* Translated by Dennis Porter. Seminar 7. New York: Norton, 1997.

———. *The Four Fundamental Concepts of Psychoanalysis.* Translated by Alan Sheridan. Seminar 11. New York: Norton, 1981.

———. *On Feminine Sexuality, the Limits of Love and Knowledge, 1972–73.* Translated by Bruce Fink. Seminar 20. New York: Norton, 1998.

———. *The Other Side of Psychoanalysis, 1969–70.* Translated by Russell Grigg. Seminar 17. New York: Norton, 2007.

———. *The Psychoses, 1955–56.* Translated by Russell Grigg. Seminar 3. New York: Norton, 1993.

Lambert, Mark. *"Troilus,* Books I–III: A Criseydan Reading." In *Critical Essays on Chaucer's* Troilus and Criseyde *and His Major Early Poems,* edited by C. David Benson, 110–27. Toronto: University of Toronto Press, 1991. Previously published in *Essays on "Troilus and Criseyde,"* edited by Mary Salu, 105–25. Cambridge: D. S. Brewer, 1979.

Laplanche, J., and J.-B. Pontalis. *The Language of Psychoanalysis.* Trans. Donald Nicholson-Smith. New York: Norton, 1973.

Larner, John. "Chaucer's Italy." In *Chaucer and the Italian Trecento,* edited by Piero Boitani, 7–32. Cambridge: Cambridge University Press, 1983.

Lavezzo, Kathy. "Chaucer and Everyday Death: *The Clerk's Tale,* Burial, and the Subject of Poverty." *Studies in the Age of Chaucer* 23 (2001): 255–87.

Leff, Gordon. *The Dissolution of the Medieval Outlook: An Essay on the Intellectual and Spiritual Change in the Fourteenth Century.* New York: Harper and Row, 1976.

Lerer, Seth. *Chaucer and His Readers: Imagining the Author in Late-Medieval England.* Princeton: Princeton University Press, 1993.

Levinas, Emmanuel. *Entre nous: On Thinking-of-the-Other.* Translated by Michael B. Smith and Barbara Harshaw. New York: Columbia University Press, 1998.

————. *Otherwise Than Being, or Beyond Essence.* Translated by Alphonso Lingis. Pittsburgh: Duquesne University Press, 1998.

————. *Time and the Other.* Translated by Richard A. Cohen. Pittsburgh: Duquesne University Press, 1987.

Lewis, C. S. "What Chaucer Really Did to *Il Filostrato*." In *Chaucer's "Troilus": Essays in Criticism,* edited by Stephen A. Barney, 37–54. Hamden, CT: Archon Books, 1980. Previously published in *Essays and Studies* 17 (1932): 56–75.

Lindenbaum, Sheila. "The Smithfield Tournament of 1390." *Journal of Medieval and Renaissance Studies* 20, no.1 (1990): 1–20.

Lupton, Julia Reinhard. *Afterlives of the Saints.* Stanford: Stanford University Press, 1996.

————. "Tragedy and Psychoanalysis: Freud and Lacan." In *A Companion to Tragedy,* edited by Rebecca Bushnell, 88–105. Malden, MA: Blackwell, 2005.

Lupton, Julia Reinhard, and Kenneth Reinhard. *After Oedipus: Shakespeare in Psychoanalysis.* Ithaca: Cornell University Press, 1993.

Maidstone, Richard. *Concordia (The Reconciliation of Richard II with London).* Edited by David R. Carlson. Translated by A. G. Rigg. Kalamazoo, MI: Medieval Institute Publications, 2003.

Mann, Jill. "Troilus' Swoon." In *Critical Essays on Chaucer's "Troilus and Criseyde" and His Major Early Poems,* edited by C. David Benson, 149–63. Toronto: University of Toronto Press, 1991. Previously published in *Chaucer Review* 14 (1980): 319–35.

Margherita, Gayle. "Criseyde's Remains: Romance and the Question of Justice." *Exemplaria* 12 (2000): 257–92.

————. *The Romance of Origins: Language and Sexual Difference in Middle English Literature.* Philadelphia: University of Pennsylvania Press, 1994.

Marx, Karl. *Capital.* Vol. 1. Translated by Eden Paul and Cedar Paul. London: Everyman's Library, 1957.

Mathews, Jana. "Land, Lepers, and the Law in *The Testament of Cresseid*." In *The Letter of the Law: Legal Practice and Literary Production in Medieval England,* edited by Emily Steiner and Candace Barrington, 40–66. Ithaca: Cornell University Press, 2002.

McAlpine, Monica E. *The Genre of "Troilus and Criseyde."* Ithaca: Cornell University Press, 1978.

McCall, John P. *Chaucer among the Gods: The Poetics of Classical Myth.* University Park: Pennsylvania State University Press, 1979.

————. "The Trojan Scene in Chaucer's *Troilus*." In *Critical Essays on Chaucer's* Troilus and Criseyde *and His Major Early Poems,* edited by C. David Benson, 57–67. Toronto: University of Toronto Press, 1991. Previously published in *ELH* 29 (1962): 263–75.

Meech, Sanford B. *Design in Chaucer's "Troilus."* New York: Greenwood Press, 1969.

Miller, Mark. *Philosophical Chaucer: Love, Sex, and Agency in the "Canterbury Tales."* Cambridge: Cambridge University Press, 2004.

Minnis, A.J. *Chaucer and Pagan Antiquity.* Woodbridge: D. S. Brewer, 1982.

Mitchell, J. Allan. *Ethics and Eventfulness in Medieval English Literature.* New York: Palgrave, 2009.

Moyaert, Paul. "Lacan on Neighborly Love: The Relation to the Thing in the Other Who Is My Neighbor." *Epoché* 1 (1996): 1–31.

Murray, Molly. "The Value of 'Eschaunge': Ransom and Substitution in *Troilus and Criseyde.*" *ELH* 69, no. 2 (2002): 335–58.

Natali, Giulia. "A Lyrical Version: Boccaccio's *Filostrato.*" In *The European Tragedy of Troilus*, edited by Piero Boitani, 49–74. Oxford: Clarendon Press, 1989.

Nolan, Barbara. *Chaucer and the Tradition of the "Roman antique."* Cambridge: Cambridge University Press, 1992.

Papka, Claudia Rattazzi. "Transgression, the End of Troilus, and the Ending of *Troilus and Criseyde.*" *Chaucer Review* 32 (1997–98): 267–81.

Patterson, Lee. *Chaucer and the Subject of History.* Madison: University of Wisconsin Press, 1991.

———. "Christian and Pagan in *The Testament of Cresseid.*" *Philological Quarterly* 52 (1973): 696–714.

———. "Introduction: Critical Historicism and Medieval Studies." In *Literary Practice and Social Change in Britain, 1380–1530*, edited by Lee Patterson, 1–14. Berkeley: University of California Press, 1990.

———. Review of *England's Empty Throne*, by Paul Strohm. *Studies in the Age of Chaucer* 22 (2000): 540–44.

Pearsall, Derek. *The Life of Geoffrey Chaucer: A Critical Biography.* Oxford: Blackwell, 1992.

———. *Old and Middle English Poetry.* London: Routledge, 1977.

———. "'Quha wait gif all that Chauceir wrait was trew?' Henryson's *Testament of Cresseid.*" In *New Perspectives on Middle English Texts: A Festschrift for R.A. Waldron*, edited by Susan Powell and Jeremy J. Smith, 169–82. Cambridge: D. S. Brewer, 2000.

———. "The *Troilus* Frontispiece and Chaucer's Audience." *Yearbook of English Studies* 7 (1977): 68–74.

Perkins, Nicholas. "Haunted Hoccleve? *The Regiment of Princes*, the Troilean Intertext, and Conversations with the Dead." *Chaucer Review* 43, no. 2 (2008): 103–39.

Prendergast, Thomas A. *Chaucer's Dead Body: From Corpse to Corpus.* New York: Routledge, 2004.

Reinhard, Kenneth. "Freud, My Neighbor." *American Imago* 54, no. 2 (1997): 165–95.

———. "Kant with Sade, Lacan with Levinas." *Modern Language Notes* 110, no. 4 (1995): 785–808.

———. "Toward a Political Theology of the Neighbor." In Slavoj Žižek, Eric L. Santner, and Kenneth Reinhard, *The Neighbor: Three Inquiries in Political Theology*, 11–75. Chicago: University of Chicago Press, 2005.

Riddy, Felicity. "'Abject Odious': Masculine and Feminine in Henryson's *Testament of Cresseid*." In *The Long Fifteenth Century: Essays for Douglas Gray*, edited by Helen Cooper and Sally Mapstone, 229–48. Oxford: Clarendon Press, 1997.

Ridley, Florence H. "A Plea for the Middle Scots." In *The Learned and the Lewed: Studies in Chaucer and Medieval Literature*, edited by Larry D. Benson, 175–96. Cambridge, MA: Harvard University Press, 1974.

Robertson, D. W., Jr. "Chaucerian Tragedy." *ELH* 19 (1952): 1–37.

———. *Chaucer's London*. New York: John Wiley and Sons, 1968.

———. *A Preface to Chaucer: Studies in Medieval Perspectives*. Princeton: Princeton University Press, 1962.

Rosenfeld, Jessica. "Narcissus after Aristotle: Love and Ethics in *Le Roman de la Rose*." *New Medieval Literatures* 9 (2007): 1–39.

Rowe, Donald W. *O Love, O Charitie! Contraries Harmonized in Chaucer's "Troilus."* Carbondale: Southern Illinois University Press, 1976.

Salter, Elizabeth. "*Troilus and Criseyde*: A Reconsideration." In *Critical Essays on Chaucer's "Troilus and Criseyde" and His Major Early Poems*, edited by C. David Benson, 92–109. Toronto: University of Toronto Press, 1991. Previously published in *Patterns of Love and Courtesy: Essays in Memory of C. S. Lewis*, edited by John Lawlor, 86–106. London: Arnold, 1966.

———. "The *Troilus* Frontispiece." In *Troilus and Criseyde: A Facsimile of Corpus Christi College Cambridge MS 61*, introduction by M. B. Parkes and Elizabeth Salter, 15–23. Cambridge: D. S. Brewer, 1978.

Salter, Elizabeth, and Derek Pearsall. "Pictorial Illustration of Late Medieval Poetic Texts: The Role of the Frontispiece or Prefatory Picture." In *Medieval Iconography and Narrative: A Symposium*, edited by Flemming G. Andersen et al., 100-123. Odense: Odense University Press, 1980.

Sanok, Catherine. "Criseyde, Cassandre, and the *Thebaid*: Women and the Theban Subtext of Chaucer's *Troilus and Criseyde*." *Studies in the Age of Chaucer* 20 (1998): 41–71.

Santner, Eric L. *On Creaturely Life: Rilke, Benjamin, Sebald*. Chicago: University of Chicago Press, 2006.

———. *On the Psychotheology of Everyday Life*. Chicago: University of Chicago Press, 2001.

Scala, Elizabeth. *Absent Narratives, Manuscript Textuality, and Literary Structure in Late Medieval England*. New York: Palgrave, 2002.

———. "Historicists and Their Discontents: Reading Psychoanalytically in Medieval Studies." *Texas Studies in Literature and Language* 44, no. 1 (2002): 108–31.

Scheps, Walter. "A Climatological Reading of Henryson's *Testament of Cresseid.*" *Studies in Scottish Literature* 15 (1980): 80–87.

Schmitt, Jean-Claude. *Ghosts in the Middle Ages: The Living and the Dead in Medieval Society.* Translated by Teresa Lavender Fagan. Chicago: University of Chicago Press, 1998.

Simpson, James. "Chaucer as a European Writer." In *The Yale Companion to Chaucer,* edited by Seth Lerer, 55–86. New Haven: Yale University Press, 2006.

———. *The Oxford English Literary History.* Vol. 2, *1350–1547: Reform and Cultural Revolution.* Oxford: Oxford University Press, 2002.

Smalley, Beryl. *English Friars and Antiquity in the Early Fourteenth Century.* New York: Barnes and Noble, 1960.

Smith, D. Vance. "Crypt and Decryption: *Erkenwald* Terminable and Interminable." *New Medieval Literatures* 5 (2002): 59–85.

Spearing, A. C. *Chaucer: "Troilus and Criseyde."* London: Edward Arnold, 1976.

———. *Criticism and Medieval Poetry.* 2nd ed. New York: Barnes and Noble, 1972.

———. *Medieval to Renaissance in English Poetry.* Cambridge: Cambridge University Press, 1985.

———. *Readings in Medieval Poetry.* Cambridge: Cambridge University Press, 1987.

———. "A Ricardian 'I': The Narrator of Troilus and Criseyde." In *Essays in Ricardian Literature in Honor of J. A. Burrow,* edited by A. J. Minnis, Charlotte C. Morse, and Thorlac Turville-Petre, 1–22. Oxford: Clarendon Press, 1997.

Spiegel, Gabrielle M. *The Past as Text: The Theory and Practice of Medieval Historiography.* Baltimore: Johns Hopkins University Press, 1997.

Stanbury, Sarah. "The Lover's Gaze in *Troilus and Criseyde.*" In *Chaucer's "Troilus and Criseyde": "Subgit to alle Poesye,"* edited by R. A. Shoaf, 224–38. Binghamton, NY: Medieval and Renaissance Texts and Studies, 1992.

Stearns, Marshall W. *Robert Henryson.* 1949. Repr., New York: Columbia University Press, 1966.

Stillinger, Thomas C. *The Song of Troilus: Lyric Authority in the Medieval Book.* Philadelphia: University of Pennsylvania Press, 1992.

Stone, Gregory B. *The Death of the Troubadour: The Late Medieval Resistance to the Renaissance.* Philadelphia: University of Pennsylvania Press, 1994.

Stones, E. L. G., ed. and trans. *Anglo-Scottish Relations, 1174–1328: Some Selected Documents.* Oxford: Clarendon Press, 1965.

Storm, Melvin. "The Intertextual Cresseida: Chaucer's Henryson or Henryson's Chaucer?" *Studies in Scottish Literature* 28 (1993): 105–22.

Strohm, Paul. *England's Empty Throne: Usurpation and the Language of Legitimation, 1399–1422.* New Haven: Yale University Press, 1998.

———. *Politique: Language of Statecraft between Chaucer and Shakespeare.* Notre Dame: University of Notre Dame Press, 2005.

———. Review of *Chaucerian Tragedy*, by Henry Ansgar Kelly. *Journal of English and Germanic Philology*, 98, no. 2 (1999): 259.

———. *Social Chaucer.* Cambridge, MA: Harvard University Press, 1989.

———. *Theory and the Premodern Text.* Minneapolis: University of Minnesota Press, 2000.

Summit, Jennifer. *Lost Property: The Woman Writer and English Literary History, 1380–1589.* Chicago: University of Chicago Press, 2000.

Taylor, Andrew. *Textual Situations: Three Medieval Manuscripts and Their Readers.* Philadelphia: University of Pennsylvania Press, 2002.

Terrell, Katherine H. "Subversive Histories: Strategies of Identity in Scottish Historiography." In *Cultural Diversity in the British Middle Ages: Archipelago, Island, England*, edited by Jeffrey Jerome Cohen, 153–72. New York: Palgrave, 2008.

Torti, Anna. "From 'History' to 'Tragedy': The Story of Troilus and Criseyde in Lydgate's *Troy Book* and Henryson's *Testament of Cresseid.*" In *The European Tragedy of Troilus*, edited by Piero Boitani, 171–98. Oxford: Clarendon Press, 1989.

Travis, Peter W. "White." *Studies in the Age of Chaucer* 22 (2000): 1–66.

Turner, Marion. *Chaucerian Conflict: Languages of Antagonism in Late Fourteenth-Century London.* Oxford: Clarendon Press, 2007.

Wack, Mary F. *Lovesickness in the Middle Ages: The "Viaticum" and Its Commentaries.* Philadelphia: University of Pennsylvania Press, 1990.

———. "Lovesickness in *Troilus.*" *Pacific Coast Philology* 19 (1984): 55–61.

Wallace, David. *Chaucer and the Early Writings of Boccaccio.* Woodbridge: D. S. Brewer, 1985.

———. *Chaucerian Polity: Absolutist Lineages and Associational Forms in England and Italy.* Stanford: Stanford University Press, 1997.

Warren, Michelle. *History on the Edge: Excalibur and the Borders of Britain, 1100–1300.* Minneapolis: University of Minnesota Press, 2000.

Waswo, Richard. "Our Ancestors, the Trojans: Inventing Cultural Identity in the Middle Ages." *Exemplaria* 7, no. 2 (1995): 269–90.

Watson, Nicholas. "Outdoing Chaucer: Lydgate's *Troy Book* and Henryson's *Testament of Cresseid* as Competitive Imitations of *Troilus and Criseyde.*" In *Shifts and Transpositions in Medieval Narrative: A Festschrift for Elspeth Kennedy*, edited by Karen Pratt, Penny Eley, and Elspeth Kennedy, 89–108. Cambridge: D. S. Brewer, 1994.

Wetherbee, Winthrop. *Chaucer and the Poets: An Essay on "Troilus and Criseyde."* Ithaca: Cornell University Press, 1984.

Windeatt, Barry. "Chaucer and the *Filostrato*." In *Chaucer and the Italian Trecento*, edited by Piero Boitani, 163–83. Cambridge: Cambridge University Press, 1983.

———. *Troilus and Criseyde.* Oxford Guides to Chaucer. Oxford: Clarendon Press, 1992.

Wood, Chauncey. *The Elements of Chaucer's "Troilus."* Durham: Duke University Press, 1984.

Wrightson, Keith. "The 'Decline of Neighbourliness' Revisited." In *Local Identities in Late Medieval and Early Modern England*, edited by Norman L. Jones and Daniel Woolf, 19–49. New York: Palgrave, 2007.

Wülfing, J. Ernst, ed. *The Laud Troy Book.* EETS, o.s., 121–22. London: Kegan Paul, 1902.

Young, Karl. *The Origin and Development of the Story of Troilus and Criseyde.* 1908. Repr., New York: Gordian Press, 1968.

Žižek, Slavoj. *For They Know Not What They Do: Enjoyment as a Political Factor.* London: Verso, 1991.

———. *The Fragile Absolute—Or, Why Is the Christian Legacy Worth Fighting For?* London: Verso, 2000.

———. *The Indivisible Remainder: An Essay on Schelling and Related Matters.* London: Verso, 1996.

———. *The Metastases of Enjoyment: Six Essays on Women and Causality.* London: Verso, 1994.

———. *The Sublime Object of Ideology.* London: Verso, 1989.

Zumthor, Paul. *Speaking of the Middle Ages.* Translated by Sarah White. Lincoln: University of Nebraska Press, 1986.

Zupančič, Alenka. *Ethics of the Real: Kant, Lacan.* London: Verso, 2000.

INDEX

Aers, David, 246n59
Afterlives of the Saints (Lupton), 149
Agamben, Giorgio, 98, 228n49
aggression, 89, 234n25
  jouissance of, 154
  and neighborliness, 14, 15, 38, 40, 48
  in Scotland-England relations,
    38, 39–40, 45–46, 47–48, 62–63,
    226n20
  and social antagonism, 165, 206,
    210
Allen, Judson Boyce, 214n8
anamorphosis, 111–12
Antigone (Sophocles), 30, 100, 101–2,
  110, 150
anxiety, 106–7, 108, 196, 197
Aquinas, Thomas, 16
art, 111–12, 251n23
Augustine, 10–11

Badiou, Alain, 86, 188–89
bare life, 56, 58, 65, 228n49
Benjamin, Walter, 17, 146, 173, 176,
  229n52
  on bare life and mere life, 228n49
  on courtiers, 170, 171, 172, 175
  on history's continuum, 92, 93
  on natural history, 25, 26, 95, 203,
    233n82
  on redemption, 70
  on self-recognition, 250n23
Benoît de Sainte-Maure, 186

Roman de Troie, 35, 89–92, 94, 96,
  97, 104, 147
Benson, C. David, 227n39
Beyond the Pleasure Principle (Freud),
  9, 11
Bisset, Baldred, 74–75
Bloom, Harold, 106, 107
Bloomfield, Josephine, 243n19
Bloomfield, Morton, 131
Boccaccio, Giovanni
  literary innovations of, 89, 92
  Teseida, 128–29, 130
  on Troy legend, 94
  unnamed by Chaucer, 190, 191, 192
  See also *Filostrato, Il*
Boethius, 215n8
Boitani, Piero, 95, 99, 235n35, 237n53
Book of the Duchess, The (Chaucer),
  139
border writing, 12, 38
Bower, Walter, 46, 48
Bowers, John, 137
Brembre, Nicholas, 201, 238n56
Brewer, Derek, 231n3
Brody, Saul, 55

Calkas, 127, 140
Canterbury Tales (Chaucer), 22, 108–9,
  138
castration, symbolic, 113, 181–82, 198,
  247n77
charity, 70, 72, 73, 76, 155

and *Nebenmensch*, 8, 9
and neighbor, 10, 137, 212
symbolic, 30, 32, 53, 100–101, 105,
   139, 149–50, 224n86
of Thing, 100–101
and transgression, 209–10
of Troilus, 53, 95, 96, 97, 101–2, 139,
   140–41, 167, 169, 235n35
Troy's destruction as, 105
and Word, 188
See also space between two deaths
deferred action, 35, 224n97
deposits of suffering, 27, 223n82
Derrida, Jacques, 191, 192
desire, 29, 54, 62, 94, 192
   as ethical gesture, 101, 237n50
   and fantasy, 13
   and gaze, 130, 240n96
   and *jouissance*, 156
   Lacan on, 237n50, 240n96
   and lack, 115, 144, 179
   law and, 188–89
   and mutability, 144
   of Other, 13, 32, 73, 96
   Troy as site of, 103
Dinshaw, Carolyn, 165, 247n63
Diomede, 113, 147, 157–58, 165, 166, 177
   as unappealing character, 193
Divina commedia (Dante), 79, 215n8
Dolar, Mladen, 117
Donaldson, E. Talbot, 120
doubt, 49–50, 67
   Lacan on, 49, 52, 227n35
Dunwal Molmutius, 74

Edward I, 74, 75
Ellis, Steve, 139
England, 79, 80
   and Scotland, 38, 39–40, 45–46,
   47–48, 62–63, 73–74, 75–76,
   226n20

social antagonisms in, 206
and Troy legend, 21–22, 74–75,
   201–2
See also London
"Ethics and Tragedy in Psychoanalysis" (Zupančič), 102
Ethics of Psychoanalysis, The (Lacan),
   68, 103–4, 111, 143, 179, 207
exchange, 209
   economy of, 9, 19, 158, 177–79, 197,
   205–6
   in history, 26, 206
extimacy, 29, 223n85

fantasy, 22–23, 190, 205
   of community, 14
   and desire, 13
   and *jouissance*, 12–13, 69, 209
   and lack, 179
   and prohibition, 116
   Sadeian, 196, 197
   sexual, 112, 114, 116, 120
   of Troilus, 72, 76
   and Troy, 152, 202, 204
Father
   betting on, 94, 123–24
   Chaucer depicted as, 31, 41–42, 43,
   204, 205
   jouissance and, 38, 60–61, 114,
   183–84, 198
   myth of primal, 42–43, 102, 159
   Troilus and Criseyde narrator as
   symbolic, 181
Federico, Sylvia, 6, 245n49
   on Troy and English nationhood,
   21–22, 23, 103
Filomena, 88, 93, 98, 99, 124, 132
Filostrato, Il (Boccaccio)
   anxiety-producing quality of, 108
   bedroom scene in, 119–22
   as canonical text, 21, 26